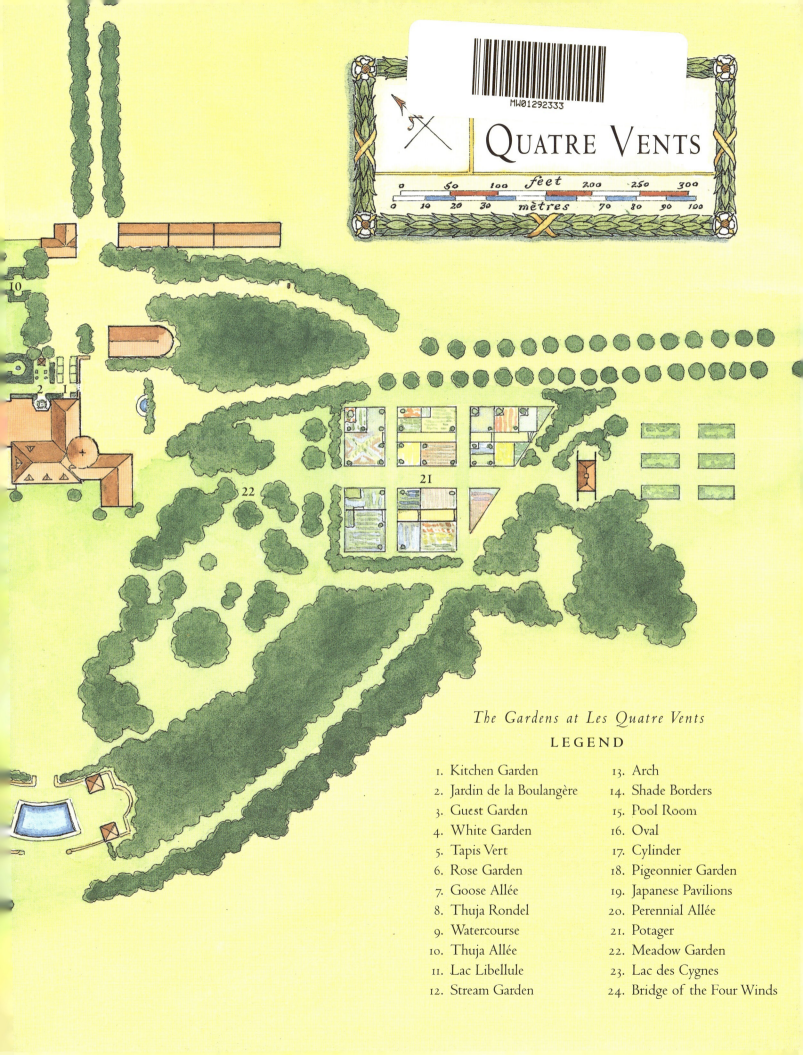

THE GREATER PERFECTION

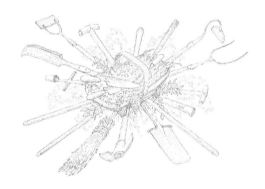

To Deborah,

Long life to those who enjoy gardens!

Paul

July 22, 2003

THE GREATER PERFECTION

The Story of the Gardens at Les Quatre Vents

FRANCIS H. CABOT

2001

A HORTUS PRESS BOOK

W.W. NORTON & COMPANY

New York   London

Copyright © 2001 by Francis H. Cabot

All rights reserved
Printed in Italy
First Edition

This book is composed in Centaur
Manufacturing by Mondadori Printing, Verona, Italy
Book design by Susan McClellan
Line drawings and maps by Nigel Hughes

Library of Congress Cataloging-in-Publication Data

Cabot, Francis H.
  The greater perfection : the story of the gardens at Les Quatre vents / Francis H. Cabot.
    p. cm.
    Includes index.
  ISBN 0-393-04189-1
    1. Les Quatre vents (La Malbaie (Quebec))—History. I. Title.

SB466.C23 Q373 2001
712'.09714'49—dc21
                                                                2001030944

W. W. Norton & Company, Inc., 500 Fifth Avenue, New York, N.Y. 10110
www.wwnorton.com

W. W. Norton & Company Ltd., Castle House, 75/76 Wells Street,
London W1T 3QT

1 2 3 4 5 6 7 8 9 0

To APC & MRK
who made it all possible

God Almighty first planted a garden; and indeed, it is the purest of human pleasures;

it is the greatest refreshment to the spirits of man;

without which buildings and palaces are but gross handy-works:

and a man shall ever see, that, when ages grow to civility and elegancy,

men come to build stately, sooner than to garden finely;

as if gardening were the greater perfection.

Francis Bacon
Of Gardens 1625

Il faut cultiver notre jardin.

Voltaire

CONTENTS

FOREWORDS
I   A Garden Rooted in the Landscape — *Laurie Olin*   8
II   A Vision of Perfection — *Penelope Hobhouse*   10

INTRODUCTION   12

I   A SENSE OF THE PLACE   16
II   THE HOUSE IN ITS SETTING   52
III   ALPINE PLANTS AND ROCKWORK   70
IV   REFURBISHING THE OLDER GARDENS   92
V   BORROWING THE LANDSCAPE   122
VI   THE STREAM GARDEN   140
VII   AN INDIRECT APPROACH   154
VIII   THE PIGEONNIER GARDENS   172
IX   A JAPANESE INTERLUDE   210
X   DEEP SHADE AND SUNNIER BORDERS   240
XI   THE WOODLAND   260
XII   POTAGER, PRAIRIE, AND PISCINE   290

AFTERWORD   310
NOTES   316
ACKNOWLEDGMENTS   319
PHOTOGRAPHY CREDITS   320
INDEX   322

D'whinnie following the antics of the ducks and geese at the far end of the Tapis Vert from a vantage point on the circular steps below the reflection pool.

FOREWORD I

A GARDEN ROOTED IN THE LANDSCAPE

Driving north, down the St. Lawrence River to La Malbaie, with heavy gray clouds pressing upon the Laurentian Mountains, you find the soils becoming thinner, the trees smaller. Birches, alders, spruce, and aspen recede into the fog with traces of snow and peach-colored leaves on the banks and rocks of the cliffs. As autumn was ending, I was making a pilgrimage to a remarkable estate and garden with great anticipation of the pleasure I was soon to have. I had seen photographs of features at Les Quatre Vents, and was curious to see the larger ensemble to which they belonged. How curious, I mused, that a great garden had been built in such a northerly place, so remote from urbanity and the more sympathetic climes in which most people indulge in horticulture.

What I found is amply described in this superb book. The story of how nine generations acquired, lived in, lost, reacquired, and more recently created the various parts of the large and rich estate that contains a finely wrought set of gardens is well told.

Like nearly all of the great gardens of the past in Western Europe and America, Les Quatre Vents is both highly personal and rooted in its context. Delightful as many parts of the garden near the house may be, a major aspect of the Cabots' garden that gives it a more serious purpose and artistic achievement is the continuing development of the surrounding woodland and agricultural elements. It was Horace Walpole in his chauvinistic essay touting the English landscape garden as the culmination of garden history who pointed out that the single most important aspect of the breakthrough in the gardens of the early eighteenth century was the elimination of walls. He praised William Kent for "calling in" the country and its distant views. Much has occurred in landscape design since then, but the notion of a garden responding to a particular sense of place — and being well connected to its situation and setting — is one of the most compelling ideas that gives character and meaning to the best designs.

Visiting Les Quatre Vents you rapidly realize that there is more to it than a collection of handsome garden rooms, water features, and pavilions. Views extend out to the surrounding fields, woods, hills, and mountains. So, too, do walks and allées. The Forêt beyond the garden proper is interlaced with several miles of drives and walks suitable for foot or horse. Wandering along them you have a feeling sought and achieved in gardens throughout history, namely that of being pleasurably lost, yet safe. Two centuries of different management of these forest "lots" has resulted in what must be at least eighteen different communities of plants. The Cabots' skill has been to make them accessible, to borrow them as extensions to the garden. Here you find spaces of all different size, shape, and color, clearings and shade, paths that are steep, paths that are gentle. The variability of the light and the bird calls, the variety and texture of the mosses and ferns compare favourably to those of the more cultivated areas of the garden near the house. The difference is largely one of the apparent artifice in each. While everything to be seen here is part of the natural ecology of the region, nowhere in the natural situation of the forest round about can one find such a concentration and particular set of situations. This is "gardening" in such a manner as to be fugitive and ephemeral. It is one pole or end of the spectrum of manipulations that comprise landscape design and gardening. Compared to the walls, steps, avenues, hedges, and herbaceous borders near the house, these woodland scenes could be mistaken for natural situations by the uninformed.

Frank and Anne Cabot's achievement is unusual today for many reasons, not least of which has been the time and resources devoted to its accomplishment. It is unusual in its great success in combining strong organization — views,

structures, linked spaces, architectural follies – with superb, even experimental horticulture. More often one find strong bones and simple-minded planting, or rich horticulture with poor or naive structure and furnishings. Frequently when both are found these days, it is a result of several different people working on a site at different times who brought their separate skills to bear. Here both are carried out with great sophistication.

The gardens at the heart of the estate present a small cosmos in the tradition of ambitious gardens through history incorporating numerous elements in different moods and styles. Think of Carmentelle's Parc Monceau with its Chinese, Moorish, Gothic, and Italianate elements, or its grand contemporary, the Désert des Retz. Yet this contemporary work on the banks of the St. Lawrence River doesn't come off as a pastiche or a zoo of pictures and themes. Each is situated within the whole in a convincing and seamless way, separated from one another visually and spatially, insuring temporal distance. A visitor must move about to reach each part. In doing so different aspects of the topography are brought into play and presented for consideration. The larger landscape has also been brought into the garden and intertwined with it through the use of native plants in the structure. The lush and robust thuja hedges that frame and shape so many of the spaces have all been dug and transplanted from the nearby hills. So, too, with the panoply of birches and maples that reach from the doorways of the house to the distant horizon. The moss and stone presented in the garden are actually part of the greater scene. Foreground and background are part of a continuum in space and time.

Les Quatre Vents is indeed in the best tradition that prompted Francis Bacon's remark that of all man's architectural and design works, it is gardens that form the greater perfection.

Laurie Olin

FOREWORD II

A VISION OF PERFECTION

FRANK CABOT IS A VISIONARY GARDENER; an amateur designer who in his own garden combines a strong "sense of place" with a quite rigid intellectual analysis of the best aspects of garden design. On one level he has created a great modern garden using all the tricks of landscape design which have evolved through centuries. Focal points, axial views, space manipulation, and borrowed scenery create a thrilling composition, in which he has freely drawn on historical precedent. Although critical of bleak historicism he has used his own visual sense to use recognizable features and "tricks" from old gardens, placing them in a new and appropriate context. French-style "rides" extend like tentacles into the forest and farmland, stitching the centre into the outlying regions and revealing distant views of the Laurentian Hills. Compartmental hedged garden rooms surrounding dark reflecting pools reveal an appreciation of Renaissance alignments as well as incorporating water steps and rills with a distinctive Islamic flavour. The design of the tall pigeonnier was the result of research into buildings of feudal France. At the bottom of a gorge buildings and foliage plants reflect an oriental influence. On quite another level, he has shown how nature works and how a contrived garden can fit into a wider landscape. With his passionate interests in plants, plant exploration, and botany, he demonstrates how a discriminating choice of plants can produce something to satisfy both aesthete and ecologist, as well as stirring the heart of the horticulturist.

This autobiography of a garden reveals much of Frank Cabot's motivation. Besides being a record of the garden's development, it demonstrates how a quite formal and theatrical layout can incorporate a composed naturalism which fits snugly into the existing lie of the land. Both

Nature and Art are triumphant. Beyond the intellectual concepts of both design and planting, the garden of Les Quatre Vents is also an appeal to the emotions. Frank Cabot has consulted Alexander Pope's dictum "let Nature never be forgot" in his own search for the "genius of the place."

Throughout the garden the constant striving for perfection ensures a constant revaluation and readjustment. Trees are lopped or pruned to keep views open, perennials annually reshuffled to maintain colour schemes, the quality and contribution of individual plants questioned. This book reveals not only the garden's inspiration but the intimate details of the maintenance required. As the years pass the fame of the garden grows. Frank and his wife Anne share it with an audience which increases annually, the Cabots drawing their own pleasure from the reaction of individuals to this extraordinary contrived landscape. The garden with all its beauty is there to stimulate emotional response, and time must be taken to allow reflection and to absorb the atmosphere. As with all great gardens, visitors are encouraged (if not urged) by the author to follow a prescribed route rather than wandering freely in order to experience in full measure the carefully manipulated elements of suspense and surprise, the intellectual appeal of design features and the delights of the decorative plantings. This book is not only the story of a garden but an essay on the finer points of gardening appreciation.

Penelope Hobhouse

INTRODUCTION

For many years visitors and garden enthusiasts asked me when I was going to write a book about Les Quatre Vents. For many years my reply was invariably "Never," since I tend to believe that there are already far too many books about gardens, and that the last thing the horticultural world needs is another — certainly not one about a single garden. But when our friend and gardening neighbour, the author Jean des Gagniers, asked if he could write a book about the garden at Les Quatre Vents, I was flattered and pleased at the prospect. I agreed to provide him with sufficient notes about the garden, its history, and its planting for him to compile his own scholarly text in French.

As soon as I began to write, however, it became clear that, for better or worse, my own book on the subject was also under way. These were to be no mere background notes: this was to be the full story. I decided to set down my own version of the evolution of the garden for posterity — lacking objectivity, of course, but as complete a record of what transpired as I could produce.

Besides, in a way the garden seemed to demand this more detailed treatment. I concluded that my record might be viewed as the garden's own autobiography, which it was my task merely to transcribe. The garden has certainly taken on a life of its own as it has matured. It has had the most profound influence on the lives of everyone intimately concerned with it, as well as influencing some who visit only occasionally. It has its own personality and story to tell, and has become very much a part of the landscape, the patrimony, and the communities that surround it. It also has a future life to consider.

Les Quatre Vents has been seventy-five years in the making, endorsing Francis Bacon's view (in the essay that gave me my book title) that stately buildings could be more readily achieved than fine gardens. It is the element of time in the life of the garden that gives us the chance to change and improve it as we constantly strive to make it perfect. Things do not happen overnight, nor can we be sure that any results we are pleased with will last. Even perfection is transitory.

Gardens come and go and change along with succeeding generations. What becomes of gardens in the longer term reflects whether their latter-day stewards have inherited their forebears' passion for the genre. Fortunately in North America more and more of the good gardens are being preserved by individuals and communities who care about them.

I hope Les Quatre Vents will continue to be a garden that gives pleasure to those who care about such things. I hope that it doesn't deteriorate once the shadow of its *patron* no longer hovers, until it becomes what Colette referred to as *"le débris d'un rêve"* and moves into what for horticulturists is the dead and dreary realm of garden history. A legal mechanism, the Charlevoix Trust, is in place to carry Les Quatre Vents into the final quarter of the new century. Whatever the state of the climate and environment at that distant moment, and whether descendants will wish to preserve what will then have been in place for over a hundred and fifty years, I would like to think that the ninth and tenth generations to enjoy the property will share the same affection for their corner of the North Shore of the St. Lawrence as those who preceded them. I would like to imagine that the scent of balsam will continue to mix with the salt air of the river and drift up the fields into the garden, along with the mist that embraces the ancient clumps of delphinium and encourages the different species of blue Tibetan poppies to proliferate.

It would be heartening if at least one member of each generation came to know and love plants in their infinite variety so that the garden's growing element was perpetually refreshed and reinvigorated by an enthusiast's hand. It would be heartening to know that future generations turned out to be equally sensitive to the aesthetics of gardens and the way they fit into their natural surroundings. But for everyone I hope that the garden will continue to provide the various joys of discovery, of peace, of whimsy, and the sense of other worlds – in particular the natural world and its inhabitants. Their pleasure in the garden and its elements will, I am sure, be a constant for many a future generation.

The biggest question I have had to face is for whom this book has been written. Although no one is likely to be interested in everything that has been included, the garden's autobiography may contain some elements, I hope, of interest to readers with different horticultural biases – just as the garden itself has aspects that interest one visitor more than another. Not everyone, for instance, will share the plantsman's penchant for citing specific plant names, or endorse my passion for primulas. But like the Emperor of Austria (whose comment on first hearing *The Abduction from the Seraglio* was "Too many notes, my dear Mozart, too many notes!"), I might answer to any reader complaining of too many primulas, or too many Latin names: "Only as many as are absolutely necessary, Your Highness." So, I suppose, the garden has resolved the question of the identity of the audience by telling its own story, and compiling something expressly for itself. I suppose that is what autobiographers often do?

Anne and I have been inordinately lucky: to have had the property in the first place; to have been the beneficiaries of my parents' devotion to it; to have had the good fortune to keep it intact, and to have had the opportunity and the resources to enlarge the garden – and, above all, to enjoy the exercise.

CHAPTER I
A SENSE OF THE PLACE

OPPOSITE

The author beside the White Garden wall in 1934.

ABOVE, RIGHT

An early involvement with plants.

I AM NOT SURE WHAT GOT ME STARTED. PERHAPS IT WAS FALLING INTO A large, raised horse trough, one of my earliest memories. Flanked by a matching pair of marble lions from China, the trough served as a decorative and functional feature in the courtyard/barnyard of Mount Murray Manor, my grandmother's summer house. The sudden submersion is still vivid more than seventy years later: the shock of the cold water, the vision of the surface light diminishing as I sank to the bottom, and the realization of what was in store for me for soaking my brand new, and best, pink suit. A photograph confirms the details just before the event but, alas, no one had the presence of mind to capture what must have been a highly entertaining aftermath.

I had been fascinated by the trough. Some sixteen feet in diameter, it was surrounded by a handsome, stout, capped limestone wall and in its center was a roughly circular rock with an irregular surface from which water bubbled — what the locals call a *roche pleureuse*. With a new appreciation of this irresistible body of water on which to launch miniature sailboats, I noticed that over the years the rock had become covered with moss and that tiny trees, mostly seedling conifers, were sprouting on it, resulting in a beautiful, natural and, in retrospect, almost Japanese scene. Perhaps it was this awareness that first kindled subconsciously my interest in gardening. In later years the trough was moved to an uncle's house, *sans* centerpiece. The memory of that charming and mossy island was sufficient to cause it to be repeated later in two water features in the garden at Les Quatre Vents, where the constant dribbling of water on stone resulted in a suitably luxuriant and mossy upholstery. Another trough with an island has recently been reincorporated in the newly restored Manor courtyard and is slowly becoming covered with moss, this time supplemented by the spray meeting overhead from the jets of two dolphins. All that is needed is the chance conifer seedling and a grandchild who delights in miniature sailboats to complete the circle.

Beside the water trough at Mount Murray Manor before the dunking in 1928. The author and his uncle Quincy Sewell Cabot.

My pink suit got a workout that summer for, shortly after its baptism, it was worn for the groundbreaking ceremony in which I dutifully tried to dig the first spadeful of the field in which the house of Les Quatre Vents was destined to materialize. The year was 1928 and the ceremony was supervised by proud grandparents, who had given that particular corner of the property to my father, and was watched by a crew of faithful, if amused, retainers who were about to undertake the real work.

I don't remember the ceremony itself, but I have a photograph of the occasion which delights me because, where now stand a house, outbuildings, and extensive gardens, there were only empty fields and woodlands in all directions. Until the house was built, this spot, known as Sunset Hill, was where family and friends would gather to picnic and catch the sun setting behind the muted cordillera of the Laurentians to the west and north. It delights me because the setting, in my mind at least, hasn't suffered from what has been placed upon it. The contrived landscape and structures blend into the surrounding fields, forests and hills, which provide a reassuring contrast to the civilized central vantage point. It delights me because I realize that for my entire life this place and its surroundings have been more important to me than anything else, with the exception of family and loved ones, and that my preoccupation just may have produced a good example of what the cultural landscape should be — a bridge between Man and Nature.

Early excursions with my beloved and long-suffering nurse Edith[1] piqued my interest and curiosity with nature. Edith, in the best English tradition, believed in the importance of taking long walks. We would set off into the hinterland, skirting the

The author breaking ground at the site on Sunset Hill with grandparents Maud and Frank Cabot (1928). In those days cellars were dug by hand and those workmen would have been paid une piastre - the equivalent of a dollar - a day.

cow pastures so as not to enrage the disagreeable Jersey bull. Some days we walked down to the beach on a road that paralleled the shoreline through ancient and majestic groves of white cedar (*Thuja occidentalis*). Other times we picked wild strawberries in the rocky meadows, climbed the sandy hillsides to pick wild raspberries or blueberries and, almost always, strolled through the balsam-scented boreal forest with its carpet of mosses, lichens, mushrooms, and wildflowers. As I grew older there were games and other children to play with, eventually leading to golf and tennis, but these obligatory activities could never hold a candle in my universe to the joys of a close association with nature. Clearing trails through the different ecosystems of the surrounding forests, camping, portaging, fishing, and hunting in the mountains, especially in the pristine wilderness, were the activities I preferred.

I have a powerful memory of a woodland copse that abuts one side of the front lawn at Les Quatre Vents. The young spruce trees colonizing the corner of the field were small enough for my father to jump over as a child at the turn of the century. Today they are virtually all gone, having succumbed to the ravages of the spruce budworm,[2] which finds mature specimens particularly to its taste, and a woodland garden, shaded by deciduous trees, has taken their place. But in 1930 the spruce were approaching their apogee. A wagon path ran through them, above a steep ravine through which rushed a brook. Somehow I managed to get in the way of a workhorse hauling a loaded tumbril and was duly run over by one of its large iron-bound wheels. While escaping without any significant injury, I was sufficiently squashed into the soft woodland duff to evoke a surprising amount of sympathy and concern from the workmen. I enjoyed being the center of their attention and, again, the memory is crystal clear – of lying on the damp ground looking up at the anxious faces of friendly folk; of tall conifers rising to the sky; of the horse nonchalantly turning its head to look back and see what all the fuss was about, and of the pervading smell of woodland soil – rich, pungent and, to this day, evocative – a magic amalgam of conifer needles, rotting leaves, and humusy sand. There was an awareness of the ravine and of the wildness of it all.

In time I forgot about the existence of the ravine and it was only some forty-five years later that I was reintroduced to it while clearing up the dead spruce trees on its rim. The childhood experience flooded back in vivid detail. At the same time came the vision of what the ravine could be as an element in the garden, an unexpected bonus – a bit of topographical lagniappe – that has now become a favored part of the whole.

That same part of the woodland became the spot where my mother would send me off into the wilderness to find presents hidden expressly for me by the fairies on birthdays and special celebrations. I must have been pretty young to swallow the idea and not object to the practice. Nevertheless, the sense of magic, of expectation, of finding something special, has lingered to this day. The woodland garden has become an exercise in discovery, not only for visiting woodland-plant enthusiasts, but for me as well. Treasures have been added to it over so many years that I have difficulty remembering what I have planted. Invariably I am joyfully surprised when I come across a forgotten introduction that has suddenly come into its own and is proudly displaying its charms. Those fairies are a persistent lot.

BACKGROUND

Jacques Cartier first sailed past the sloping woodlands on the north shore of the St. Lawrence, where Les Quatre Vents is located, in the autumn of 1535. He continued some eighty miles further upriver to the site of the future citadel of Quebec before returning to France, but it wasn't until 1608 that Samuel de Champlain systematically explored this great inland sea, giving names to the bays and coves and the rivers that flow into it.

Champlain must have arrived to anchor in our bay at high tide, just as it was getting dark, for he had a rude awakening when his ship keeled over in the middle of the night, stranded on a mud flat. He is reported to have said "*Quelle salle baie!*" and proceeded to name it La Malbaie. In recent years raw sewage flowing into the bay from the small

OPPOSITE, ABOVE

The North Shore of the St. Lawrence from just above Quebec to the Saguenay Fjord.

BELOW

A late eighteenth-century rendering of La Malbaie and its seigneuries.

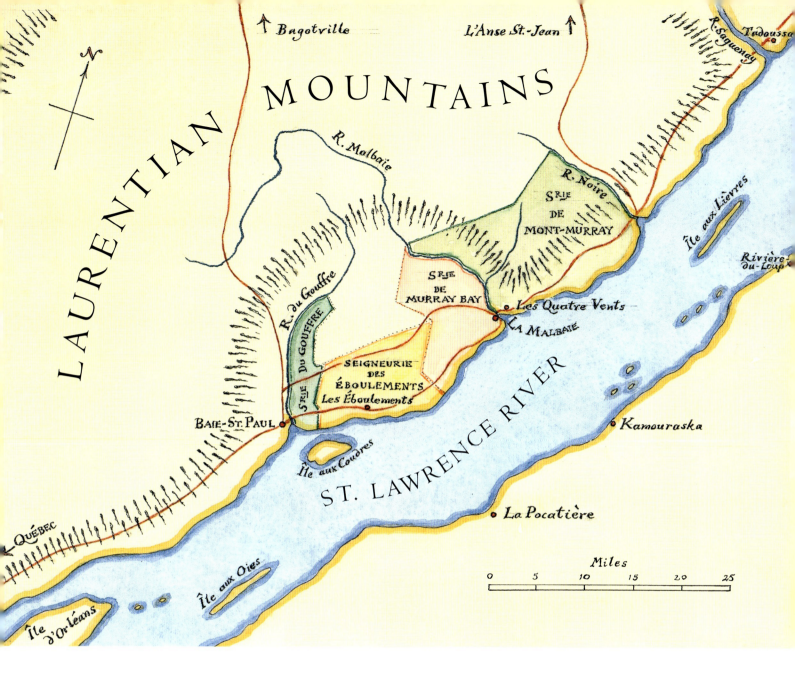

communities that surround it have reinforced the appropriateness of Champlain's epithet. At low tide in the heat of summer it has been a Malbaie indeed.

When Louis XIV undertook the settlement of La Nouvelle France he parcelled out large tracts of land, known as seigneuries, to those of his favored subjects who were willing to undertake the uncertain business of colonizing these distant territories. These seigneuries were similar to the patents granted to the Livingston and Philipse families along the east bank of the Hudson and, in some cases, covered hundreds of square miles. The seigneuries were different, however, in that they adhered to the feudal system of seventeenth-century France, with the tenant colonists obliged to use the *moulin banal*, or communal grist mill, and to share the proceeds with the seigneur, a practice that was abandoned in 1854.

The Seigneurie de la Malbaie, consisting ultimately of 150 square miles, along with many other seigneuries, was granted to Jean Bourdon, Surveyor General of the Colony of New France in 1653 and passed back and forth between the crown and various individuals for the next century. At the time of the English conquest of New France in 1758, the few habitations at La Malbaie were put to the torch by a British force on their way up river to attack the citadel of Quebec. The Seigneurie of La Malbaie was appropriated by General Murray, who had succeeded to the command of the occupation forces and the new British territory after General Wolfe's death on the Plains of Abraham. Murray divided the property into two parcels and granted them for a pittance to two of his favorite officers: the sixty-square-mile Seigneurie of Murray's Bay on the southern side of the bay went to Lieutenant John Nairne and a ninety-square-mile Seigneurie of Mount Murray, on its northern side, to Lieutenant Malcolm Fraser. La Malbaie and the Rivière Malbaie soon came to be known as Murray's Bay, or Murray Bay, and the Murray River.

Nairne built a Manor House in 1762. He and his descendants married their countrymen, the descendants returning to England for their education, with the sons fighting in English wars and systematically perishing. The last female member of the family died without issue in 1884, leaving the large property to a friend who, in turn, bequeathed it to his half brother whose family enjoyed the property for some years but who, regrettably, sold off bits and pieces of their windfall during their tenure so that by 1960 nothing of this historic site remained.[3]

Malcolm Fraser, on the other hand, lived a more North American life. He continued his military career, defending Quebec during the American Revolution and serving during the war of 1812. He was also commercially active, establishing colonists on his land and acquiring a second seigneurie on the south shore of the St. Lawrence near Rivière-du-Loup. He and his descendants married local French women and he established separate families on both of his seigneuries, commuting between them across the fourteen miles of the often choppy St. Lawrence in a rowboat.

In the 1780s Malcolm Fraser built a modest house on his seigneurie's Beach Farm, in a protected field along the bay at the point where it joined the St. Lawrence and where eels are now harvested in weirs each October. Scant evidence remains of the contrived landscape between the house site and the beach, channeling the eye to different views of the river/sea. His son, William Malcolm, built a suitably commodious Manor House on a bluff overlooking Beach Farm and the bay and river in the mid-1820s.

It was from William's great-nephew, John Fraser Reeve, that my great-grandfather, George T. Bonner, purchased the Seigneurie of Mount Murray in 1902 for $50,000.

George Bonner was proud of the fact that his ancestors were of "good yeoman stock." His father, John, emigrated in 1813 from Monkwearmouth, near Durham, to Quebec, where he established a lumber business. In 1842 George Bonner, aged five, and his siblings were sent downriver from Quebec to spend the summer on Beach Farm below the Frasers' Mount Murray Manor, to escape a cholera epidemic in the city. From then on he returned regularly. When he married he brought his new wife Isabel Sewell to a rented cottage in the village of Pointe-au-Pic in 1870. Isabel was a descendant of two early Chief Justices of Lower Canada, including Jonathan Sewell and his father-in-law, the historian William Smith who had formerly been Chief Justice of the New York Colony. The Bonners built their own summer house (which still exists as 'Le Barachois') in 1898, and played an active role in the beginnings of the summer colony.

Bonner was a childhood friend of John Fraser Reeve, the last male heir of Malcolm Fraser to live in Mount Murray Manor, and together they enjoyed the summer pleasures of the St. Lawrence riverfront life afforded by the seigneurie, which had originally stretched for some fifteen miles along the north shore to the village of St. Siméon at the mouth of the Rivière Noire. Limestone cliffs and outcroppings result in a rich flora along the shore, with giant white cedars and clumps of the fairy orchid (*Calypso bulbosa*) poking their colorful heads in late May through carpets of moss. An extraordinarily varied geology can be traced along the beach's edge, evidence of the impact of the asteroid that created La Malbaie and its surroundings in the first instance, and

On the Beach, Murray Bay
J.B. Wilkinson (1871).

The beach road circa 1900. The view is essentially unchanged today.

on a more everyday level providing a marvelous playground for children, with tidal pools and fossilized rocks to scramble over.

Bonner left Quebec in 1852 for New York at the age of fifteen to live with his elder brother John (who later became the editor of the *New York Times*) and to make his way in the world. Starting out as an errand boy in a chemist's shop, he went to work for de Coppet, a brokerage firm, where his knowledge of French led to his handling of the firm's business with France. He ended up with his own successful firm and was able to retire in 1877, at the age of forty, and devote much of the rest of his life to salmon fishing. He and his friend William Paterson of Montreal would abandon their families and spend much of their summers fishing the great rivers of the Gaspé, bringing along a bottle of champagne to celebrate the first salmon weighing over forty pounds. (In those days the Murray River, which constituted the southern boundary of the seigneurie for a length of six miles, was a superb salmon river. At one point Bonner took a 53-pound salmon from its waters.) Unfortunately, he did not believe that either women or children should be associated with salmon fishing, with the consequences that his three daughters and their offspring had little exposure to the sport of kings.

ABOVE

A thoroughly idealized version of beach life at Murray Bay at the turn of the century. The water temperature rarely gets above 45° F.

RIGHT

George Bonner's acquisition of Mount Murray was considered to be news by the New York Herald *in 1902.*

Towards the end of the century Bonner hoped to acquire the island of Anticosti in the northern St. Lawrence when it was offered at auction. However he was outbidden by Monsieur "Chocolat" Meunier, who acquired the island, with its seven salmon rivers, for $125,000. In 1902, still chagrined at having lost the chance to acquire his dream, he ran into his childhood friend, John Fraser Reeve, in the bar of the Garrison Club in Quebec. Reeve, childless and in deteriorating health, told him to stop grumbling and suggested that he could buy the Seigneurie de Mont-Murray for $50,000 instead. Bonner jumped at the chance and, since he had recently built a commodious summer cottage across the bay, proceeded to give the property to his eldest daughter, Maud, who had married my grandfather and namesake, Francis Higginson Cabot, and was in the process of raising four children.

In due course Maud's younger sisters, Mabel and Isabel, lobbied for equal treatment. Despite my grandmother's entreaties, her father opted to sell off the great bulk of the seigneurie's land and forests for some $250,000, which became Mabel and Isabel's share of the spoils.

George Bonner was very much a builder of the summer community across the bay, interesting his friends in shorefront property adjacent to his summer house and being a principal founder of what is said to be one of the oldest golf clubs in North America. Fortunately, an attempt to develop part of the seigneurie's acreage for summer homes never got off the ground and the dramatic cedar and spruce forests that drape

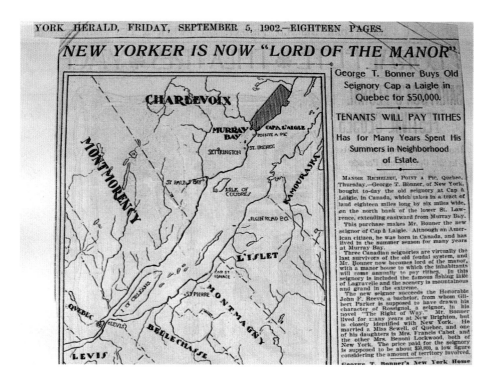

the hilly shore and limestone cliffs along the St. Lawrence remain inviolate.

Maud Cabot still owned Mount Murray Manor and some 500 surrounding acres, and proceeded to enjoy the life of chatelaine to the fullest extent, reveling in the summer colony activities and spending as much time in the woods as she could, trout fishing and hunting. (It was only in her later years that she finally got a chance to fish for salmon.) My grandfather was definitely the quieter and more subdued spouse, and acquiesced as "Mootzie," as she was known to her family, dominated the lives of those who let her get away with it. My father was the exception. He had regularly won scholarships at Harvard and, with a $3,000 loan from his father, quickly achieved financial independence. Maud, a suffragette and founding member of New York's Colony Club, put the family on the map. In Boston other family members referred to our branch as the Bonner Cabots.

OPPOSITE

George and Isabel Sewell Bonner on the front lawn of their Pointe-au-Pic house in 1898.

RIGHT

Maud Cabot at the Pointe-au-Pic house in 1901 with the author's father, Higgie, and his younger brother, George Bonner Cabot, dressed for church.

ABOVE, LEFT

"Snake" fences in the fields above the Manor barnyard.

ABOVE, RIGHT

Beach Farm below Mount Murray Manor.

Tuesday teas at the Manor were an important part of the weekly round from late June through mid-September. The summer residents showed up *en masse* with their guests for garden-strolling, tennis, and the occasional icy plunge in the dark waters of a deep circular pool overseen by a version of Verrocchio's *Boy with a Dolphin*. In mid-season there could be up to a hundred guests, and the long dining-room table proffered a Victorian's dream of what tea should be.

Iced tea and hot tea were dispensed at opposite ends of the table. I took more interest in the former on hot summer afternoons and have spent much of my life trying to reproduce the delicious brew served up by Sarah Mulhern, Mootzie's factotum. Sarah had started working as a barmaid in Ireland before ending up in my grandmother's employ, for the rest of her life as it turned out. Sarah would make the iced tea on a Monday, leaving it to steep overnight in a pail with the halved lemons whose juice had been added to the brew along with sugar and a touch of mint. By Tuesday afternoon the dark mixture, poured over ice with a slice of lemon, was the ultimate refreshment. Sarah also produced her version of the local specialty, *sucre à la crème*, a wicked combination under any circumstances but thoroughly lethal when the sugar was shaved from the darkest of brown sugar bars and cooked with Jersey cream. So lethal, in fact, that any effort to match Sarah's creation has been abandoned in favor of longevity.

The sideboard, in turn, held the berries of the season accompanied by Jersey cream so thick that a spoon was needed to transfer it to one's plate. Berried fruits from northern gardens and fields have an incomparable taste. The amber-colored "white"

Higgie with his father Frank on the Pointe-au-Pic beach circa 1899.

raspberries of late July were probably the best and, with sugar and a dollop of that life-threatening cream, may have been as close to ambrosia as one can get.

Mootzie ran a very tight, if comfortably nourished, ship. She would rise at 5:00 am when morning tea was brought to her room, and worked on her correspondence until breakfast was served, promptly, at 7:30. After breakfast, dressed in a skirt, sports jacket and tie and a straw fedora hat, she would be off to the extensive cutting garden to gather flowers. The Manor rooms were filled with the scents of summer: fragrant lilacs, and then peonies, spires of delphiniums, bowls of sweet peas, and meadow flowers in abundance.

The house guests were usually women and almost invariably forceful women, some younger, some older. I knew what stage of summer was at hand by who was there. Mary Cabot Wheelwright, the Bostonian who did much to preserve the Navajo culture in New Mexico, was a July regular. So was another spinster, Mary Lee of Chestnut Hill, Massachusetts and Westport, New York. Mary had written the prize-winning *It's*

a Great War, chronicling her World War One experiences as an ambulance driver in the Red Cross in France. She loved to tell the story of going to a Harvard lecture on her book and hearing the speaker point out the strong influence James Joyce's *Ulysses* had on her work. This amused her no end since she had never read any of Joyce's books. Mary was a great camper and source of woods lore, as well as a brilliant correspondent. She also introduced me at the age of twelve to my first cigarette.

Another devotee of the North Woods was Bessie Stevens, who would come to the Manor each September and go off for an extended camping trip with Maud in that best of seasons. There were partridge and trout in abundance, canvas tents with floors of freshly picked and fragrant balsam boughs to cushion the sleeping bags, camp fires

Maud and Frank Cabot enjoying a winter picnic in the Forêt, *circa 1910.*

ABOVE

Mount Murray Manor in 1915.

OVERLEAF

The Manor as it is today. After the house was rebuilt in the early 1990s, the property was screened from the increasingly noisy main road with forested berms. A lake and Italianate garden, with a "cup and saucer," now replace the former vegetable garden and a field.

of spruce and fir, poetry to be read and pipes to be smoked. Bessie was tall and wonderfully handsome with striking white hair. I was sufficiently overcome by this engaging and powerful figure in my twelfth summer to ask for her hand in marriage, despite well over sixty years difference in our ages. She let me down easily and we remained the best of friends.

There is no stronger sense of place than that where one spends one's summers as a child. The Smiths and the Sewells established deep roots here in Quebec at the end of the eighteenth century, as did their descendants, and the Bonners and Cabots, after them. Now that nine generations of the family have been consistently exposed to this corner of North America it is small wonder that we have a deep attachment to it.

SURROUNDINGS

It was a meteorite that violently changed the topography of what is now Charlevoix County some 350,000,000 years ago. Its explosive impact on the mountainous mass that skirts the north shore of the St. Lawrence as it widens dramatically above Quebec resulted in a peak ring within a circular crater. The rim of the crater now consists of two river valleys that curve down to the St. Lawrence. La Seigneurie de Mont-Murray, and Les Quatre Vents within it, are located along its northern edge where the Rivière Malbaie flows into La Malbaie.

Charlevoix County is considered to be the "Switzerland" of Quebec. Here the granite mass of the Laurentians, clothed in the spruce and fir mantle of the boreal forest, meets the salt-water coastline for the first time and is at its most dramatic. These two elements — boreal forest and salt water — are the norm until one reaches the tundra and permafrost of Labrador. They dominate the ecological and horticultural life of the region and are responsible for the deep winter snow cover and cool, foggy summers that so enhance the performance and durability of perennials. The fact that Les Quatre Vents is situated in the rim of the crater, near the St. Lawrence at a point where it has become an inland sea, means that it enjoys a Zone 4 maritime climate tucked into a land mass where Zone 3 is the rule, another benign factor in its favor.

In the eighteenth century the seigneurial *censitaires* cleared the boreal forest in the less mountainous portions of Charlevoix. Family farms in long, thin strips running from the shore to the wooded hills enabled the *habitant* to have access to the river and its harvest of fish, to cultivate fields for his family's nourishment and the support of his livestock, and to use the trees from his woodlot for lumber and fuel. Once a riverfront area was colonized, a road was built along its forested border and a new *rang* would be established, this time without access to the St. Lawrence, but often incorporating a river or stream filled with trout and suitable for the occasional mill.

Before World War Two, one of my parents' favorite after-dinner pastimes, in the long twilights of early summer, was to take their guests on a twelve-mile drive in their open Buick touring car up one side of the Murray River valley to Clermont and back down the other. They passed mostly farms with the occasional mill, dairy, forge, or general store; there was no traffic other than the occasional horse and buggy or Model A Ford. Some of the farmhouses dated from the eighteenth century and the fields were enclosed with "snake" fences of split cedar. The houses were heated by birch firewood, stacked in cord after cord outside the kitchen wing behind the outdoor oven or *four à pain*, and lit by kerosene lanterns that would twinkle through the open doors and windows. Often a family could be glimpsed seated around the kitchen table. There were herds of cattle, flocks of sheep, gaggles of barnyard fowl, great shaggy work horses and oxen — the whole an apparent idyll of a peaceful, bucolic existence. It could just as well have

OPPOSITE

Echium vulgare *(an indicator of poor soil) adds a touch of July color to a meadow grazed by Highland cattle.*

ABOVE

Calypso bulbosa, *the fairy orchid.*

The old haybarn in the Pinière, one of the seigneurie's hillside pastures, with a view across the valley of the Malbaie River.

been a corner of Normandy.[4] Charlevoix County's population peaked in the early nineteenth century, reaching over 35,000. Today things are different. The bulk of the land has reverted to secondary forest, the family farm is a rarity and the young leave to seek employment elsewhere.

The predominant ecological influence in Charlevoix is the boreal forest and the many ecosystems within it. In those that have developed in the secondary growth forests, one can observe the rate of ecological change virtually as it happens. I never cease to wonder at the changeability of the forests.

For a number of years, before becoming hopelessly involved in the making and maintaining of gardens, I spent my holidays cutting horse trails through the seigneurie's and adjoining forests to give my wife Anne, a devoted equestrian, a choice for her daily rides. I was able to induce my mother, before she died in 1965, to purchase adjacent, abandoned farms. The price in those days was irresistible, some few dollars per acre for the most part, and in time the seigneurie's acreage was more than doubled and now constitutes several square miles. Not only did the enlarged unit

A horse trail in the Forêt *runs through a mixed conifer forest carpeted with caribou moss* (Cladinia sp.)

provide a haven for the local fauna (bears, wolves, moose in more recent years, and – at the turn of the millennium – a cougar) but, since each strip had its own farm road running the length of the property, it was a simple matter to cut trails at different points across the parallel strips so that a network of riding and walking trails emerged in great variety. Each neighboring farm owner had handled his woodlot and farmland differently during the two centuries that the forest had been worked, with the result that every two or three *arpents*[5] of width of each farm means, today, a different eco-system. There must be at least fifteen distinct habitats in all on the property from climax forests of a single species, such as birch (*Betula papyrifera*), jack pine (*Pinus banksiana*), red pine (*Pinus resinosa*), white spruce (*Picea glauca*), black spruce (*Picea mariana*), or balsam fir (*Abies balsamea*), to mixed forests with majestic white or red pines towering over aspen, birch, larch, maple, mountain ash, and amelanchier. The shrubs, groundcovers, mosses, wildflowers, and fungi vary widely in each ecosystem as a consequence of the diversity of soils and the amount of light, providing lessons in plant association.

PREVIOUS

A kilometer-long paper birch allée forms a golden swath in October along a farm road.

OPPOSITE

A woodland trail in the Forêt *running through a patch of* Cornus canadensis *carpeting a stand of balsam fir (*Abies balsamea*).*

BELOW

The choicest member of the Pyrolaceae, Moneses uniflora, *with a species of* Marasmius.

The trail-cutting not only satisfied some primal urge, as well as releasing the frustrations that beset all of us, but it also revealed how the forest works; where the partridge, foxes, and hares are likely to be; which ecosystem each wildflower, especially one of the ground orchids, prefers. The natural succession, with seedlings of fir suddenly appearing in sheets in certain habitats while spruce seedlings appear in others, is a marvel full of promise that the deciduous trees, which colonize after a conifer forest has been harvested, are about to acquire the evergreen contrast that so enhances their beauty through the seasons. All this happens so fast in woodlands building towards climax; the raw trail is soon covered with moss and needs clearing and, suddenly, it is a different place.

I remember one golden and brisk August afternoon when I had been cutting a random, winding trail through dense woods and suddenly came upon an ancient farm road leading back towards the river. The road and the floor of the surrounding woodlands of mature black spruce were a carpet of bright green moss filled with unknown and bizarre mushrooms. The road was branched over leaving only a waist-high clearance below the branches as far as the eye could see, indicating that it hadn't been used for many, many years. When the branches were lifted, and a tunnel high enough for horse and rider established, the mossy road was dubbed "Fairy Land," an enchanted setting.[6] Two species of rattlesnake plaintain (*Goodyera repens* and *tesselata*) made stunning clumps along its edges, dark green, variegated jewels set against the bright green background.

Fairy Land became the preferred destination on all rides and, while the mature white spruce in the surrounding woodlands succumbed to the spruce budworm, the mature black spruce surrounding Fairy Land appeared to be immune. Or so we thought until one summer, when sunlight began to appear in patches in that normally shady dell. Deciduous seedlings followed and, all at once, Fairy Land was gone; the dead trees harvested, the slash burned, and a forest of impenetrable seedling birches and mountain maple (*Acer spicatum*) established, so thick that it was impossible to tell whether the orchids and the moss were still there. I suspect that they are, however, and ten years after the demise of Fairy Land and almost thirty years after its discovery, the occasional seedling conifer appears in the new young forest, a hint of what lies ahead when the moss returns and the goodyera reappear.

There is another spot in the forest, a plateau with a stand of mature *Pinus banksiana* and a thick carpet of pine needles on almost pure sand, which is an indicator that it once skirted a glacial moraine. The plateau looks out over a steep hillside across the seigneurie's fields to the Murray River and its "bad bay" and the villages on the far shore, indistinct except for the steeple of the handsome Pointe-au-Pic church which punctuates the headland as it slants down to the deep, icy, turbulent main channel of the St. Lawrence. The plateau, with its soft needles, provides the ideal spot for an extended canter as well as a jump ride and slopes imperceptibly up into a stand of

mature red pine. The setting is an ideal habitat for the pink ladyslipper (*Cypripedium acaule*) which appears in hundreds, if not thousands, in every shade from the darkest maroon to the most pristine white. The alliterative opportunity was too good to pass up and it was dubbed "Ladyslipper Slope."

That was some forty years ago and it is now apparent that the plants in the colony,

The view from Les Quatre Vents' upper fields, overlooking the bay and village of Pointe-au-Pic with Cap-aux-Oies in the background jutting into the St. Lawrence.

which is about four acres in extent, move to those places that best suit them, where the exposure, the shade cover and the light are just right for their growth. In some spots, young seedling spruce and fir are appearing and the ladyslipper clumps that once were thick in those areas have dwindled, with other areas once empty now filled with plants. With such a subtle ecology, no wonder the species is virtually untransplantable, no matter how much of the surrounding soil accompanies it. I am experimenting in the spots where the volume of plants has dwindled, cutting back the new growth of young conifers to see if the area will be recolonized. It would seem logical that one could manage the habitat, but then what would happen when the pines reached senility or suffered a blowdown and there was nothing left at all? Should nature just take its course? The pines, after all, are themselves aliens, planted as a crop in a sandy field by a farmer over a hundred years ago.

A woodland has its own life-cycle. We have seen an ecosystem on the limestone bluff known as Pointe-à-Gaz that was completely wiped out. Pictures of this bluff at the turn of the last century show majestic towering spruce and cedar arching over a road along the beachfront. When the lot of managing the seigneurie fell to me in the 1960s there was no more impressive forest on the property. I shall never forget climbing up to the brow of the overhanging plateau through centuries of rotting,

PREVIOUS

*The pink ladyslipper (*Cypripedium acaule*) flourishes on "Ladyslipper Slope."*

LEFT

Calypso bulbosa, *the choicest and rarest of the ground orchids.*

mossy fallen tree trunks in late May one year and coming upon a drift of the fairy orchid (*Calypso bulbosa*) carpeting the mossy forest floor as far as the eye could see. It was a breathtaking sight: up to that point I had seen the elusive calypso only very occasionally as an isolated single clump in the deepest of forests. These covered several acres, running through a stand of mature white cedar mixed with a few mature spruce on a limestone outcrop buried under deep moss. Here were thousands of them, many of them white-flowered.

The spruce were getting to the point where they were slowly dying of senility. This proved too tempting for a new, young farm manager who saw value being wasted and, unbeknownst to me, proceeded to harvest the mature spruce one winter, proudly announcing the receipt of $10,000 for the timber the next spring. The manager, now in his fifties, is still with us and we couldn't enjoy or manage the property without him. It is a testament to his tenacity and resilience that he survived the fury of our reaction to the desecration of this magical corner of the property. Mary Lee, who continued coming for summer visits well after the death of Mootzie and my parents, castigated me unmercifully for having allowed the destruction of something that was irreplaceable and guilt, despite the circumstances, weighed heavily on my soul.

To some extent the guilt was later assuaged by the loss of *all* mature spruce on the seigneurie, wherever situated, due to spruce budworm. Mootzie's dictum never to harvest trees on the property resulted in a sea change to the landscape, with the dark green forests turning first a sickly brown and then a bleak grey as the insect destroyed the habitat. The dead trees were harvested within three years to salvage some of their value

An autumn view from the Pinière towards the Laurentians with a stand of aspen in the middle ground.

and to clear the forests so that one could walk through them. (The alternative was to wait a century or two while the fallen trunks slowly settled to the ground and rotted.) The manager had merely done something which would have been necessary in a few years in any event. I can only hope that Mary Lee's indomitable, but now ethereal, spirit can somehow sense this mitigation.

Nevertheless, the consequences of interfering with an ecosystem were ineradicably driven home. Once the spruce were gone many of the giant cedars began to succumb to gales and the calypso plateau was rendered inaccessible. Now we are pleased when we can find a hundred in bloom at the beginning and end of the wagon road to the beach. Once or twice I have scrambled through the tangle of giant, fallen trunks to the edge of the bluff and seen the occasional surviving calypso in the midst of the chaos. The task of clearing the area is herculean: I only hope that some descendant who cares will undertake the job and be rewarded by the joyful response of the calypso as their habitat is made rehabitable.

After British friends have had a thorough look at the garden, we make a point of walking them for half a day through some of the forest ecosystems (it would take several days to do the lot) to give them a feel of the boreal woodland, so different from the ones they are used to. Rosemary Verey, who first came in 1983, was struck by the number of great botanists and plant hunters who were commemorated in the flora. Not only the great Linnaeus, in the twinflower (*Linnaea borealis*) that carpets the woodlands, and Peter Kalm, whose travels in Quebec in 1749 stopped a few miles short of the seigneurie, in the sheep laurel (*Kalmia angustifolia*), but the English explorers: John Goodyer, in the three species of goodyera (*oblongifolia*, *repens*, and *tesselata*), and Sir Joseph Banks, in the stands of *Pinus banksiana* (Charlevoix County boasts the southernmost outposts of this genus). John Bartram of Pennsylvania is commemorated in that choicest of the serviceberries, the shrubby *Amelanchier bartramiana*, which is found in the Laurentians and the higher elevations of the Appalachians but is hardly ever found, alas, in gardens since it is very difficult to propagate from seed or cuttings.[7]

It is worth taking the trouble to try and establish *Amelanchier bartramiana* in the garden, however, not only in honor of John Bartram but for its large, oval fruits and white flowers, the largest of the genus, as well as for its leaves, which vary from bronze to pale green as they emerge in the spring and turn to burnished orange in late September. It grows slowly, attaining a maximum height of five to six feet at maturity and is compact with a sympathetic and slightly irregular outline such as one finds in specimens of ancient English box.

The natural woodlands are the dominating feature of the property and a world unto themselves, filled with the scents and the sounds of untrammeled nature — the pungency of balsam and thuja, the wind in the treetops, the song of the wood thrush and the hoot of the great horned owl. They provide a kaleidoscope of color from the delicate leaves of early spring to the pyrotechnics of autumn, the evergreen component anchoring the whole, a perfect contrast during the long white winter when animal tracks are all that mar the surface of the deep snow.

It is when one emerges from this magical woodland world that one discovers the rest; looking over the fields to the Murray River winding down its valley some six miles from the pulp mill in the neighboring town, beyond which its long and happy course can be traced back through the gorges and high mountains in the distance; looking across the bay, alternating between mud flats and a shimmering high tide, and the wooded hills above it; looking out over the great St. Lawrence to the villages on the south shore, some fourteen miles away, glinting in the afternoon sun; looking down towards the complex of gardens and structures that make up Les Quatre Vents, with horses and sheep and Highland cattle grazing in the surrounding fields.

ABOVE

In July the Forêt *is carpeted with the dainty twinflower (*Linnaea borealis*), a circumboreal plant named in honor of the great Carl von Linné.*

PREVIOUS

Highland cattle graze in a meadow against the backdrop of the Laurentians.

*Bunchberry or ground cornel (*Cornus canadensis*) enlivens the boreal forest. The handsome flowers are followed by clusters of red berries. In mid-September the foliage turns a dark gray-purple. Where the habitat is to its liking it becomes a rapacious colonizer.*

The French say: "*La nuit porte conseil,*" meaning that waking often brings the solution to some pressing problem that was on one's mind when one went to bed. I like to think: "*Le site porte conseil.*" What we learn from our surroundings when we watch and listen carefully and patiently is invaluable. I find that a solution to questions about how to deal with the landscape, within or outside the garden, will gradually reveal itself. I have listened intently for twenty-five years and, striving for the Greater Perfection, have derived the purest of pleasures from doing so. I am still listening. There is so much to hear.

Having wandered through the boreal forest and become aware of its importance to the setting and the garden within it, we should have somewhat of a sense of place. It is time, at last, to focus on the contrived landscape.

CHAPTER II
THE HOUSE
IN ITS SETTING

OPPOSITE

A view of Les Quatre Vents and its surroundings from the south. Lupines have begun naturalizing in the arc of meadow below the house and garden

ABOVE, RIGHT

The four à pain *in the Bread Garden.*

THE POINTS OF THE COMPASS WARRANT CONSIDERATION WHEN YOU ARE siting a prospective house. There are sensible folk who appreciate the importance of nestling the building into a site protected from the winds, forsaking panoramic views for the peace and quiet of a sheltered nook. Not so my father. The winds were either incidental or unconsidered when it came to implanting his dream house on Sunset Hill. I have a vision of him as an adolescent, wandering up to Sunset Hill from Mount Murray Manor and determining that one day he would build *his* house so that it could enjoy both the panoramic view to the west and the view across the bay towards Pointe-au-Pic.[8] His instinctive choice of a site would lead to an elaborate series of gardens, inextricably linked to the alignment he had chosen, that over the years (especially the last thirty years) has encroached upon a great deal of the surrounding farmland. The "capabilities" of this landscape were developed initially by a professional architect brought on to the scene after the house had been built, then enhanced by a talented and artistic garden landscaper. They have been completed by an enthusiastic autodidact obsessed with plants, whose enthusiasm has spread to pursuing the art of linking the gardens to their natural surroundings. As a consequence, despite the inconstant winds that attack the site from every direction (the head gardener, Raynald Bergeron, claims the place should have been called Les Huit Vents), a series of axes and vistas, of framing devices and revealed views, has resulted in a complex but unified garden landscape.

In the beginning things were more simple. My father always claimed that he designed the summer house he built on Sunset Hill on the back of an envelope. Begun in 1928 (when that sod was turned), it was a simple rectangular two-story box to which was soon added a guest and servants' wing. The house was surrounded by fields, pastures, and unobstructed views in all directions. To the west lay Sunset Hill's superb 180-degree panorama of the Laurentians. Southwards the view was down towards the

The original house in the mid-1930s after the addition of a wing, terraces, and steps designed by Eddie Mathews.

bay and the village. Up a gentle slope to the north past a service area lay fields and farmland. The house was approached along an entrance allée of Lombardy poplars (*Populus nigra* 'Italica') on the eastern boundary, and in that direction looked down across vegetable gardens to the St. Lawrence. A single row of poplars continued past the house and garage court to a stream beyond that cut across the property.

The silhouette of this long line of tall, fastigiate poplars, so reminiscent of France, was a prominent feature of the landscape for seventy years, until their senile condition and state of decrepitude resulted in their removal in 1998. Young paper birches were planted between them some years ago and will eventually take their place. At the same time, a parallel farm road was planted with Lombardy poplars. While the poplars sustain the silhouette from a distance, they have no impact on the driveway, and the drive up to the house now seems to me an alien experience, an approach to a completely different place. Seventy years of driving through that tall, narrow allée cannot easily be forgotten. The newer plantings will, in the end, make it right once again and will become something for descendants to look forward to. It is more or less decreed that each generation should plant trees for its successor.

Poplars of one sort or another will always be a part of Les Quatre Vents. But that first house was a house in a field surrounded by unimpeded views, not a house with a garden. There was nothing to anchor it to the landscape. Today all that has changed. You are allowed to discover that encompassing landscape only gradually. First you glimpse it in views from the house. When you walk through the front door and enter

ABOVE

On the right young birches have been planted between the senescent Lombardy poplars of the entrance allée. Due to the mature Amelanchier canadensis on the left, the planting of an allée of matching birch awaits the removal of the Lombardies.

RIGHT

The entrance allée in 1936.

the living room, a large, tall bay window reveals the dominant western view over the foreground of the reflection pool on the terrace and the Tapis Vert. The original wide view of the mountains is partly screened and framed by trees so that you see only glimpses of the Laurentians beyond the Tapis Vert. The panoramic view awaits further discovery once you are well into the garden.

By framing a view and directing the eye, paradoxically limiting what can be seen, you create an appetite for more. Because it is not omnipresent, the view (however wonderful) is never too much of a good thing. Additionally, the simplicity of the unimpeded vista leads one to think of the whole rather than the parts; to focus on the link with nature rather than on the details of the garden elements. The unimpeded vista yields the illusion that the garden has no boundary, that what one sees is the totality, reinforcing the principle propounded in many of the great English gardens and in the borrowed scenery (*shakkei*) of the best Japanese gardens, that the garden is merely an antechamber to the wider landscape.

Since the Tapis Vert's broad green swath and bordering hedges are all that one notices from the living room's west-facing window in addition to the distant fields, forests and hills, it means that the discovery of the garden, and of its parallel and transverse elements, requires exploration. This invitation to explore, with the delights and surprises that should ensue, may be the most important ingredient for any garden. It is a *central* part of the visit to the garden at Les Quatre Vents.

The first stage in the process of structuring the garden took place in the 1930s, when my mother's brother Edward J. (Eddie) Mathews, an accomplished architect, took charge of creating the skeletal framework that would link the house to its surroundings. From his vision any number of consequences flow. He established the firm platform which anchors the building to the ground – the sound horizontal base of terraces and steps on which the house sits comfortably in the uneven terrain. However, his most commanding achievement was to strengthen the east-west axis on which the house was built. His treatment of this axis forms the backbone of the garden and has influenced every subsequent development. It runs directly through the house from the mountains in the west all the way to the eastern horizon. From windows in the east of the house it follows a path leading through an orchard, bisecting the vegetable garden and carrying on through a breezeway in a garden shed and through fruit and nursery beds on its way towards the St. Lawrence. To the west the house is firmly anchored, on a slight rise, in the center of the main axis. Horizontals such as the reflection pool terrace provide the platform for the building and the visual base for vertical accents such as trees and hedges that direct the eye and contain the view. This horizontality is strengthened by the wall and steps that now end the terrace, in place of the original slope that flowed down to a rectangle planted with perennials smack in the middle of the axis.

ABOVE

The author's uncle, Eddie Mathews, was responsible for the skeletal framework that linked the house to its setting and influenced all further additions.

OPPOSITE

Oblivious of the sunset over the Tapis Vert, D'whinnie monitors the chipmunks that scurry around the reflection pool terrace.

OPPOSITE

The spine of Les Quatre Vents' landscape runs from the center of the Potager, where Anne's scarecrows hold sway, through the house to the Tapis Vert.

BELOW

Sheep grazing in the field below a curving meadow seeded with lupines, with Eddie Mathews' 1936 barn complex in the background.

The "stroke of genius" in the view to the west is that no distractions impede the vista. Beyond the reflecting pool in the terrace foreground the eye travels unhindered over the carpet of plain green lawn specified by Eddie Mathews (and immediately christened the "Tapis Vert" by my mother) towards the distant hills, alighting briefly on the shaggy Highland cattle who pose on axis and animate the pastoral scene. Over the years the wide view has been progressively narrowed and restricted to that portion of the Laurentians that lies directly in line with the restricted vista of the Tapis Vert. Periodically the vista requires some adjustment to keep it sufficiently open, but it remains the *raison d'être* of all later expansion and lies at the heart of the story of the garden.

Much has changed since Eddie Mathews was at work in the 1930s — above all, the house at the core of this landscape has been replaced. But the framework of the gardens he decreed around the house remains essentially the same today, although the stonework and planting have been redone, and additional hedges have been planted. He laid out the Tapis Vert, and designed the long stone wall and steps that flank it and support the White Garden at the higher level, balanced by a Blue Garden on the opposite side of the Tapis Vert. My mother spent the next three decades working on these gardens and improving their plantings. Eddie Mathews' tool house (known as the Cabane) is still in place, and his swimming-pool and barn complexes are almost exactly as he designed them in 1936.

If the vistas and the landscape are constants, the building from which they are seen is quite different. The 1928 house was struck by lightning and burnt to the ground on May 5, 1956, destroying not only all my parents' summer belongings, furniture, and memorabilia, but all the family portraits and possessions that my father had inherited from Mootzie, who had died the year before. Fortunately no one was living in the house. Somehow the fire did not strike us as particularly disastrous at the time. It happened three months after my father died just short of his sixtieth birthday following an agonizing two-year struggle with esophageal cancer. This mortal loss was so overwhelming that the loss of mere possessions seemed of little consequence to any of us.

Shortly before his death my father had doubled the insurance on the original house. The Korean War was in full force at the time and, since the house burned so soon after his death, there was an exorbitant rate of tax on the insurance proceeds unless they were to be invested in a new house within twelve months. It was almost as if my father had directed the thunderbolt to divert my mother by keeping her mind off her troubles.[9]

Her brother Eddie Mathews, a design partner of Skidmore, Owings and Merrill, was now busy designing major skyscrapers, cultural landmarks, and corporate headquarters around North America and therefore unable to take on any residential projects.[10] Mother sought out her friend Frederick Rhinelander (Freddie) King, who produced an elegant and classic French structure to be superimposed on the footprint of the rambling and rather simple first house. The restoration resulted in the controlling axis becoming far more evident than it had been in the original structure. You could now stand in the middle of the sizable living room and enjoy both the western view through the bay window and the view to the east running through the entry hall and library and out through a tall French window where it follows the path towards the Potager down to the garden shed known as the Doodle-Doo.

I realize now that the importance of the house, a clearly French display of architectural pretension, may well have dictated the grandeur of the landscape and horticultural developments that were to come. The opportunity to indulge in appropriately grand garden schemes might not have been undertaken had the replacement house been more conventional. This was a chance to draw on the garden traditions of the Old World, given the unlimited encroachable space in the surrounding fields and the appealing panorama to the west.

In addition to the large western bay window, the living room has three tall French doors surmounted with window transoms leading out on to the front lawn. This slopes down to a grassy terrace and the southern view of the bay, with the village and the summer resort on the far bank, much of which has been planted out. Standing on the square stone platform outside the central door you see the woodland garden copse, hiding the village, at a 45-degree angle on the right, a view of the bay directly ahead over the top of a distant low hedge and, at a 45-degree angle to the left, a glimpse,

Les Quatre Vents overlooks La Malbaie at ebbing tide with the summer resort of Pointe-au-Pic in the distance.

THE GREATER PERFECTION

THE HOUSE IN ITS SETTING

under some Scots pines (*Pinus sylvestris*) in the near distance, of the Pointe-au-Pic headland with its handsome church and deepwater wharf jutting into the St. Lawrence.

Again, that view started out as panoramic and over the years was channeled and divided so that you are now drawn well down the lawn towards the view before discovering the panorama. A major staircase down to the swimming pool and terrace then comes as a complete surprise.

NEW GARDEN SPACES TO THE NORTH

THE NORTHERN SIDE OF THE HOUSE, WHICH INCLUDES THE KITCHEN, dining room and guest wing, has been treated entirely differently. The landscape backdrop of fields and distant wooded ridge has been completely obscured by a series of garden rooms that provide a different view for each window of the north façade. While there is formality, as well as modest vistas and glimpses of further areas to explore, these are essentially enclosed, inward-looking spaces separated by "walls" of clipped *Thuja occidentalis*, commonly called cedar or thuja.

When Freddie King re-created the house on the original concrete foundations, he switched the use of the two wings flanking the central component. What had been the servants' wing, a low one-story structure set back to the right of the western vista, became a three-bedroom guest wing, while the former guest room/living room wing to the east became a library/master-bedroom suite. The servants' quarters in the new house moved upstairs to an apartment over the living room. Originally the area just to the north of the house had been a cobblestone alley service court with woodshed, dairy, and laundry facing the servants' wing. Since the wind had been blowing from the northwest during the fire, the *pompiers* had been able to save the dairy and laundry. In due course these small, detached units were moved to the north into an empty field where they have served successively as a children's house, *garçonnière*, and overflow guest cottage. My mother turned the freed-up space into an herb garden of sorts, and an ancient outdoor bread oven – the *four à pain* – was moved from one of the seigneurie's tenant houses to be near the kitchen door.

When we inherited the property and, after some twelve years of living with it, began to improve and extend the garden, this north side of the house was one of the first areas to be dealt with. It was a puzzling space. The view to the fields was diffuse and not particularly inspiring and the cobblestone ramp up to the higher level of the garage court had lost its *raison d'être*. There was little incentive to be on that side of the house, at the time accessible only from the kitchen. Once altered, the north façade, running from east to west, consisted of the kitchen door, indented French doors off

The stepped, raised beds of the Salad Garden are conveniently to hand a few paces outside the kitchen door.

the dining room and the doors and windows of the three guest bedrooms, terminating in a tall, thick wall extending from the wing to the Cabane, with an opening into the garden proper.

A geometric treatment of a space next to a house is almost invariably the most satisfactory solution. Straight lines and right-angle corners, or arcs of a circle, fit naturally next to the geometric mass and are a logical transition to unstructured or open spaces. In this instance we divided the rectangular space adjacent to the north façade (thirty by a hundred feet) into three separate "garden rooms," that ran from the wall and the toolshed in the west to a new stone wall, matching its western counterpart, between the new complex and the entrance court to the east. The garden visitor now enters through a doorway in the wall bounding the entrance court and traverses the three gardens, each quite different in both theme and appearance.

THE SALAD GARDEN

A COBBLESTONE RAMP opposite the kitchen door leads up a slope to the higher level of the garage court. The ramp is flanked by a double set of three stepped raised beds filled with *fines herbes* and salad greens. The plantings in each rectangle are a designed pattern, a tapestry that Anne varies from year to year. Next to the kitchen proper and flanking the kitchen door, two squarish raised beds fashioned out of stout treated lumber, as in the case of the salad beds, are filled with gritty scree and limestone rocks, as a repository for alpines that tolerate the partial shade from the house.

One disadvantage is that Phyllodoce and Plucky-Lucky, our two cats, prefer the raised salad garden beds over any other spot for their *toilette* in the great outdoors, wreaking havoc with seedling shallots and mâche. Anne's response to this challenge has been a cumbersome and elaborate restraining system of sturdy wood and wire frames to be placed over the emerging seedlings until the mature plants fill the space.

THE BREAD AND KNOT GARDEN

ONCE THE SALAD GARDEN was in place, the interior of the north façade rectangle was levelled to the grade of the house. The cobblestones were extended to the space opposite the dining room, and the *four à pain*, now caparisoned with a roof compatible with its surroundings, was placed on axis with the French doors leading from the dining room into a knot garden designed by Anne, the weaver in the family, and filling the indented half-hexagon between the kitchen and the guest wing.

To frame this new space (promptly dubbed the Jardin de la Boulangère) and separate it from the Salad Garden, thuja hedges of varying heights in the foreground, and higher to the rear and the sides of the bread oven, were installed so that the space appeared to be a direct extension of the dining room. A pair of little-leaf lindens (*Tilia cordata*), trimmed to echo the lines of the bread oven's roof and underplanted with lily

OPPOSITE

The Bread Garden with its oven and topiary loaves viewed from the dining room window over Anne's Knot Garden. Its threads are composed of Buxus microphylla *var.* koreana, Berberis thunbergii atropurpurea, Thuja occidentalis *'Tom Thumb,' and* Chamaecyparis pisifera filifera *'Nana'.*

of the valley (*Convallaria majalis*), flank the oven. Shorter thujas, placed in planting beds in the cobblestones, are kept trimmed to simulate loaves of the local staple, *pain à l'eau*, as well as the classic Quebec *habitant* galette (a delicious, round, sweet loaf filled with raisins).

This Jardin de la Boulangère is functional as well as decorative. The oven is made from clay gathered from the mud flats in the bay plastered over a frame of alder saplings which rests on a raised brick base. Anne is the *boulangère*, marshalling descendants and guests every ten days or so to help in the process of baking bread. They begin in the morning after breakfast, kneading dough in the *huche* or kneading trough and "punching" it in early afternoon. A fire is built in the airtight interior and left to burn down to glowing cinders which Anne rakes from the oven floor into a wheelbarrow. The *boulangère* waits until she can hold her fist inside the oven for a count of fifteen before the loaves are placed for the 45-minute baking that renders them a delicate golden brown, attended by the haunting aroma of bakeries. The process finishes gloriously when the loaves are brought into the kitchen to cool on racks and be brushed with butter. Then they are wrapped in a towel and placed in the cool room for a day or two before being consumed at their very best.

The Bread and Knot Garden is a surprise to the visitor; the former somewhat puzzling until the topiaries are seen as loaves, and the latter an unusual sight in Quebec but whose logic and decorative appeal becomes apparent as it is considered. The woven knot that Anne created has a fringe filled with white *fraises des bois*, which display thoroughly albino but nonetheless delicious small, pointed berries through much of July and whose jam is a conversation piece. The plant is a prolific colonizer and arrived as a house present from Allen Paterson, the former Director of the Chelsea Physic Garden in London and the Royal Botanic Garden in Hamilton, Ontario. He spied it at a roadside nursery while tied up in a traffic jam in Scotland and hopped out of his car to acquire it (as passionate plant collectors are wont to do.)

Anne placed panels of different colored gravel between the interstices of her knot to enhance the contrasting textures of the plants used for its warp and woof. This worked admirably, except for the adventitious weeds that kept appearing, and there must have been something about the "woof" aspect because our late, beloved cairn terrier, Frizzle, would regularly bury the body parts of slaughtered woodchucks under the gravel so that they would ripen for his later delectation. More than once the serenity of the garden was shattered by screams of disgust as Anne's weeding uncovered the bloodied head of an unfortunate victim, Medusa-like among the ordered sinews of her knot. Now porous plastic underlies the gravel, suppressing the weeds, and woodchuck burials have moved to another venue.

The Guest Garden with its upholstered topiary furnishings.

THE GUEST GARDEN

ROSEMARY VEREY'S FIRST ANTHOLOGY, *The Englishwoman's Garden*, a volume in which the owner of each garden writes her own descriptive essay, was published about the time we were considering what to do with this space. I found it to be full of inspiring ideas, beautifully reflected in the excellent photographs.

One particularly intriguing garden was that of Shute, belonging to Anne and Michael Tree, which had been worked on over the years by Geoffrey Jellicoe. Its imaginative features included a topiary bedroom, replete with four-poster bed, adjacent to the house. Given the climatic limitations imposed by the deep and often icy snow drifts of the boreal winter, there was no way the four-poster bed could be duplicated at Les Quatre Vents, but the feeling of a furnished room could be achieved using the tough and reliable local thuja or "cedar" which was readily available for the digging in nearby abandoned fields.

A stylish architectural element from Eddie Mathews' 1936 swimming-pool surround (see pages 300-301), consisting of a curving banquette attached to a curved

THE HOUSE IN ITS SETTING   67

wall, was duly reproduced as thuja hedge and centered on the middle guest-bedroom window. A shaped cocktail table was planted in front of it and a pair of shaped lindens, repeating the Bread Garden feature, behind it. Thuja masses, shaped to resemble giant, overstuffed armchair, were incorporated to complete the room.

As it happened, this configuration left a corner of the space nearest to the hedge hiding the bread oven unused. There we created a Cup Garden, a miniature version of the idea behind the landscape at Innisfree. The thuja surround was shaped to form the sides of the cup sweeping down to a circular bottom of grass, with a circular four-foot pool in its center. The surface of the pool was made to be flush with the grass, with water gently bubbling out of a round, mossy central stone (another echo of that childhood dunking). This soothing feature is hidden from the casual visitor who walks straight ahead towards the garden proper, but awaits discovery by the curious, who generally exclaim with pleasure on finding the peaceful pool, for all I know recalling something from their childhood as well.

The point about the Guest Garden is that it is devoid of horticultural excitement. It is a garden of shades of green: the grass, the dark green thuja furnishings and walls, and the brilliant green of the mossy stone. It is a place for relaxation, whether viewed from within the garden or from the guest-room windows (in each case the rooms look out to the terrace and reflection pool on the south façade as well), a place to recover from the sometimes strenuous social exertions of the summer colony across the way. These outdoor rooms soothe the nerves and are a shield against the north wind.

The traverse to the Guest Garden is along a narrow corridor that runs directly from the door in the entrance court wall towards a dolphin spouting into a scallop shell against the far wall. The corridor blocks any view of the Cup Garden water feature and leads one into the center of the "furnished" room. The open door in the left hand corner of the far wall gives just a hint of the gardens that lie beyond.

Some years after making this series of garden rooms off the north façade I was delighted to note that Lockwood de Forest had used the same device at his wonderful house in Santa Barbara. To the side of the house he placed a discrete, small garden off each room, creating a suitably varied outdoor extension of each interior that complemented its function. With the area in front of his house simply a green lawn and with an informal garden well in the distance and a Japanese style atrium filling the center of the house, it was an inspiring example of how a garden could serve as an adjunct to the interior.

While, in the normal course, the visitor has no choice but to go through the far door and across through hawthorn hedges to the White Garden, we can move at will and approach the garden as a house guest would from the living room or from the door of one of the guest rooms opening on to the covered terrace where one can lunch and, very occasionally, dine in mid-summer.

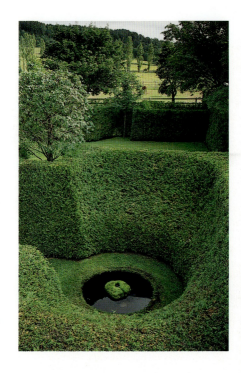

ABOVE

A Cup Garden pool with a roche pleureuse in a corner of the Guest Garden.

OPPOSITE

An overview of the Bread Garden and Guest Garden.

CHAPTER III
ALPINE PLANTS AND ROCKWORK

OPPOSITE

The "campanula moment" in mid-July enlivens the walls and circular steps supporting the reflection pool terrace. Campanula cochlearifolia *in its blue and white forms predominates.*

ABOVE, RIGHT

Primula marginata.

WHO KNOWS WHY A CERTAIN TYPE OF PLANT TURNS OUT TO HAVE such irresistible appeal to an individual? Why should African violets or rhododendrons or bromeliads become so firmly entrenched in the enthusiast's affections to the point where little else matters? In my case alpine plants were the hook that dragged me from a normal existence into a lifelong involvement with, and attachment to, plants. In 1951 my first sight of *Armeria juniperifolia* 'Bevan's Variety', a particularly neat, sessile, and seductive form of the familiar sea-thrift of Britain and Europe, was a revelation. I was consumed with admiration as the diminutive, grassy tuft produced a myriad of enchanting, pale pink tufted flowers that obscured their origin and were equally beautiful when their dried and generously opened pods filled with shiny, black seeds. For me there was no turning back.

It so happened that one of our first major undertakings at Les Quatre Vents was doing something about the stony structures in the garden in which alpines, incidentally, prefer to grow. By the 1970s we realized that the garden needed major rehabilitation (and also that it could be expanded to advantage). In the early 1930s Eddie Mathews had surrounded the then rather modest house with terraces, walls and steps that made a visual and practical link between the building and the garden. After some forty years it was clear that much of the stonework needed major attention. The dry walls to the north and east of the Tapis Vert were ramshackle and on the verge of collapse. Terraces and steps planted during my parents' tenure were full of ineradicable weeds and coarser plants that had seeded in uninvited and overwhelmed anything choice. Keeping the roughest semblance of order required tiresome and regular hours of difficult weeding to the exclusion of any other garden activity. We had just completed a five-year program of creating raised stone beds and walled gardens at Stonecrop, our garden in Cold Spring, New York, and had more or less learned how to achieve satisfactory results.

The underpinnings of the terrace, too, were in sore need of attention. The double retaining walls between this upper terrace and the Tapis Vert were particularly decrepit and well on their way to pulling the terrace down with them. The covered terrace under the roof of the servants' wing of the original house was part of Eddie Mathews' design. When the house was rebuilt after the fire, the terrace was expanded and raised a step or two to tie into the new floor grade. Fortunately, one of Eddie's elegant trellised columns fell clear of the blaze and served as a model for the new gallery. All the terraces and walls are made of random-size square-cut limestone from a local quarry, and flow in an ingenious and complex combination and variety of steps from the house level to the Tapis Vert. A four-inch-deep reflection pool sits flush in its limestone setting and corresponds in width to the living room. The deep blue color of the pool interior (it is known as *le Bassin Bleu*) enhances the mirror effect, reflecting the sunsets and northern twilights through the bay window so that they illuminate the living room's cove ceiling.

The corner of the stepped, covered terrace is anchored by a clump of thuja, shaped into a rounded bun (a form that is used with both thuja and crataegus in the various terraces around the house) with just enough room to walk between the clump and the reflection pool.

The bay window is separated from the pool by a twenty-foot-wide grassy strip. At its southern end is a terraced *rocaille*, with alpines planted in square or rectangular planting pockets placed at random throughout the terrace. We have used this way of planting alpines wherever a terrace exists. It was a last resort after trying to give alpine plants the conditions they revel in without having to deal with the endless weeding that ensues from planting a rock garden in this northern climate.

Our learning curve began with that seductive sea-thrift. It appeared in our first

ABOVE, LEFT

The terraces and steps in 1936 with the then servants' wing. The Cabane toolhouse and its companion Lombardy poplar are in the background.

ABOVE, RIGHT

The same view in the early 1970s with weed-infested steps and crumbling walls. The servants' wing has become the guest pavilion. A corner of the reflection pool is just visible on the right.

OPPOSITE

A recent autumnal view of the Bassin Bleu. *The reflection pool is four inches deep and its surface lies flush with the surrounding limestone terrace studded with alpines in planting pockets.*

OPPOSITE

A pair of Dianthus *'La Bourboule' reveling in their planting pockets in the limestone of the reflection pool terrace.*

garden after Anne had been taken to a nursery near Walpole, Massachusetts, by Hallie Long, an experienced gardener and wildflower enthusiast, who guided our initial endeavors and saw to it that we started with a beginner's dozen of rock garden plants. By so doing Hallie inadvertently started us down a path that, with guidance from the wonderful Elizabeth Hall, the beloved librarian of the New York Botanical Garden at the time, led us to the American Rock Garden Society. Here we experienced the joy of learning from *aficionados* and legendary horticulturists about a limitless world of alpine jewels from the world's mountainous crown. We also learned the ways and means of growing them. This meant, in essence, trying to duplicate the extreme conditions under which alpines thrive. They are used to struggling for their existence — enduring broiling sun, cloudbursts, freezing nights, continual winds, and long winter dormancy under deep snow — in gravel screes where, if there is any soil, their roots have to search deeply to find it.

Most alpines fare better in a Zone 4 climate than they would in a warmer zone, but so do weeds, especially in a gravelly scree. We gradually learned how to cope with them in the conditions we could offer.

The *rocaille* at Les Quatre Vents was our proving ground. It started out as a low, dry wall flush with and terminating the grassy strip in front of the bay window. A narrow bed for alpines was then placed between the wall and the grassy strip. This was subsequently improved and widened and turned into a simulated moraine, with water delivered in a perforated pipe 15 inches under the scree (a practice I have reluctantly concluded, after being inordinately proud of it, is not worth the effort). Limestone rocks were then buried so that they protruded from the scree, providing a cool root run for the alpines. In each instance, after a year of relative calm while the newly planted alpines grew on promisingly, the bed turned into a thicket of weeds with the most pernicious — the local cerastium and vetch — embedding their own roots in the very core of the root systems of the new plants to assure their ineradicability.

The solution came about when the terrace had to be redone, along with the stone steps and walls throughout the garden. It was based on the theory that the less scree surface exposed, the less chance for weeds to become established. Planting pockets, some four to six inches square, would be created in and about the cemented stone surfaces and would vary in intensity depending on whether the terrace or step surface was to be used for walking or merely as a setting for plants.

The rebuilt terraces consist of four inch thick rectangles of the locally quarried limestone laid on a six-inch base of reinforced concrete poured, in turn, on a thick layer of gravel spread over a sandy soil base. Placing a vertical plastic four-inch pipe through all these layers when the gravel is laid and the cement poured, and then retracting it before the cement sets completely, leaves a deep narrow pocket. Filling the pocket with an overwhelmingly gritty mix (we use 75% limestone shale chips and 25% humus, with

The Greater Perfection

the richest mixture at the base of the hole), results in the ideal, well-drained medium for the roots of an alpine to probe on its way to becoming deep-rooted and content. Of course, weeds often do appear before the plant has filled the surface of the pocket (which we top with one to two inches of pure stone chips) but they are quickly noticed and easily removed. In time, cushions of happy plants bloom their sessile heads off and, if something starts to grow out of their midst, it will probably be a promiscuous alpine such as a dwarf aquilegia, an alpine poppy, or an inquisitive campanula, which are tolerable commensalists.

The *rocaille* now has steps leading down from the terrace level to the sloping south lawn with the terrace to each side a sheet of limestone pocked with individual plants, the ultimate stony bed for finicky alpines. The planted pocket treatment is used throughout the steps below the reflection pool and terrace as well and the plants are thriving. For an alpine divorced from its native habitat it is the next best thing to being planted in the face of a wall.

ABOVE, LEFT

The easy Aquilegia buergeriana *has a tendency to appear in the middle of clumps of other species in the terrace plantings.*

ABOVE, RIGHT

A happy specimen of Adonis vernalis, *a gift from Joel Spingarn, at Stonecrop.*

OPPOSITE

An example of Cono's rockwork around the pool above the Rock Ledge at Stonecrop.

BUILDING WALLS

A FEW INDIVIDUALS ARE, INSTINCTIVELY, GOOD BUILDERS OF WALLS. One day in the mid-1970s, while driving north on Route 9 near Cold Spring, I saw some handsome terraces under construction and came to a screeching halt. The terraces were the creation of Cono Reale, who was busy turning the hillside behind his house into a landscape reminiscent of Capo d'Orlando, his native village on

the north coast of Sicily. An agricultural engineer turned self-taught mason, Cono took one look at the rounded fieldstone walls that needed rebuilding around the garden in Cold Spring, rubbed his hands with glee and announced in an authoritative, if almost unintelligible, Benito Mussolini manner, "There is a great deal of work to be done around here. You better believe it!"

We worked closely together for the next twelve years and I learned much from the process. Cono had the native Italian flair for construction and his association with both Stonecrop and Les Quatre Vents was enormously positive. His sensitive eye and innate sense of proportion meant that his modifications and adjustments to my ideas on how a bit of rock ledge was to be placed, how a wall was to be configured, or how a garden pool designed, invariably turned out to be an improvement over the initial concept. There is no substitute for the hands-on artisan with aesthetic sensibility working with the gardener. Having gone through the learning process with Cono, we subsequently followed this route in developing our gardens and eschewed professional help except when it came to the proportions and detailed working drawings for important hardscape and structures.

At Stonecrop, one of my dreams had always been to create some rectangular free-standing raised stone beds with alpines filling crevices on all exposures. It was in the course of that process, working with Cono, that I learned the principles of wall building with square-cut fieldstone and could apply my knowledge of the preferences and idiosyncrasies of alpine plants.[11]

It was a symbiotic process. While I was observing the principles that underlie the making of a solid and well-laid wall, Cono soon learned how to handle the plants and identify which were best suited for a particular crevice. Since Stonecrop always had a wide variety of alpines it was an easy matter to assemble plants as the walls rose and to draw on this available reservoir as needed. The walls and raised stone beds went up rapidly early each spring during the month or so before it became too hot and dry to risk exposing the plants' roots to such an extent.

At Les Quatre Vents life was more complicated. Planting had to be done in August when Cono would come with his family and spend his "vacation" rebuilding the dilapidated framework of walls. This process took a painful seven years to complete: wall building, if done properly, is slow work. Steps are even more demanding.

The plants for Les Quatre Vents' walls were brought up from Stonecrop each spring, dutifully dipped in a toxic mix under the eye of a phytosanitary inspector with the USDA. Upon arrival in Quebec they would again be inspected by a specialist to ensure that no evil insect or plague had inadvertently accompanied them. The plants would then be nurtured in pots through the summer until mid-August (early autumn in Zone 4) and planted in the courses of the newly laid and much improved retaining walls.

The principal problem was that the really choice plants resented their toxic dunking

BELOW

The choice Potentilla nitida *from the Swiss Alps blooming happily in a terrace planting pocket, a result we never achieved at Stonecrop.*

ABOVE

The circumboreal mountain avens Dryas octopetala *is content in the face of the White Garden wall.*

The Rock-Garden Wall-Builder's 10 Commandments

- On a 6-inch layer of gravel, build a solid foundation course of large square-cut stones that barely protrudes above ground level.

- Place square-cut stones in courses, rising in a slight "batter," so that the finished wall slopes gradually back from the base to allow moisture to reach all crevices. Avoid aligning vertical joints to keep erosion of soil in the joints to a minimum.

- As each course is added, fill in just behind the wall with large rocks of any shape so as to reinforce the façade and reduce the likelihood of instability.

- Pack gritty scree mixture (75% poultry grit, rock chips, or coarse sand; 25% organic matter) between courses, in joints, and behind the façade and compact it thoroughly by tamping and watering as each course is laid.

- Plant the crevices between and above each rock with the smallest feasible specimen, making sure it has a good, established root system preferably reaching back to the soil mixture. Between courses press the root mass down as flat as possible and barely cover with gritty scree mix. (Keep roots constantly moist throughout the process.)

- Use small flakes and chips of stone (tapped in as wedges) to fill gaps in the front of crevices, once a course is planted, to reduce erosion and ensure that the plant's crown remains in place.

- The soil in the crevices need only be sufficient to fill the minimal air spaces between square-cut rock surfaces. Use almost all grit with a small amount of organic matter. The richer mixture in the center awaits the plant's hardworking roots. Once these become well-anchored and produce a healthy mat of plant at the surface, the plant will look exactly as if it were growing in its alpine setting.

- Indulge the exposure preferences of the plants: saxifrages and ramondas on north-facing walls, Mediterranean species facing south and west.

- Assemble twice as many plants (in great variety) as you think you'll need. Overplant! A number of plants will succumb over the first two years. Be sure to include non-invasive campanulas; they will outlast most species and will obligingly fill in the empty spaces left behind.

- Early spring and early fall are the best times for planting.

Ramonda myconi *in the north-facing terrace wall.*

Campanula cochlearifolia *and a small encrusted saxifrage.*

and quietly died, so some other way had to be found to get them to Quebec alive. Strangely, it turned out that declaring them at the border as house plants seemed to be acceptable to all concerned and thus the more fragile species traveled contentedly without the toxic shock, despite the demeaning title.

THE WHITE GARDEN WALL

THE FIRST ELEMENT TO BE COMPLETED WAS THE RETAINING WALL supporting the White Garden. The following spring, where there had been desultory blooming of a few banal plants the year before, we witnessed with joy an explosion of white-flowering alpines from early May through late July. The whiteness of that garden's flowers not only filled the perennial portion of the beds, but now swept down to the scree area behind the wall, over the top of the wall and throughout the interstices of the wall itself.

Not everything still survives. Many true alpines prefer a mostly northern exposure and casualties were inevitable in this southwest-facing wall. Nevertheless, some twenty years later, a respectable series of waves of bloom still draw one to the wall for closer inspection after seeing it from the reflection pool terrace. The first wave consists of several of the neater varieties of arabis (*androsacea, bryoides olympica,* x *kellereri* and x *sturii*) which revel in the site, followed by *Schivereckia podolica, Dryas octopetala, Iberis saxatilis,* and *Phlox subulata* 'Ellie B' and 'Schneewittchen', followed by a wave of white-flowered dianthus, *Gypsophila repens* 'Alba' and *tenuifolia, Silene alpestris* 'Flore Pleno',

Rebuilding the White Garden wall in the late 1970s, clearly showing the wide strip of sheet metal used to separate the different soil conditions required by the perennials and alpines.

The rebuilt White Garden wall and steps showing the transition from perennial to alpine plantings. The bulk of the alpines in the wall have flowered and been cut back and the Campanula cochlearifolia *'Alba', in bud, is just about to whiten the walls in its turn.*

Campanula betulifolia and, finally, a three-week display of Campanula cochlearifolia 'Alba' which does its inquisitive best to usurp every inch of available space.

By the end of July the plants in the wall are cut back severely so that their remnants have a chance to consolidate their position in the limestone courses, storing up energy for the coming winter. Above them, old favorites such as Achillea ptarmica 'Boule de Neige', Rosa rugosa 'Alba', Papaver sendtneri, and intermediate-size dianthus and campanulas draw the eye away from the wall to the upper beds and the spires of the white delphinium.

The weakness of this wall is its southwestern exposure and we have found it necessary to drape it with burlap so as to minimize winter damage. I enjoy the ritual in early spring when the protective covering is removed and the wall surface checked for signs of life. Before one knows it, the gray-brown tuffets have revived. With the dead bits excised, the wall becomes a tapestry of green and white, requiring trimming and dead-heading as each genus, exhausted from its orgy of bloom, begs to have its seed-heads and stems removed so that it can present a reasonably orderly front while it rebuilds its energies for next year's extravaganza.

THE TERRACE WALLS AND CIRCULAR STEPS

Once the White Garden wall, steps, and plantings had been resuscitated, the reconstruction of the more important walls and steps designed by Eddie Mathews leading from the reflection pool terrace followed. The retaining walls as seen from the Tapis Vert consisted of double walls of varying heights that bulged, were generally askew, and had begun to affect the terrace which they supported.

To cure the problem, both walls and all steps, and much of the terrace skirting the periphery of the pool, had to be removed before the rebuilding could begin. Fortunately the foundations under the reflection pool were sound. Also sound was the terrace to the south of the pool, filled with cubes of thuja specified by Eddie Mathews, as well as his stylish, broad, shallow steps that lead from the grass terrace in front of the house down to the level of the south lawn.

"Maestro" Cono rebuilding the rear of the two walls supporting the terrace, now underpinned by a reinforced concrete base.

The rebuilt terrace walls and steps in their entirety in late June.

As every other bit of stone was removed, its location was carefully noted. Special care was taken to preserve the capstones of the right-hand wall which had accumulated over the years a sympathetic patina of lichens on their exposed surfaces.

The steps consisted of eight concentric semicircles descending from an intermediate terrace level some eighteen inches below the reflection pool surface and centered on the Tapis Vert. The dry steps were filled with "old-fashioned" pinks that somehow or other had survived the incursions of creeping thyme, of the aggressive indigenous cerastium, as well as of every other weed known to the region, and were a nightmare to maintain.

But, once past the pain and trouble of the major disassembly, and with the pinks transplanted to a holding area for an uncertain future, the rebuilding became a positive experience full of promise. Biting the bullet and starting over again, rather than just

ABOVE

Primula aureata, *collected near the Rupina-La in the Ghurka Himal of Central Nepal, failed to appreciate the Quebec climate, succumbing after its first winter. Here it is shown in the alpine house at Stonecrop.*

OPPOSITE

Primula marginata *'Kesselring's Variety' and* Saxifraga apiculata *enjoy the north-facing terrace wall site.*

BELOW

A dark blue campanula takes over after Campanula pilosa *(in the lower right corner) has finished blooming.*

patching up, meant correcting the problems in their entirety and for posterity as well. The first priority was to instal reinforced concrete footings to ensure the integrity of the pool, support the terrace, and form a solid base for the circular steps.

It was at this point that the idea of the planting pockets with the deep, gravelly rootrun became the obvious way to achieve the effect of planted dry steps that had been a familiar and pleasing, if frustrating, aspect of the descent to the Tapis Vert. This time the only place for weeds to become established would be in the planting pockets themselves, a much easier field of battle for the gardener. So pockets were built in, tucked against the edge of the surmounting step, starting at each end of a given semicircle and spaced about two feet apart. Since each step had a different circumference this meant that no two pockets in a pair of adjoining steps were aligned with one another, lending a suitably random effect to the whole.

Once the solution of re-creating a relatively weed-free version of the planted steps had been found, it was an obvious ploy to extend the practice to the terrace itself, along with its associated steps and landings, and create a new sort of hardscape for alpines, a rock garden in a formal setting where the plants can be walked among and admired, or viewed at eye level from below, with ease. In time, the plants provide the informal softening that relieves the severity and enhances the charm of the terrace, an agreeably serendipitous result. This practice has now become our norm in comparable settings where alpines are concerned.

The walls to either side of the steps were then reconstituted. The higher section of the interior wall, resting solidly on its invisible concrete base, was rebuilt without plants but with the mortar between the stones set far in so that it was invisible, with inviting crevices in which stray seeds of such ubiquitous and easy plants as *Campanula carpatica* could become established. The lower front wall was laid in courses and planted with alpines, as in the case of the White Garden wall. It was at this point that the lack of a readily available supply of alpines in variety became apparent. The only option was to divide the few plants we had to hand and spread them throughout the wall surfaces.

When I had been gathering plants for this purpose the previous spring, I hadn't considered that the wall faced squarely northwest and received a limited amount of sunshine along with the brunt of the prevailing winds – the ideal exposure for many saxifrage species. We must have had well over one hundred saxifrage varieties at Stonecrop, but only two in hand to plant at Les Quatre Vents: the easy and very early *Saxifraga apiculata* and a choice small-rosetted, encrusted saxifrage whose name has long since fled my mental inventory. Both have thrived, the former producing enormous hummocks down the face of the wall and behaving as if it were an aubrieta in Devon, while the smaller encrusted species slowly but surely spreads, filling increasingly distant interstices with its neat and sparkling habit.

A clump of *Primula marginata* 'Kesselring's Variety' was on hand when the front walls were built, dug from the nearby Woodland Garden. It was torn into five tiny bits and lodged here and there across the fifty feet of wall. Today those bits have spread throughout the nearby cracks, turning into fountains of bloom worthy of their forebears in the Maritime Alps, each clump filled with myriads of flowers each May. They are a joy to behold. 'Kesselring's Variety' is a fine version of that many-formed species, but it can't compare with 'Amethyst', 'Beamish', 'Prichard's Variety', 'Stonecrop Blue', or that choicest of all, *Primula marginata* 'Linda Pope' and its rarely seen white form. It galls me that *all* of those varieties were available at Stonecrop and, with a little forethought, could have been spread throughout the wall with spectacular results. As it is, we did what we could with *Dryas octopetala, Draba rigida, Sedum middendorfianum* (which never warranted such choice company and which must be trimmed regularly to stay in scale), the charming *Ramonda myconi,* and the occasional campanula species.

Of course it could be redone again – this time with all those saxifrages and primulas that should have been incorporated in the first instance and, in five years, it would be the wonder of the wall-garden world. But no; those incomparably happy specimens of saxifrage and primula would have to be scrapped or divided into unneeded plants and, besides, Cono is back in Sicily. It will never be what it might have been, but then it's *pas mal!* E. B. Anderson put it succinctly in his glorious book *Seven Gardens*: "It takes two lifetimes to grow alpines – the first to gain experience, the second to cultivate them." I would add a third: to achieve perfection.

Between the two walls lay a space for the *ideal,* narrow scree bed, over three feet deep with a northwest exposure and limestone rocks on all sides, something the alpine plant enthusiast dreams about for all those choice and ungrowable plants that *just* might make it in a cool northern setting. The next spring a host of such plants was duly imported from the Alpine House at Stonecrop and planted among carefully laid paving of small limestone slabs buried into the scree surface. Here was a spot where Kabschia saxifrages would thrive and *Gypsophila aretioides* 'Caucasica' would form dense, low, tiny hummocks, enjoying the shady exposure, the cool, moist root-run under the limestone slabs and the gritty scree that stretched so deeply below it. With luck the gypsophila might grow into dinner-plate-size hummocks that might even have a flower or two by the middle of the twenty-first century. Here too was a spot to experiment with aretian androsaces, *Dicentra peregrina,* and *Aquilegia jonesii,* with every hope of success.

The plants went in, grew happily the first summer and, for the most part, were nowhere to be found the next spring. Why? Was it something about the winter? Did they dislike being planted on the level, in lieu of the well-drained site occasioned by a vertical wall? Had they too much winter sun, or not enough snow cover due to wind patterns? Was it a message to keep one's aspirations on a more attainable level and not to taunt the horticultural gods?

The circular steps and terrace plantings in late June with the alpine (as opposed to old-fashioned) pinks in bloom. The campanulas in the scree wall beds are a blur of green. Hieracium villosum's pale and dainty yellow daisies are encouraged to spread throughout the front lawn in the background.

Of course, some of the plants survived, mostly campanulas, and one in particular, *Campanula cochlearifolia* in its blue, white and intermediate forms, appeared to thrive. All was not lost! Or, in retrospect, was it? Today that charming, brash, totally invasive, stoloniferous campanula has taken over the scree bed in its entirety and run down into the front wall. It has seeded itself into the leafmass of the alpines in the planted pockets, associating adventitiously with the aquilegias, dianthus, penstemon, potentillas, and other campanulas with its insistent and irresistible charm and getting away with it because it is a visual delight. For three weeks in July it turns the whole façade into a low froth of blue and white fairy bells, intermingling with the other plants and showing off to such an extent that, upon discovering the display, you are hard put not to catch your breath and be filled with joy.

The down side is that during the rest of the year, the scree bed is pretty much a dull and uniform fuzz of green. Also, because of cochlearifolia's insatiable curiosity and winning ways, one must be prepared in early spring to rescue *Androsace sempervivoides* before its rosettes are strangled and *Penstemon campanulatus (pulchellus)*, which has stopped even trying to bloom: too shy and compliant in the face of such horticultural chutzpah. The rescue means lifting the mass of plant and roots out of the plant pocket (along with any scree soil that may contain bits of campanula root), picking or even washing out the campanula roots from the host plant's root mass and then replanting it, or a bit of it, in hopes that close and regular inspection will prevent a recurrence.

Some dwarf aquilegias behave the same way, imposing themselves in the middle of another alpine and blatantly showing off, uninvited. They are less rapacious, however, and not so unwelcome, having a commensal, as opposed to usurpative, approach to sharing the same space.

THE CORNER CIRCULAR STEPS

Between the White Garden wall and the corner of the Guest Wing a series of four wide, steep steps had always led from the Tapis Vert up to the stretch of lawn running to the Cabane toolhouse. Here was a spot that could contain a more appealing stone staircase — as well as a host of plant pockets for additional alpines, this time with a southwestern exposure.

It seemed inappropriate to emulate the handsome circular steps leading from the reflection pool down to the Tapis Vert. The challenge was to incorporate a steep set of steps in a restricted space that would supplement and harmonize with the existing walls without protruding into the Tapis Vert.

The solution was the use of a classic device, a set of concentric circles, set in the middle of a stepped-back, solid wall with the smallest circle, a full one, in the center and midway up the rising steps. Convex semicircles descend to grade below it and concave semicircles rise to grade above it. The wall and staircase have small terraces, both at their base and their top, just wide enough to encompass the largest semicircle, and planting pockets, filled with alpines, are dispersed throughout. Potted standard *Syringa* 'Palibin' bracket the steps and *Clematis macropetala* tumbles down the face of the wall on either side. Behind the staircase a thuja hedge with an opening blocks the view from the upper level and forms an appropriate backdrop for the structure. After descending the White Garden steps on to the Tapis Vert, one notices the staircase in the corner. It is also apparent as one walks around the reflection pool and descends the protruding, central circular steps.

The proportions and final design were worked out *in situ* with Cono and provide a stagey corner setting for the plants within it. When it was first completed I had reservations that it might be too "busy," too much of a good thing and a distraction from the neighboring garden walls. Now that it has aged a bit and is softened with plants, tubs, and vines, and backed with the solid, dark green of a thuja hedge, I feel reassured that it is not unduly obtrusive. The contented alpines within it appear to enjoy being presented in an appropriately elegant setting.

OPPOSITE

The corner circular steps with the Syringa 'Palibin' standards in bloom. These steps provide additional pockets for alpines and lead to the Cabane toolhouse.

OVERLEAF

The walls and steps in mid-July.

CHAPTER IV
REFURBISHING THE OLDER GARDENS

OPPOSITE

A view of the White Garden and Tapis Vert from the Rose Garden. Roses come into bloom as the pinks go over and a Crambe cordifolia towers over the White Garden.

ABOVE, RIGHT

One of the roses in the perennial beds at Les Quatre Vents.

ESSENTIALLY, THE FRAMEWORK OF THE GARDENS TO THE WEST OF the house remains identical to that decreed by Eddie Mathews. His aesthetic directions and spatial layouts were never questioned in the family and were followed to the letter. His powerful axial features such as the Tapis Vert and the placement of the original gardens, along with his handsome walls, terraces and steps, have stood the test of time and are what characterize the essence of the place to most visitors. The bones were good and there was never a thought of modifying them. In fact they served as the core reference for all the garden expansion that began in the mid 1970s. Even that acme of garden taste, Russell Page, approved Eddie's layout, although he questioned aspects of the details, especially the plantings, with waspish acuity.

It was not only the rock work that had to be rebuilt but all my mother's garden beds had to be completely redone and the hedging revitalized as well. Fortunately, the perennials, which last forever in a northern climate, were salvageable and the shrub framework, now grown to maturity after forty years, was fine. The passage of time, that essential element in a garden's stature, had endowed Eddie Mathews' classical vision with a timelessness that is more often sought after than realized.

Let's approach these elements of the core of the garden as the visitor does, leaving the Guest Garden through the far door. A hawthorn hedge screens the Cabane to the right, while a thuja hedge screens the complex of circular steps and wall gardens that lie to the left, below the reflection pool terrace.

THE WHITE GARDEN

In the early 1930s Vita Sackville-West was writing about the extraordinary gardens that she and Harold Nicolson were creating at Sissinghurst. My mother was one of the many who were inspired to follow their example in planning her gardens at Les Quatre Vents, albeit on a very modest scale when compared to Sissinghurst's crowning feature, that best of all white gardens.

In the center of a rectangular space, raised four feet above the level of the Tapis Vert, Eddie Mathews placed a simple oval pool fed from an eighteen-inch canal in the center of its longer axis. The canal leads from a statue of Pan — more Peter Pan than the goat-legged figure of mythology — playing his pipes within a deeply recessed niche formed by columnar chamaecyparis and rounded thuja.

The pool was designed so that the water would be level with the surrounding lawn and filled with white water lilies. The lawn edge soon completely obscured the narrow

OPPOSITE

A bird's-eye view of the rectangular White Garden in early July with Cono's steps, invaded by Campanula cochlearifolia *'Alba', leading up to the flush oval pool.*

ABOVE

The White Garden bench under a bower of philadelphus is seen through white delphiniums and Campanula latifolia *'Alba'.*

concrete pool edge, rendering the water surface a mirror set in a green frame. All subsequent pools on the property have been modeled upon this simple idea. Water flush with the surrounding surface is far more striking than a pool with a stone surround that draws attention to itself, or a pool with the level of water below the surrounding grade, which lessens its impact and gives it an unnatural and contrived look.

The seventy years that have elapsed since Pan began to pipe water into the canal have taken their toll. One of the pipes has broken off and it is a regular chore to ensure that Pan is not totally obscured within his evergreen setting. It is important that he be seen, for he is the focal point at one end of the principal transverse axis that runs along the short canal, across the oval pool *between* the white water lilies, down a flight of steps, across the Tapis Vert, down more steps through the Rose Garden, on down a long, stepped-terrace path between the beds of the Perennial Allée and, finally, across a grassy circle to a raised fountain set in a semicircle of maturing thuja edging the taller trees of the Woodland Garden.

The Cabane and its Poplar Companion

The cabane in the mid-1930s.

The tool house was sufficiently separate from the original house for Eddie Mathews to indulge his creativity. He designed a stylish modern building with a lot of character. Now filled with the clutter of years of benign neglect by generations too preoccupied to make it neat except in the rainiest weather, the Cabane serves as a gathering place for those working in the garden. Here the orders for the day are given after a strategic early-morning council. The dogs check it out regularly, ever mindful of the possibility of a handout during laughter-filled morning and afternoon breaks.

The Cabane's most appealing quality, however, is its intimate embrace by the trunk of a Lombardy poplar that was left in place when it was built almost seventy years ago. The tree has simply grown around the jutting roof in an accommodating manner, lending an air of age and adaptability to the setting. These two disparate elements, building and tree, support one another in a symbiotic way and seem quite pleased with the result. During my lifetime they have always been a unit and I choose not to think of the loneliness the Cabane will feel once its partner's time has come. I suppose the compromise will be to cut off the trunk above the juncture and then seal it to minimize the rate of decomposition so that these two friends, now both inanimate, can remain joined well into the new century, comforted by their continuing bond.

The cabane today.

White lupine and Dictamnus albus *frame steps leading down to the Tapis Vert and the transverse axis that runs through the Rose Garden to the Perennial Allée.*

If you stand in front of the White Garden pool, at the head of the steps leading down to the Tapis Vert, your eye is carried down the axis to the just-visible fountain in the distance. The Rose Garden, framed by hawthorn and thuja hedges, is in full view, but there is only a hint of the double perennial borders, which are partially obscured by a tall hawthorn hedge. At the same time one is exposed to the full extent of the Tapis Vert, which runs at right angles to the steps and, for the first time, you notice on the left the circular steps and walled alpine beds that flank and support the reflection pool terrace.

The White Garden beds form a rectangle that frames the oval pool. At the narrow ends of the rectangle they comprise white-flowered syringa, philadelphus, and viburnum, with the occasional white-flowered clematis climbing through them. A white garden bench centers the longitudinal axis. The perennial beds on either side are edged with the successive blooms of *Sanguinaria canadensis* forma *multiplex*,[12] *Primula denticulata* 'Alba', *Bergenia* 'Silberlicht', *Aquilegia flabellata* var. *pumila* 'Alba', *Fritillaria meleagris* 'Alba', *Lamium maculatum* 'White Nancy', and a succession of white lilies. The beds' interiors include white forms of *Geranium phaeum*, *pratense*, and *sylvaticum*, *Dicentra spectabilis*, *Dictamnus albus*,

peony, delphinium, campanula, and phlox along with *Cimicifuga racemosa*,[13] and *Aconitum septentrionale* 'Ivorine' interplanted with white-flowered annuals. Tall white martagon lilies poke their heads above the foliage of the cimicifuga, while the blossoms of *Clematis recta* appear in the midst of the surrounding hawthorn hedge, a serendipitous plus, in this instance, from this aggressive colonizer.

An unfortunate condition of this garden has been its proximity to the single row of Lombardy poplars that was planted in the late 1920s and that ran along what was then the property line from near the house to the stream on the west side of the garden. Today the only survivors of this row, aside from the Lombardy bonded to the Cabane, are the five aging Lombardies next to the White Garden. They serve as a rather ragged and somewhat too broad background for the axis viewed from the fountain at the woodland's edge up through the Perennial Allée and Rose Garden to the diminutive Pan centered at their base. The plants near them also require constant watering and fertilization. Poplars are voracious feeders and absorbers of moisture and we can vouch for the fact that their roots extend an astonishing distance from the base of their trunks (some say a distance equivalent to their height) if there is moisture to be had.

As a consequence, for years we have found ourselves in a catch-22 situation. The more the perennials are fertilized and watered to assure their survival, the longer the Lombardies' longevity. Until recently, their health and majestic presence overruled any chance of their removal. Now, after seventy years of making their statement, they are faltering and becoming ragged as the autumnal gall that makes them exude a powdery substance (which disfigures the water features in the garden) recurs with increased intensity. Despite a recent topping and pruning, it seems unlikely that they will endure for very long into the new century. In 1984 we planted three young Lombardy poplars directly behind Pan so that, when the time comes to remove the remnants of the row, the fastigiate accent will remain – this time centered on axis. The three trees should create sufficient mass to anchor that important focal point. Once again, the change to what has been a given of the landscape will be dramatic. If needed, more trees can be added.

Because of the poplar roots, we found ourselves digging and redoing the perennial beds in the White Garden more frequently than anywhere else. The last time this upheaval took place, after cutting the extensive mass of poplar roots that had been reveling in the rich soil, we edged the poplar side of the beds with a three-foot-deep band of sheet metal, which seems to have limited the problem. It will be interesting to see how the plants respond once the older trees are removed.

Another deep band of sheet metal divides the portion of the White Garden beds fronting the Tapis Vert, and planted with perennials, from a scree-filled section adjacent to them behind the dry walls. In this two-foot-wide scree, white-flowering alpines and perennials and annuals of intermediate height are grown, bringing the mantle of bloom down to the sessile crevice plants blooming at the wall's surface.

A view across the White Garden's oval pool in late July when Cimicifuga racemosa *is in bloom.*

THE GREATER PERFECTION

THE ROSE GARDEN

IN THE BEGINNING, WHAT IS NOW THE ROSE GARDEN WAS A RECTANGULAR, enclosed Blue Garden flanking the Tapis Vert and echoing the elevated White Garden across the way. I remember noticing the Blue Garden as a child, filled with Siberian iris, delphinium, and campanula. This memory is perhaps prompted by a watercolor by Robert Cauchon, a painting that was elsewhere during the fire and is our only record of the garden.[14]

It was Pat Morgan, an artist, teacher, and, above all, inspired landscape designer, who after my father's death extended the transverse allée from the White Garden down a long perennial allée to the woodland and created a sunken Rose Garden where the Blue Garden had been. At least, the lawn space within it was sunken. The rose beds, supported by walls made of thin limestone slabs, remain at the level of the Tapis Vert.

I have any number of gaps in my horticultural capabilities and one of them is roses. I believe this stems from spending my gardening years in climatic zones where roses had rough going. On our windy hill at Stonecrop, climbing roses and hybrid teas rarely survive, although shrub roses fare rather better. At Les Quatre Vents many of the perpetual and floribunda roses perish in a winter without adequate snow cover, leaving gaping holes to be filled from the limited supplies of a local nursery.

It is not that I don't find roses beautiful or life-enhancing — were it possible, Les Quatre Vents' walls would be covered with 'Gloire de Dijon' and the Kiftsgate rose would fill a corner of the vegetable and picking garden. It's just that there have been too many discouraging losses, despite herculean efforts to provide winter protection. I

LEFT

Robert Cauchon's watercolor of the Blue Garden in 1936.

BELOW

Pat Morgan, October 1981.

OPPOSITE

A view of the Rose Garden at the moment when the underplanting of pinks dominates the scene in late June, before roses other than the shrub types have bloomed.

OPPOSITE, BELOW

Pat Morgan's design for the Rose Garden, 1957. The circular steps were never installed where specified, but were added instead at the entrance from the Tapis Vert in 1982.

100   CHAPTER IV

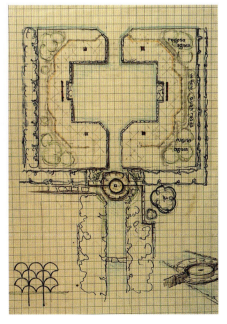

succumbed to Will Tillotson's prose fantasy on old-fashioned roses. In fact I became emotionally involved with 'Bishop Darlington', an endearing Penzance rose that enjoyed a protected corner near the kitchen door at Stonecrop and, invariably, bore the last rose of the season, its single amber and apricot flowers scenting the October twilight. Regrettably, the Bishop was done in by the Quebec winter.

But, aside from some shrub and species roses (its hard to improve on *Rosa glauca* as a companion plant) and obliging performers such as 'Bonica', which fit so agreeably in amongst other perennials, I gladly leave the chore of encouraging the roses to Anne, who has the patience and temperament to deal with them. I would infinitely rather cope with more obliging plants and view the roses from a respectful distance. I do care, however, how the Rose Garden looks and will do anything to avoid the bare-earth approach that one so often finds in North American rose gardens, with the roses displayed in serried ranks, devoid of companion plantings.

When the expansion of the garden had begun in earnest, we enjoyed a sort of horticultural summit in 1983, with a party of house guests consisting of Mary McCarthy (a keen garden enthusiast), her husband Jim West, her friend Eleanor Perenyi, and Rosemary and David Verey. One outcome was Rosemary Verey's suggestion that our roses

should be underplanted with *Lamium maculatum* as a solution to the bare-earth problem.

Later that summer we were visited by Russell Page, who announced categorically that pinks were the plants to use to cover the ground beneath roses.

I mentioned Rosemary Verey's suggestion of lamium.

"Only pinks."

What about *Thymus lanuginosus*?

"*Only* pinks!"

What about that gray artemisia?

"*Only* pinks!!"

Not surprisingly, the Rose Garden today is underplanted only with pinks — those old-fashioned dianthus that were rescued from the weedy, dry-laid circular steps — and never was there a more felicitous combination. The pinks (probably forms of *Dianthus Allwoodii* group) bloom before the roses and for three weeks make a solid mosaic of intermingled pink, white, cream, and rose blossoms, filling the garden with color and perfuming the air around it with the heady scent of cloves. Then, as the blossoms go over and the pinks are given a proper haircut, the roses come into bloom, their vivid colors set against, and enhanced by, the foil of the gray, blue-green carpet beneath them.

ABOVE

Once the pinks are dead-headed their foliage provides a gray-green foil for the roses in late July.

OPPOSITE

A view of the White Garden from the Rose Garden.

OVERLEAF

The transition from the Rose Garden to the Perennial Allée. The blue borderline notes of Campanula persicifolia *and* Clematis integrifolia *are echoed in the towering geranium and* Campanula lactiflora *in the Allée.*

THE TAPIS VERT

At the outset the Tapis Vert was bordered by high solid fences of white cedar (thuja) posts. It was gently terraced into three levels and had two shallow stone borders running across it at equidistant intervals between the reflection pool terrace and a festooned and swagged, roped apse at its terminus, just before the slope tumbled into a deep, open ravine.

I suppose the cedar fences were there not only to frame the space, but also to act as a windbreak until hedges could be established, for the site was swept by those all too familiar winds from all directions. In time a double hedge was planted consisting of the local hawthorn (*Crataegus flabellata*) dug from the fields, with a lower, inside hedge of *Berberis thunbergii* next to it, and the cedar posts and rope festoons were banished. Shortly before my mother's death the ravine was dammed to make a small lake below where the apse had been. When we inherited the property we removed the two stone borders and today the green sward flows unimpeded towards the view, with only the skeleton of the snake fence around the adjoining field as an interruption.

When we were about to tackle the reflection pool terrace, walls, and steps at Les Quatre Vents, a number of other general landscape questions concerned me. Were we doing the right thing to rebuild the existing walls between the pool and the Tapis Vert? Was there a way to correct the awkward slope in the entrance court? How were we to screen the shopping center and other horrors that had sprouted across the bay, where the Nairne seigneurie had once been?

I decided to call Russell Page, who was spending a good deal of his time at Pepsico in those days, developing that grand corporate landscape around massive and important

ABOVE

Currie Mathews Cabot, the author's mother, in her White Garden circa 1935.

BELOW, LEFT

The view from the reflection pool terrace over the Tapis Vert to the hills in 1936.

BELOW, RIGHT

Looking up the stepped Tapis Vert towards the house in 1932, before the reflection pool terrace was installed.

Highland cattle obligingly resting on axis with the Tapis Vert on a damp day in late June.

modern sculptures. He jumped at the idea of an excursion to Quebec and the prospect of *perdrix aux choux*.

We had originally met Russell when his protégé and successor, François Goffinet, brought him to Stonecrop. This was not a professional visit, but I did ask his advice about landscaping a new lagoon we had created. He took one bewildered look at all the alpines and raised stone beds and pronounced that the new feature should be kept as simple as possible in view of all the horticultural excitement nearby. It was good advice.

Russell Page stayed at Les Quatre Vents for two nights and one long, exhausting day, which reduced me to a nervous wreck. Every hour of daylight was devoted to touring, examining and discussing every aspect and element of the garden we were about to rehabilitate and expand. I was privileged to have the eminent author of *The Education of a Gardener* giving me the most intensive one-day individually tutored crash-course in garden design. By the end of it I was considering taking up my unfortunate game of golf once again as a less threatening avocation.

Examining a winding path that led from the White Garden to what had been a hidden picking garden behind the hawthorn hedge, Russell Page queried: "Why on earth is there a path from here to there?"

"It's always been there!"

"But *why*?"

Looking at Eddie Mathews' ingenious arrangement of steps around the reflection pool terrace: "It just won't do!"

Looking at any vista, especially if it led down to the water's edge, where there were plantings that intervened: "Get rid of that fuzz!"

Looking at many of the elements I had grown up with: "What possessed them to do *that*?"

There was constructive and helpful advice as well. I should stop worrying about screening the changes in the view across the bay, since I was the only person it bothered. The way to get rid of an ungainly hump in the middle of the sloping south lawn was to start a new slope thirty feet above and behind it. There were too many shrubs in the White Garden beds. They should be replaced with perennials. The arc of the south lawn should be broken up by planting trees at strategic spots: "One here; and one here!" I dutifully obliged.

Again and again: "Get rid of that *fuzz!*"

Everywhere I looked, sure enough there was fuzz.

It was a wonderful, practical seminar in some of the basics of landscape design and although it was thoroughly gruelling I just wish it had lasted longer, for every forceful point has become part of my frame of reference. Today there is no fuzz anywhere.

We measured the reflection pool steps and the entrance court and Russell promised to work on improving them. At the end of our long day, settling comfortably into his second whiskey, Russell took pity and threw a rope to the drowning sailor. "Well, you know, it really isn't all that bad." He went on: "If it were my place I would remove the snake fence from the vista and replace it with a ha-ha to keep out the livestock." *Perdrix aux choux* was duly produced, we were regaled with tales of the projects he had worked on, and parted as friends.

After some time had gone by and there was not so much as a bill for his travel expenses, I wrote and sent him a sum adequate to cover them and asked him to bill me for his time. No bill was ever sent, but I received a charming thank you letter for reimbursing him. It wasn't too many months later that he died.

I had promised to send Mary McCarthy and Eleanor Perenyi a full report on Russell's visit. Mary wrote back: "Don't you dare replace that fence with a ha-ha! Your garden would lose its naiveté." Mary McCarthy won out. The snake fence, which I had begun to think of as a bit of horizontal fuzz, is still there and the appealing thought of a ha-ha, now that I was well on my way to becoming an unfuzzed vista purist, was shelved, awaiting the right time and place.

The snake fence, with the occasional contented and shaggy cow looking over it towards the house, belonged there and was the *right* link between the house and the field. Naiveté lent a quality to the garden that might be extinguished if a professional took over. It seemed wisest to muddle through as best one could.

OPPOSITE

A wild-duck-in-flight's-eye view of the core of Les Quatre Vents.

OVERLEAF

The reflection pool terrace and the Tapis Vert in late June.

The Greater Perfection

110   Chapter IV

If a garden is to reflect the spirit of the creator it really has to be the result of a personal rather than a professional effort. The amateur, of course, can benefit from the advice of professionals or can become quasi-professional through study and observation. However, it is unlikely that the numinous quality one senses in a successful amateur's or autodidact's garden can be found in a bought and paid for, professionally designed garden, no matter how illustrious the designer.

The Tapis Vert is at the heart of Les Quatre Vents' landscape, an unchanging green carpet from the moment the warblers swarm in May until the first snow falls. In midsummer the Toulouse geese parade daily at its foot near the lake, flapping their wings, and enjoying the naiveté of the scene.

THE GOOSE ALLÉE

THOSE GEESE WERE SUPPOSED TO FLAP THEIR WINGS AT THE END OF the new perennial allée behind the hawthorn hedge parallel to the Tapis Vert. In this first expansion of the inherited landscape (and at the time the only one contemplated) they did just that when the allée was built in 1979 and gave the new element its name. However, once the allée was completed and the plantings had matured, they abandoned it for the more open Tapis Vert, where they were visible from the living room, driving the dogs to distraction. In the end we resorted to a fiberglass goose, placed at the far corner of the grass path through the allée.

The idea behind the Goose Allée was to make the most of what had once been a hidden picking garden and to add a second perennial allée filled with plants for which there was no room in the original main allée flanking the transverse axis from Pan to the woodland fountain. The new allée would also enjoy an orientation at right-angles to the main allée, providing a new set of conditions with different angles of sunlight and shade for the plants.

The picking garden contained mostly annuals. From my childhood I remember a forest of larkspur bordered by the single row of Lombardies along its perimeter. By the time of my mother's death in 1965 the trees, which had not been constantly watered and manured as in the case of their counterparts bordering the White Garden, were becoming increasingly decrepit and unsightly. Over the next ten years I was more preoccupied with cutting woodland paths and horse trails in the nearby Forêt than with the garden and they were removed one by one. The neighboring field, now part of the property and used as a horse pasture, dominated the view from the now-abandoned picking-garden space.

If a perennial allée was to be placed in the space it would need to be contained by matching hedges and shut off from the wide-ranging view of fields and wooded ridge in the distance. The old snake fence was removed along with the giant and tenacious

An overview of the upper part of the Goose Allée showing its relationship to the ensemble.

Lombardy stumps. Young hawthorns were brought in from the fields one spring, a trench was dug and, instantly, there was a framework for the perennial beds, albeit a lop-sided one. Rehabilitating the hawthorn hedges bordering the Tapis Vert (by cutting them back severely, manuring them heavily, and shaping them carefully each season to keep them narrower at the top than at the base) had turned them into tall, thick walls that had become something to be proud of.

The gardener at Les Quatre Vents during my mother's time was our neighbor David Lapointe. He had been there close to thirty-five years when she died. He was a good gardener with aesthetic sensibilities, but he had my mother's number. Every other spring he would threaten to leave, and mother, who depended on him, would cave in to whatever his demands might be. He was not the most active individual, and when we inherited Les Quatre Vents and faced the hard work of expanding the garden, I elected to give him early retirement and offered him his final year off with full pay until the government pension kicked in. It was an option he embraced with more energy and enthusiasm than I'd ever noted before.

Expansion was now possible because we had recently succeeded in acquiring the neighboring land. During his lifetime my father had acquired Kelley Desmeules' property but had balked at the high price ($25 an acre!) that the Lapointe family was asking for their land, which included the wooded ridge that overlooked Les Quatre Vents to the north. David Lapointe's father then proceeded to harvest the mature red pines on the ridge. (Fortunately the younger specimens grew to maturity in the intervening half-century and the view is back to where it was.) After both our fathers had died, David and I continued the negotiations for a decade without coming to agreement. Just before mother's death I made a final offer of $75 per acre, which was once again declined. Discouraged, I told David that was the end of it, turned away and was about to drive off when he came after me and accepted the offer after all. The lesson was clear: if all one wants is one's neighbor's land, it should not be too apparent.[15]

Since the ridge was now secure and the surroundings were not about to change, there was every reason to work on enlarging the garden. With the new matching hedge in place, the perennial beds were dug (in retrospect nowhere nearly well and deeply enough) with a grass path separating them, and with two transverse grass paths leading from openings in the hedge by the Tapis Vert cutting the central path at right angles and the perennial beds themselves into three sections each. The transverse paths carried on through openings in the new matching hedge to the now unfenced neighboring field.

The new hedge grew like Topsy and it wasn't long before the beds were filled with healthy, mature perennial clumps. Given the long, narrow rectangular space, bracketed by nine-foot hedges, we decided to enhance the tunnel effect by massing the hedge sides of the beds with as many tall and fastigiate plants as possible.

In the spring the first bit of color comes from interplantings of *Doronicum orientale*

ABOVE

Primula vulgaris ssp. *sibthorpii* mixed with *P.* 'Wanda' *and* Scilla siberica, a combination used by H. F. duPont at Winterthur.

OPPOSITE

Campanula latifolia *and* Astrantia major.

and *Brunnera macrophylla* bordering the transverse paths, with their sprightly mixture of yellow and blue. At the end near the lake the scented blossoms of *Daphne mezereum* are complemented by a mixed underplanting of primulas (*P. vulgaris* ssp. *sibthorpii* and *P.* 'Wanda') and *Scilla siberica*, a combination we first saw in the woodland garden at Winterthur. The rest of the perennials come to life and, in the briefest of intervals, what appeared to be an almost empty and sparsely planted bed is filled with foliage except for the spaces where annuals are to go and where questionably hardy plants such as *Anemone hupehensis* and *Aster* x *frikartii* have succumbed to a bad winter.

The matching beds have an overall symmetry, with *Aruncus dioicus* in each corner of the rectangular space adjoining *Cimicifuga racemosa*. In this way from late June into August a succession of tall, white spires provide corner accents. Tall clumps of *Thalictrum aquilegifolium* in shades of light and dark lavender and the palest of grays are dispersed throughout the beds, along with the taller campanulas such as latifolia and lactiflora, *Centaurea dealbata*, tree and herbaceous peonies, filipendulas and the like. In addition to the aruncus and cimicifuga, monkshood and delphinium contribute the fastigiate quality that characterizes the plants in the Goose Allée. There are varieties of monkshood that carry the bloom from June through October. The tableau starts with the durable, pristine white spires of *Aconitum septentrionale* 'Ivorine' set against handsome dark foliage, surely one of the most satisfying of border perennials, surprising us all with its earlier-than-expected appearance in June when the Quatre Vents borders are just getting going. 'Ivorine' is followed by *A. compactum* 'Carneum' which blooms vigorously some weeks later in a tattletale shade of pink; not exactly what was in the mind's eye, but still a useful transition to the blue monkshood that takes over in August. One of the best of these is *A. tauricum* 'Bressingham Spire', a wonderful compact variety with the truest of blue spires.

Aconitum henryi follows, with its tall loose spires of intense dark violet-blue towering over the rest of the garden and complementing the bright yellow of *Rudbeckia maxima*, which enjoys equal stature. This monkshood is sufficiently vigorous to require periodic curbing, but worth it for it lasts well into September, a welcome substitute for the delphinium spires dead-headed in early August. *A. carmichaelii*, with the rich blue flowers of its 'Arendsii' form, along with the blue and white *A.* x *bicolor*, are used sparingly. They are shown to best effect massed by the lake and are an essential part of the picking garden.

The monkshood tableau ends with a tall, late-blooming variant of *carmichaelii*, known as *A. carmichaelii* var. *wilsonii* 'Kelmscott', which blooms until the hard frosts of mid-October, looking rather lonely and isolated as its fellow perennials call it a day and begin hunkering down for the winter. Ideally, 'Kelmscott' should be mixed with *Chrysanthemum uliginosum* and *Cimicifuga simplex*, plants which rarely, if ever, bloom in our short Zone 4 season.

The Greater Perfection

118   Chapter IV

PREVIOUS

The bench at the east end of the Goose Allée with Lavatera cachemirica *doing its utmost to top the delphinium spires.*

OPPOSITE

Delphiniums thrive in Les Quatre Vents' cool, moist maritime climate and individual clumps appear to last forever, certainly longer than we mortals. They get bigger, better and showier each year, outdoing themselves in a cool, rainy season after a real winter with deep, long-lasting snow cover. It is so different from the struggles of trying to induce delphiniums to survive for more than a few seasons further south.

The delphiniums, on the other hand, bloom from mid-July to early August, the very center of the season, and constitute the perennial borders' apotheosis. The Goose Allée has only Pacific Hybrids, many of them grown from hand-pollinated seed distributed by the Delphinium Society. The tall clumps march down either side of the allée and proudly display their dramatic spires that, in a good year, reach up to nine feet before they are clobbered by the inevitable August thundershower.

In the Goose Allée the delphinium plantings are separated into different color groups — purest white and truest blue in the beds nearest the appletree seat at the upper end of the allée; lavenders, pinks, and grays in the central section; and deep purples at the far end. The only trouble we have experienced was a year when the delphinium leafhopper suddenly appeared and proceeded to decimate the spires overnight. The next year the insects were discouraged by Sevin and since then have chosen not to return, no doubt because we resort to precautionary spraying as well as regular checking to ensure the spires are bug-free.

For the garden at Les Quatre Vents the delphiniums' apotheosis represents the turning point of summer. We make no effort to sustain the intensity and mass of their blossoms after this point in their companion plantings. The last two weeks in August are the window when the perennial beds can be reworked and improved, executing the strategies and switches noted earlier in the season so that the reconfigured border and its transplants can be in place by September 1st and enjoy six cool growing weeks before the really hard frosts set in.

I find orchestrating the perennial beds the most stressful part of gardening at Les Quatre Vents. They never seem to be right or, if they are, then the next year is a different story; the tall *Lavatera cachemirica* that so well complemented the pale blue delphinium has vanished and it will take a year, if one is lucky, to replace it. More often than not serendipity rules and there are brilliantly successful combinations that were never intended, while the most deliberate juxtaposition turns out to be disappointing. My goal is to create a series of moments from May into August, maybe five in all, when the plant combinations blossom in an harmonious blend, a succession of well-orchestrated themes. The musical simile is apt: a perennial border should provide a series of themes and movements which, together, form a horticultural symphony.

Gardening involves so many other appealing things (such as pruning espaliers or dividing primulas) devoid of the mental anguish that composing a perennial border entails, and where one's judgments and tastes aren't so blatantly exposed. I've reached the point where I steer visitors quickly by the perennial areas and discourage them from walking between the beds so that they see the whole more or less from a distance, as a mass of plants and color, and are unable to focus on the individual plants.

The Goose Allée has had two drawbacks, one of which is now corrected. In the autumn of 1996 and the following spring, some seventeen years after they were begun, we redug the beds, this time correctly. We dug a two-foot-deep trench, removing all the root debris from the poplars and the hawthorn hedges and placing a thirty-inch galvanized sheet-metal barrier between the hedges and the beds. The sandy soil was enriched with compost, moisture-retaining peat moss, and copious amounts of rotted cow manure, and the plants were divided and replaced. A few plants, such as the coarse *Centaurea macrocephala* and some strident ligularias that clearly weren't team players, were consigned to other parts of the garden.

In the early spring the beds look empty and I wonder how they can possibly be filled with plants. A month later I can see which plants are too close together after all, and where there are gaping holes, for the *second* year. The ideal hole-filler drifted into our inventory of plants, thanks to Thompson & Morgan: *Nicandra physaloides*, known as the apple-of-Peru or, more readily, the shoo-fly plant. Characterized by large oval leaves and one-inch, wheel-shaped, pale blue flowers followed by a berry enclosed in a papery, lantern-shaped bract, it quickly grows into a handsome four-foot umbrella obscuring whatever is beneath or nearby. It works wonders and is so effective that I invariably forget that there is a hole to be filled when late August rolls around.

The second drawback may be uncorrectable. The beds are too narrow — only five feet wide; they really should be at least half that much again. I knew that before I started, but was seduced by the channeled vista (or was it a case of tunnel vision?). There is no way of enlarging the beds — except, perhaps, by doing away with the center path to leave a narrow, possibly winding, dirt path for access. But then could the vista to the bole of the paper birch at the end of the allée be maintained? And would the more gradual descent from the dizzying heights of the delphiniums and cimicifugas towering on either side be an anticlimax?

Or do these doubts matter to anyone other than the gardener striving for that Greater Perfection? A great ploy in this situation is to be able to divert the audience's attention elsewhere. The hedged thuja path leading from the Goose Allée towards the Rondel is an even narrower corridor, and by urging visitors into it, I keep them from looking too closely at the deficiencies (at any given moment) of the planting in the Allée. It is easy to proclaim by way of diversion that so much lies ahead to see that it would be better to return for further inspection after the tour is completed. In 1997 a stately urn was added as a terminal focal point that lures the visitor in for a closer look.

But we are getting ahead of ourselves. There was empty space out there to the north begging for attention.

The Goose Allée with the paper birch at the west end of the allée, near Lac Libellule, where mauve and purple tones predominate.

CHAPTER V
BORROWING THE LANDSCAPE

OPPOSITE

The basins and canals of the Watercourse step down to Lac Libellule. Behind the obliging swan, a turtle is poised to spout water back towards the viewer.

ABOVE, RIGHT

Antonia looks out over Lac Libellule.

TO AN EXTENT THE NEIGHBORING FIELDS HAD ALWAYS BEEN A bit of borrowed landscape for the original gardens, a peaceful, open counterpoint to the formal compartments and enclosures amongst trees and hedges whose hidden intricacies had to be discovered through exploration. Over the years we had made incursions into the farmland by planting saplings forming allées of trees that crisscrossed the landscape. The farm roads that extend from river to wooded hills through each of the neighboring farms acquired by Les Quatre Vents lend themselves to allées. A note of formality near the house was long ago established by the typically French use of a Lombardy poplars along our entrance drive and delineating our property line. We planted Lombardy poplars along what had originally been Kelley Desmeules' farm road to maintain this traditional silhouette when we realized that the senescent trees along the entrance drive were destined for removal. These formal allées immediately tied the agricultural surround to the core of the contrived landscape.

We also ventured farther afield. For a number of years beginning in the late 1960s, we chose to plant as many birch saplings as we could to form an allée along the road that cuts across the long, narrow strips of farms abutting Les Quatre Vents that had been acquired in the preceding decade. We found the native paper birch (*Betula papyrifera*) to be far and away the best allée tree. It grows in abundance in the woodlands and is a deciduous colonizer in abandoned fields. Easily dug and transplanted once the frost is gone and before the buds burgeon, five- to seven-foot saplings with an adequate sod can be removed in the morning and planted in the afternoon. We continued during each spring planting window until the allée was complete and the road turned a corner into the forest at the last farm strip. Today much of that allée is approaching maturity. The birches are forming an extended arch and we soon shall have a birch arcade, a kilometer in length, leading across the fields behind the house and up a significant hill to an upper plateau (only discovered after climbing the hill) and on into the distance.

Back near the house another, shorter tunnel is in progress. Between the garage court and the new Lombardy allée, we have planted the Amur maple (*Acer ginnala*) whose Zone 2 hardiness rating enables it to survive in the exposed, windswept site behind the house. These maples are slow-growing and somewhat brittle, but are the first to show color, a brilliant red, in the autumn. In due course the Amur maple allée will form a tunnel twenty-five feet high.

But enough of the allées and the air of formality they lend to the surrounding landscape and the pasture where Anne's horses graze. We are primarily concerned with the expansion of the garden proper. Now that the Lombardies had been removed where they impinged on the Goose Allée, it was an obvious next step to devise a suitable use for the adjacent, horticulturally-promising *lebensraum* that was waiting patiently to become part of the garden. In the meantime we had been exposed to the effects and consequences of the formal compartments and partitions of clipped yew so ingeniously deployed at Sissinghurst and Hidcote. Plagiarism was in the air again.

At first the rectangular space adjacent to the Goose Allée was an empty field sloping down to the lake, its only occupant the former dairy and laundry, lately a *garçonnière*, salvaged from the fire. A fence extending from the far side of the garage court, and running down to the corner of the little lake before turning up towards the farm road along the stream, left a generous rectangle measuring some 280 x 120 feet, a natural adjunct to the garden.

ABOVE

The second poplar allée planted along the farm road.

OPPOSITE

The riding ring, paddocks, and sheds that Anne has established for her horses ensure that the northern margin of the garden will stay where it belongs.

THE RONDEL

IN 1978 WE VISITED SISSINGHURST IN MIDSUMMER, WHEN IT SEEMED AS if every plant in the garden was in bloom. It was not only the floriferous perennial beds that we sought to emulate, however. Harold Nicolson's hedged corridors and "Rondel" were two elements that made a particular impression.

Rondel in French means a fifteenth-century short poem of thirteen lines using two rhymes throughout. The English used the word in the eighteenth century to denote a circle or circular object such as a fortified round tower. To the English ear it has a nice frenchified ring and seems to suit a garden. The French, when they hear it used for a garden feature, merely look puzzled.

In any event, the first thought that came to mind when looking at the empty slope next to the Goose Allée was to appropriate Harold Nicolson's design and create a long, hedged corridor with one of his "rondels," or hedged circles, off to one side on the left, and the *garçonnière*, ultimately to be screened by the mature hedge, off to the right. We

The Greater Perfection

would, of necessity, resort to using the local thuja rather than the yew of our role model.

Once the future thuja corridors and Rondel and surrounding spaces were staked, our manager Jean-Claude Bernier,[16] at twenty-four hours' notice, was able to produce the thousand or more field-dug specimens of thuja required. Within another twenty-four hours the trenches were dug, the small trees planted and there was the outline, albeit only three feet high, of the future complex – a bit of ordered geometry adjacent to the Goose Allée coming to life in an empty field.

The hedge trees were planted in a single row in a trench twelve inches deep into which equal parts of peat moss (well-soaked with the twenty-fold volume of water that it can absorb) were mixed with "*terre forte*," a rich clay soil available from the fields bordering the Malbaie River. After recovering from their first winter, with very few casualties, they grew rapidly and before long they had thickened into respectable walls that obscured the surroundings. The *garçonnière* soon vanished and the now-obscured little lake could suddenly be "discovered" through the openings leading into the Rondel. This, in turn, was an element "discovered" only when one was drawn into it to examine a sundial set in an old French millstone at its center.

A transverse axis through the center of the Rondel, which is set within a square, hedged frame, leads in turn to secret corner rooms, each planted with a paper birch. These corners are ideal places to sit and read and relax, shaded from the sun, surrounded by tall, green walls and shielded from the crowd of garden visitors.

Later, when statues were sprinkled throughout the garden (almost invariably seconds

BELOW, LEFT

The beginnings of the Rondel behind the newly-planted hawthorn hedge of the Goose Allée in 1978.

BELOW, RIGHT

Le p'tit bonhomme and Antonia staring at one another when the Rondel's thuja were first planted.

RIGHT

An overview of the center of the Rondel.

BELOW

The Goddess of Flowers from Kenneth Lynch's emporium of statuary.

from Kenneth Lynch's considerable repertoire of composition stone facsimiles), a writhing Asiatic Goddess of Flowers, with arms akimbo, garlands, and a wasp waist, was installed against the Goose Allée's hawthorn hedge, as the focal point of this transverse axis. A visit to Kenneth Lynch in Wilton, Connecticut by someone susceptible to garden statuary, as I am, is comparable to a chocaholic's exposure to a fine Swiss *chocolatier*. The enthusiast wants one of everything – a bit of the frieze from the Parthenon, dolphins and scallop shells in every size and configuration, statues of the muses or the four seasons, putti; there is no end to it, except that the prices are justifiably steep and daunting. Not so the seconds, which lie obscured in a corner of the inventory yard, agreeably aged by moss and encroaching vegetation. Blemishes such as the occasional broken nose or truncated arm lend a far more convincing air of antiquity to the pieces than that possessed by the newly-produced "firsts," which take years to mellow.

In the center of the main thuja corridor, a curved niche was added to incorporate a statue of a suitably battered putto denoting winter. Known endearingly by all and sundry as *le p'tit bonhomme*, the now-mossy figure is perched on a large block of limestone with beveled corners and looks through the Rondel across the millstone sundial to the little lake. In due course, to keep him company, we placed an equally battered head of Antonia, Claudius' mother, on a plinth on the far shore of the lake, where she is surrounded by naturalized perennials and mugo pines, with a Lombardy poplar serving as an exclamation point on axis against the snake fence in the near distance behind her.

THE THUJA ALLÉE

In this same open field, once past the Garçonnière, a different landscape solution was required. Here the field swept unhindered from the garage court down to the upper end of the little lake. In the late 1960s Pat Morgan sketched a pseudo-Chinese bridge to serve as a means of crossing the stream that fed the lake, thereby completing a walk around it. Made of plywood and painted cinnabar red, the bridge also served as an obvious focal point on which to frame a long allée from the garage court.

In Charlevoix County rhubarb grows with abandon and forms statuesque, large-leaved clumps. For some unremembered reason before the Rondel was started (maybe it was the lack of anything else on hand or a first example of my addiction to large-leaved plants), I elected to put in a double border of rhubarb some forty feet long alongside a broad pathway. With the beginnings of the Rondel in place, and just below the rhubarb allée, I then planted a double row of thuja specimens (shapely trees as opposed to hedge material) in an arbitrary, spaced, quincunx pattern, separated in turn by a twenty-foot strip of lawn. At the same time, as backing for the right-hand row of

OPPOSITE

A classical urn terminates the cross-axis corridor leading from the Goose Allée through the Rondel to the Thuja Allée.

BELOW

The Thuja Allée in late September. The vista extends down the sloping lawn, across Lac Libellule, over a sod bridge, and through the Arch to the hills and fields beyond.

thujas, a row of sugar maples was planted along the fence of the neighboring field extending from the garage court to the end of the little lake.

Some time later we installed thuja hedges as backing for the rhubarb allée and much later, in the early 90s, a mirror-image of the perimeter hedging of the north façade garden was placed on either side of a ten-foot strip of lawn extending to the edge of the garage court.

Today the allée extends about an eighth of a mile, running from the garage court down to the little lake, across a curved sod bridge that replaced the pseudo-Chinese plywood one, along an allée incorporated into the lower end of the Stream Garden, to the tall Arch installed in 1988 and, finally, across fields to the distant hills. In 1997 an additional 220 feet were added by placing a silhouette statue of Phoebe and her dog on a silhouette plinth beyond the garage court under the allée of maples lining the garage entrance road. Visitors entering the garage court from the entrance drive, and passing Phoebe on their right, see the allée axis in its entirety with the Arch silhouetted against the hills in the distance.

The silhouetted Phoebe was suggested by Nigel Hughes, the talented watercolorist and painter of tropical birds, who created her as a maquette with a buzz saw and a sheet of plywood. Phoebe was later reproduced in quarter-inch sheet steel and painted a brilliant white so that she can be seen from the opposite end of the allée under the Arch. Nigel's new statuary genre has caught on and is appearing in a number of British gardens, including Hadspen in Somerset and Aberglasney in Carmarthenshire. It is an effective way of lending excitement and interest to a terminal focal point.

If one is obsessed with greenery in general and with green spaces and textures in particular, as I am, it is worth reentering the garden from the garage court and walking the full length of the allée down to the little lake. You walk first through the matching thuja plantings, which echo the shapes of the thuja framework of the Guest Garden and enjoy similar punctuation by shaped little-leaf lindens, then into the broader and peaceful rhubarb allée, with its backdrop of spaced, clipped thuja specimens. This leads into an even broader swath with flanking quincunxes of clipped thujas that increase in size as the land falls away to the lake (free, of course, of any obstructive "fuzz"). As you head for the lake you find first the urn on your right hand and the corridor leading back to the Goose Allée on your left. Further on you come upon a transverse axis to the left leading across the center of the Rondel to the writhing Goddess of Flowers. Below this you encounter another transverse axis leading to the left along the outer lower hedge of the Rondel to a second entry to the Goose Allée before finally arriving at the lake's edge, with the roof of the Pigeonnier looming mysteriously in the distance at ten o'clock.

The allée is another "naive" element in that the path down it is not level all the way, but begins to list to the left as it approaches the lake. If you look carefully, you

The Thuja Allée quincunx, with a mantle of snow, in February.

The Pigeonnier roof as seen from Lac Libellule.

notice that it is a bit askew as well and doesn't quite line up until one is below the rhubarb allée. The imperfection of the list to the left, however, gives it a certain charm and offsets its lack of perfect alignment.

I never noticed the list until it was pointed out to me by Jean Carlhian, the distinguished architect and creator of the "garden" that unites the architecturally disparate elements flanking the Smithsonian Institution's "castle" in Washington, D.C. in an extraordinarily harmonious whole (in my view the most successful bit of urban landscape created in the United States in the last half of the twentieth century). Nor did I notice that the mature thuja quincunx had resulted in a totally unexpected series of diagonal vistas, at once interesting and appealing (and, I suppose, the consequence

of geometry), until Jean forced me to look at them. I would give anything for an architect's eye and latterly have regretted that I never studied the discipline.

However, I did elect to top the shaped thuja so that, while specimens become larger and taller as the allée slopes down to the lake, their pointed tops are level, enhancing the regularity of the allée and the illusion of length. I was also intrigued by the now very occasional glimpses of the horse pasture through gaps in the formality of the new plantings, a contrasting juxtaposition that was appealing and that illustrated the principle of linking the two landscapes by almost obscuring the one from the other.

THE WATERCOURSE

I ALSO CHOSE TO PLAGIARIZE ANOTHER OF GEOFFREY JELLICOE'S ELEMENTS at Shute, portrayed in Rosemary Verey's *The Englishwoman's Garden*, consisting of a series of rectangular pools and canals conveying water down a gentle slope. This idea was not there at the outset when the Rondel and Thuja Allée were created. Rather it just happened that there was enough space between the two (with only a little bit of adjustment) to incorporate such a watercourse, and it suddenly dawned on me that this would be a logical use for that space.

Again, discovery and surprise play an important role. Visitors are not conscious of the water feature until they emerge from the narrow thuja corridor leading from the Goose Allée and actually cross the narrow canal in the center of the Watercourse.

On the right, at the upper end, a dolphin (surrounded by thuja specimens that obscure the *garçonnière*) spouts water into a canal that leads to two pools at successively lower levels before falling into the canal just crossed. To the left are three more successively descending pools and canals that carry the water to a point in line with the lower edge of the Rondel hedges, where it disappears below ground and emerges at the lake edge next to a gunnera. Across the lake, on axis, a turtle in front of a paper birch spouts a *jet d'eau* back towards the dolphin. Decorative rhubarbs bracket the descending basins periodically and, where the water disappears, frame a transverse path to the Goose Allée.

The pools are filled with white water lilies which, alas, don't really bloom until midsummer but, nevertheless, enhance the vista. Now that the tall, flanking thuja specimens have reached maturity there are often gasps of pleasure when the Watercourse is first taken in by the surprised visitor.

Once across the canal and facing the urn in its thuja niche, we come into the center of the Thuja Allée with the Arch and Phoebe as terminal focal points on either hand. Now is the time to turn left and walk down the allée to take a closer look at the little lake.

The Watercourse, framed by shaped thuja, descends the gentle slope in a series of pools and canals.

LAC LIBELLULE

In 1961 Pat Morgan, at my mother's request, put a dam across the ravine at the end of the Tapis Vert. The red pine, spruce, willow, and thujas specified in his design have now grown to maturity, the bands of *Iris sibirica* 'Perry's Blue' and the yellow *Iris pseudacorus* have been divided and reestablished any number of times, and the simple and charming Japanese bridge across the outlet over the dam, one of Pat Morgan's more lasting creations, has once again undergone a face lift.

The dragonflies that buzz over it in midsummer gave us the name for the new lake: we dubbed it Lac Libellule (although Lac des Libellules might have been more correct.) It is home to many creatures, including trout, muskrat, the least bittern, blue herons, puddle ducks, and geese and, increasingly, wild mallards. The muskrats systematically denude the Siberian iris of their leaves as the summer progresses and the ducklings no longer need the cover to hide from predators.

ABOVE

The view back towards the house over Lac Libellule.

OPPPOSITE

Antonia and friends surrounded by Pinus mugo *and* Thermopsis caroliniana.

The Greater Perfection

Chapter V

OPPOSITE

A seated Kwan Ying keeps watch over Lac Libellule.

ABOVE

Ducks enjoy the shelter of the Japanese bridge above Lac Libellule's dam.

OVERLEAF

Chamaenerion angustifolium album has become established on the slope behind Lac Libellule's dam.

There is no better compliment, or more satisfactory enhancement, than when a wild creature elects to settle in and enjoy the contrived landscape. In the early 90s, for the first time, a wild mallard chose to raise her young on the lake and take advantage of the feed trough placed there for the domestic waterfowl. Each subsequent year there have been more mallards, presumably offspring from the initial family, and the wild duck population has increased logarithmically as a consequence, spilling out into other bodies of water throughout the garden and giving the dogs the endless challenge of a tempting quarry that is invariably just out of reach. The tiny ducklings are irresistible, scooting across the surface at high speeds in May as a host of warblers dart around the lake's edge. By June they become active divers and, when the cedar waxwings pass through in midsummer, they are beginning to show color. By late August they begin to fly to nearby ponds, circling the garden, the house and the Pigeonnier at breakneck speed, and returning to land in the lake with a great swoosh and splash. In the fall their presence attracts itinerant black duck and blue wing teal on their journey south and then there is the crisp October morning when they are all gone, leaving the domestic waterfowl behind, as if they knew that those remaining in this sheltered and well-nourished environment would be consigned to the freezer.

The approaches to Lac Libellule are intensely formal, whether via the Tapis Vert or the Thuja Allée. The excitement of "discovering" the lake is enhanced by the sense that here is a completely new aspect, that it is a different sort of garden to what might be expected. The mood here is naturalistic and informal. And there is that intriguing glimpse of the Pigeonnier roof and finial peeking over the trees.

In addition to the bust of Antonia and the spouting turtle, a wasp-waisted seated Kwan Ying, another one of Kenneth Lynch's seconds, sits tranquilly beneath a paper birch at the end of the Goose Allée, inscrutable and unmoved by the antics of the ducklings. She is seen best from the opposite bank. Also from this vantage point the Rondel, Watercourse and Thuja Allée are clearly viewed on the facing slope, as are the lakeside plantings of monkshood, ostrich fern, Siberian iris, rhubarb, and our token and very slow-growing gunnera, which spends the winter dry and dormant, well insulated within its plywood box. It is surprising that more North American gardeners don't try their hand at growing it.[17]

Lac Libellule was created by damming a winding stream and curves gracefully at its upper end, achieving that desirable characteristic of not being entirely visible from all vantage points. The straight line of the dam has become a narrow stone pathway softened by Pat Morgan's Japanese bridge. The slope below the dam is filled with plants including aruncus, dogbane (*Dorycnium hirsutum*), heracleum, lupines, rhubarb, Siberian and pseudacorus iris, and a forest of the white-flowered *Chamaenerion angustifolium album* whose showy spires illuminate late July and early August.[18]

The ducks and drakes arrive in late April. Both disappear in short order and the presumption is that they've left for wilder surroundings. But then, suddenly, there is a mother duck with a flotilla of ducklings scooting around and then another, and another. Usually four families in all remain in the lake, with some forty ducklings. I don't know in which northern feeding ground the drakes spend their summers. I like to think that they return on their way south and fly away with their families to their winter haunts. Many of the same birds come back each season, in greater numbers as the adopted flock grows. Those daily feedings are too good to pass up.

The puddle ducks and geese occasionally become itinerants, traveling from one part of the garden to another. One year the Toulouse geese migrated to the swimming pool and it took the concerted efforts of dogs and grandchildren to force them back to their home base in an hilarious chase through the woodland. Often I would be surprised weeding as they surreptitiously traipsed back in a single file. I'm glad they took an interest in the garden's diversions in their short life. That Christmas they tasted particularly succulent.

CHAPTER VI
THE STREAM GARDEN

OPPOSITE

A Highland cow is framed in the "Lutyens" Arch against the Laurentian backdrop. A sod bridge spans the upper end of Lac Libellule.

ABOVE

An upstream view of the Moon Bridge in its wooden incarnation.

ONCE THE RECTANGULAR SPACE NEXT TO THE GOOSE ALLÉE HAD become part of the garden, the new plantings of thuja and sugar maples bordered the fence that separated it from the neighboring field. Used as a horse pasture, the field was an agreeable adjunct to the garden, with the horses watching curiously as the plantings gave form and structure to what previously had been an enticing, if unattainable, green lawn.

With the good fortune of having a stream running through the property, the dynamic element a garden needs, it seemed an obvious next step to extend the contrived landscape further up on either side of the stream. Fences ran up both sides of the stream, which wound its way down the gentle slope through clumps of alders, rendering the transition to Lac Libellule rather abrupt and unnatural. The first task was to move the fences away from the stream for about a hundred feet on either side.

As a child I was introduced to the alder thickets along this stretch of the stream by the much older sons of our neighbor Kelley Desmeules, who used to take me fishing with them. The stream was only two or three feet at its widest so the fishing was about as rudimentary as it could be. We would cut an alder branch, tie a string on the end and bait a hook with worms with invariable success, except that the brook trout were minuscule and anything but "keepers." Nevertheless it was the perfect pastime for a summer afternoon. The Desmeules boys also taught me how to make a whistle from an alder branch by tapping and removing a cylinder of bark and then fashioning a mouthpiece vent and blowhole. We would sing a special song during the long tapping exercise.

It was not without qualms that I decreed that the stream banks be cleared of all vegetation and the stream shaped into a series of descending pools from the farm road downward. A diversion from the topmost pond allowed a secondary loop to flow through its own set of somewhat larger pools and a bog, before returning to the main stream.

With the water elements in place it was time to plant the area. Small specimens of paper birch, shadbush, spruce, pine, larch, aspen, sugar maples, and mountain ash were dug that first spring and grouped in different sections of the new area around a winding set of newly-laid broad lawn paths running up and down both sides of the stream. Transverse paths periodically crossed the stream, over a bridge where necessary, and were planted with non-indigenous trees and shrubs. There is a mugo pine path, a crabapple path (*Malus* 'Hopa'), a hawthorn path (*Crataegus* 'Toba') and an arctic willow path. After many tries, we have established a single red maple along the stream.

The Stream Garden is low-maintenance. Only the paths and, in late July, the areas of meadow after the flowers have finished, need upkeep. The few cultivated plantings consist of sweeps of Siberian iris. Here also is another "Rondel," this time a ring of Lombardy poplars about thirty-six feet in diameter, towering around a grassy circle. This Rondel is a sort of arboreal Stonehenge, a place for virgins to dance by the light of the moon or for young and carefree children (more easily come by these days) to lie flat on their backs and watch the clouds go scudding by across the opening at the top of the wavy, leafy columns. A large clump of *Petasites japonicus* var. *giganteus* in the stream bed terminates a short vista that runs across the Rondel.

This giant form of petasites, the lazy man's gunnera, is used abundantly at Les

OPPOSITE

A sea of Petasites japonicus *var.* giganteus *covers the bank below the farm road that cuts through the Stream Garden. When the pond was first shaped in the stream bed, three small shoots of petasites were planted around it, one behind and one on each side. Today a sloping, curved wall of huge leaves has filled all available space, obscuring the steep bank supporting the farm road and drawing the attention of anyone heading towards the Music Pavilion.*

BELOW

A young red maple should reach maturity by the time the Pinus mugo *specimens on the far bank, whose needles are pinched annually, have melded into a solid bank of dark green.*

Quatre Vents since the scale of the garden can accommodate its rampant urge to colonize its surroundings. Petasites sends out stoloniferous shoots six feet in length in any direction where root masses of trees and shrubs do not already exist or where there is no artificial barrier to contain the roots. Known as the Japanese butter burr, or *Fuki*, the leaf stems can be eaten in the spring when they shoot above its nondescript and messy flowers.[19] Their three-foot-wide leaves make a striking impact and we have massed them in appropriate settings along the stream bed.

THE MUSIC PAVILION

IF YOU WALK UP THE STREAM FROM THE LOMBARDY RONDEL AND CROSS a bridge flanked by pairs of crabapples you come face-to-face with the Music Pavilion. This octagonal structure was the first folly we incorporated into the garden at Les Quatre Vents. A strictly homemade effort, it took advantage of the intrinsic talents and architectural sense of the local carpenters.

A windowed French door, leading into the Guest Garden from one of the guest rooms, was replicated eight times and then assembled on a wooden platform to form an octagon. That was the easy part. Having difficulty visualizing proportion and worried about getting the roof just right, I had to resort to making maquettes of different roof styles and sizes and then hoisting them up over the octagon with a backhoe to see which looked best. The system, if cumbersome, worked, but I'm not sure it was less expensive than using the services of an architect.

Once finished, the new folly, sited in what had been an open pasture, could be seen for miles around and elicited curiosity on all fronts. Today it is obscured by indigenous plantings and blends into the woodland background. Lines of aspen (*Populus tremuloides*), which radiate into the distance from each point of the octagon, are particularly apparent in fall when the aspen leaves turn to gold and shimmer against the clear blue of the autumnal sky. The interior is finished almost entirely in the blond wood of yellow birch (*Betula alleghanensis*) and, serendipitously, it has turned into an acoustic delight thanks to the turret ceiling. It is furnished with six chairs and an hexagonal music stand modeled on an eighteenth-century double music stand with candle holders. The top part of the music stand can be hoisted from its single center support so as to serve as a chandelier.

The Music Pavilion serves as a functional folly and is used for chamber music and Anne's recorder jam sessions. On special garden days it is a delight to be lured to the structure by the sound of Bach or Corelli. On a hot summer's day, with the Pavilion's windowed French doors open, the music follows the water down through the stream garden and across Lac Libellule to the floor of the Ravine, where it can be clearly heard above the babble of the brook.

BELOW

Setting the roof on the Music Pavilion, and the finished product in 1981.

OPPOSITE

The Music Pavilion, here framed by Syringa prestoniae (S. reflexa x S. villosa) hybrids is at the center of lines of aspen (Populus tremuloides) that radiate from its corners.

THE GREATER PERFECTION

THE STREAM GARDEN 145

THE GREATER PERFECTION

Walking up the slope from the Music Pavilion one emerges on to the farm road which, on the right hand, is bracketed by a now towering allée of Lombardy poplars destined to endure at least to the middle of this century. On the right there is a view over an inverted thuja arch overlooking the sea of petasites and down the stream to the bridges and ponds below, the Pigeonnier roof just apparent in the distance.

THE MOON BRIDGE

LOOKING UPSTREAM ACROSS THE ROAD, AND OVER A MATCHING INVERTED thuja arch,[20] one is surprised to find a Chinese Moon Bridge arching across the far end of a small circular pond. The prototype exists as one of a pair of Moon Bridges, their arches some twenty feet in diameter, in Seven Star Park in Guilin, one of China's more appealing cities, in Guang Xi Autonomous Region.

Barry Ferguson was responsible for our introduction to Moon Bridges; first by showing slides of them in a lecture on China and then by organizing a tour of the Botanic Gardens of Southern China, which we enthusiastically joined. Later, armed with a set of photographs that captured every detail of the bridges, I sketched a version, in this instance with a twelve-foot-diameter arch, that would fit into the

OPPOSITE

The Moon Bridge in its concrete incarnation against an October background of aspen. The Amur maple (Acer ginnala) provides scarlet accents and Rodgersia aesculifolia clothes the stream bank in the center distance.

BELOW

One of Kenneth Lynch's buddhas sits astride the overflow in the Moon Bridge pond.

THE STREAM GARDEN

The Greater Perfection

topography of the upper stream above the farm road. After a backhoe spent a week fashioning a deep circular pond within the bowl-like banks of the stream, a wooden dam was installed next to the road. Working from the photographs and my rough sketch, two local carpenters proceeded to re-create a bit of Guilin at the upper end of the small pond during the summer of 1986.

In Guilin the bridges had been made of either stone or a stone-like cement and had flat approaches on either side. At Les Quatre Vents our first effort was in wood. The topography was such that the only way to incorporate the bridge in its allotted space was to build stairs down to it from the banks on either side. This, in turn, led to a doubling of the length of the bridge and a delightful undulating effect arising out of the extension of the railings and panels and the posts to accommodate them. This serpentine aspect rendered our version more interesting than its prototype and turned it into a Dragon Moon Bridge, something for the Chinese to emulate in their turn (in the unlikely event that one doesn't already exist).

The Moon Bridge in its wooden incarnation. Primula florindae *is in the foreground, with* Rodgersia aesculifolia *on the far bank behind the bridge.*

ABOVE

Three simple wooden dams with two-foot-wide spillways step down the stream, containing a series of ponds and creating interest and drama for those looking up the stream from the center of the Moon Bridge, with the early fall color of Acer ginnala *and* Rodgersia aesculifolia *animating the scene.*

OVERLEAF

Plumes of Astilboides tabularis *in the foreground are echoed by the spires of* Aruncus aethusifolius *on the bank and near the bridge.*

Aruncus aethusifolius, *Iris sibirica*, *Primula florindae*, and *Astilboides tabularis* are planted amongst clumps of indigenous *Juniperus communis* around the pond's edge and below the birches and mature thujas that encircle it. Upstream of the bridge the stream emerges from a deep gorge filled on its less steep side with aspen. On this upstream side *Acer ginnala* are underplanted with a mass of *Rodgersia aesculifolia*, which fill the riparian space as they do alongside the rivers in the Wolong Valley in Szechuan.

The Moon Bridge is enclosed within a woodland so that the eye can only follow the stream bed up or down. Originally it was exposed so that one could see the St. Lawrence on the one hand and the Laurentians on the other. It was Jean Carlhian's invaluable suggestion to contain the Moon Bridge experience, excluding any extraneous views. This was achieved by creating a circular walk within a mixture of spruce, birch, shadbush, and thuja, and thickly planting the banks of the pond with thuja specimens. The experience now is exclusively that of discovering and traversing the Moon Bridge.

There is a path off the circle, leading to vantage points above the Moon Bridge where one can best appreciate its undulations, seen against a background of golden aspen, scarlet *Acer ginnala*, and dark green thuja. For the first fifteen years of its life the wooden Moon Bridge was painted two shades of blue with white trim. Over the winter and spring of 1998 it was replaced with a reinforced concrete version which appears more Chinese than ever in its gray stone-like configuration, and will be even more so once it weathers and accumulates mosses.

THE ARCH

A PATH TO THE WEST OF THE MUSIC PAVILION WINDS ALONG THE snake fence through lines of aspen, Preston hybrid lilacs (*Syringa reflexa* x *S. villosa*), Japanese larches (*Larix leptolepis*), and purple osier (*Salix purpurea*). Most of the view is obscured by the plantings, but there are two viewpoints, in each case under a sugar maple. Here one can admire the Highland cattle and a 180-degree panorama of the village of La Malbaie, the Laurentians, and the forested ridge to the north.

The path continues down to the main vista running from the garage court to the Arch and emerges within a hundred feet of the Arch, now immense at close range.

The Arch was inspired by a photograph taken by Mick Hales of the arch designed by Sir Edwin Lutyens for the end of a long vista in the Royal Mughal Gardens in the Viceroy's Palace in New Delhi. Lutyens' arch was flanked by ficus trees and framed a view of the Himalayas. At Les Quatre Vents the Arch is flanked by Lombardy poplars and frames a view of the Laurentians. The portion of the nearby vista leading to it is bordered by conifers, interspersed with *Acer ginnala*, *Amelanchier canadensis*, and *Betula papyrifera* to provide autumnal excitement when viewing the Arch from the Thuja Allée.

Franklin Faust, a retired art professor and designer of garden structures, took Mick Hales' photograph and produced a model of a version adapted for its Quebec setting. The model was then reproduced on a grand scale out of treated British Columbia fir. The top of the structure is thirty-eight feet high. At the start it towered over the young trees and shrubs and stuck out like a particularly sore thumb. Anne reacted rather strongly, felt it had been a mistake, and referred to it as "Frank's erection." The general reaction was invariably intense curiosity. I explained its function to the francophones as a feature that could serve as a guillotine, and to anglophones that it represented Anglo-Saxon dominance over the countryside. Both groups seemed pleased.

Imagine my shock when eight years later, shortly after my seventy-first birthday, a particularly gusty tempest blew down the Arch, which had rotted at the base, taking two of the Lombardy poplars with it. It was disturbing since the surrounding plantings were reaching maturity and were finally in scale with the Arch. The symbolism was disheartening as well. Did it signify the end of an era, the start of the slow decline? Was it a message from the horticultural gods that it was time to stop trying to do what George Kaufman, in a comment on Moss Hart's country place in Bucks County, Pennsylvania, described as "doing what God would have done, if he'd had the money"?

Happily, it turned out the end was not at hand after all. The Arch was reconstituted with a steel frame embedded in subterranean concrete and faced with British Columbia red cedar, and two replacement Lombardies filled the ranks of their fallen comrades. It should last for a long time and I find the resuscitated structure, with its implicit symbolism, a comfort and satisfaction.

ABOVE

The resurrection of the Arch after its collapse in 1996.

OPPOSITE

The Arch, flanked by Lombardy poplars, frames a view of the Laurentians.

CHAPTER VII
AN INDIRECT APPROACH

OPPOSITE

*The lower and newer of the two rope bridges is suspended high over the Ravine floor, which is filled with rodgersia in variety as well as other large-leaved plants and ostrich fern (*Matteuccia struthiopteris*).*

ABOVE, RIGHT

A strikingly spotted form of Lilium martagon *that appeared one day in the garden.*

From the Arch it is a stone's throw to Lac Libellule for an overview of the structured thuja plantings on the far bank and the waterfowl on the lake, and – in a moment – a splendid view back over the lake and the Tapis Vert towards the house. The Pigeonnier roof, first glimpsed from the foot of the Thuja Allée, is even more apparent now. We are on the west side of the lake, and you can sense its gravitational pull.

Wherever possible I choose to prolong the suspense. In this instance, to make a detour through unknown territory is the appropriate preparation. I like people not only to come upon the Pigeonnier as a complete surprise, but to view it from a particular direction – over its reflection pool from the east end of its long vista. To achieve this I guide visitors away from the Pigeonnier and back towards the house to new experiences and sensations that are so diverting that they will forget the very existence of the Pigeonnier until they come upon it. The digression entails exposure to perennial plantings in shade, before entering the edge of the Woodland for a challenging traverse that will require total concentration. First we cross the little Japanese bridge on the dam, duck under a mature spruce and veer to the right, where we come upon a new world of large, curving shade borders that recede along the edge of a woodland. At the far end of the space, which is roughly parallel with the Tapis Vert, the area is blocked by the lilac and thuja screen at the rear of the Rose Garden and by the main Perennial Allée, both of which run at right angles. Access to the Perennial Allée is deferred to achieve yet more suspense. Tree peonies and species peonies are planted on the slope beneath the hawthorn hedge and there is a clump of three exotic Asian birches, all that remain of a large order placed with Hilliers in the 1960s, their identification labels long vanished.[21]

OPPOSITE

The mauve corner of the Shade Borders in mid-June. Allium aflatunense *mixes with 'Mariette' tulips. In the background the blue blossoms of* Camassia leichtlinii *'Caerulea' contrast with the white ones of* Sorbus americana *overhead.*

BELOW, LEFT

White-fruited actaea contrasts with the red plumes of Astilbe 'Fanal' in the foreground with the converse combination to the rear.

BELOW, RIGHT

White and pale pink astilbes contrast with red-fruited actaea. Both these photographs reflect the appearance of the Shade Borders before lilies and tulips were added to the mix.

THE SHADE BORDERS

THESE CURVING BORDERS SKIRTING THE WOODLAND WERE DEVELOPED contemporaneously with the Stream Garden. There are four in all, separated by small paths leading into the Woodland. They face northeast and are shielded most of the day from direct sunlight by the high canopy of birch leaves overhead. They turned out to be an object lesson not only in learning what will thrive in shady conditions but also in how to mix plants in a border and in the importance of trial and error, however slow and painful, in arriving at a successful result.

There was considerable space to fill; the borders extend for some two hundred feet and, where their curving edges permit, are as much as fifteen feet deep.

The first fall, I tore apart the few clumps of polyantha and juliana primula hybrids that had been dotted around the perennial border in my mother's time. They grew like Topsy once they were divided. I did the same with the few clumps of astilbe and hosta from the same source. As a backdrop I divided an ancient clump of goatsbeard (*Aruncus dioicus*), literally chopping it into smaller sections with an ax, and interspersing the planted divisions with transplanted clumps of Solomon's seal (*Polygonatum biflorum*) and ostrich fern (*Matteuccia struthiopteris*) dug from the nearby woods. I concluded this was going to be easy gardening and waited smugly for the next spring.

The results were painfully disappointing and I was suitably humbled. The primula hybrids bloomed their heads off and flourished, but the colors were a terrible jumble. The astilbe followed the same pattern, and the hostas were, well, just hostas, with generally ungainly blossoms. The only plantings that seemed appropriate were the Solomon's seal, ostrich fern, and goatsbeard, which rapidly filled their allotted spaces. The overall expanse was only sparsely filled and was generally a sorry sight.

That autumn I tried again, rearranging and dividing the primulas, hostas, and astilbes and introducing some snakeroot (*Cimicifuga racemosa*) to keep the goatsbeard company. Despite these changes, the next summer showed very little improvement. The planting still seemed an unsatisfactory jumble. The primulas were fat and happy but I found their hybrid exuberance and flower forms a bit gross, while the astilbe blossoms set my teeth on edge with a clashing juxtaposition of colors. Furthermore, the natural woodland plants were taking over, with the ostrich ferns shooting long runners out in all directions. To add insult to injury, other woodland plants were seeding at random in the improved soil of the borders, especially the ubiquitous baneberries in their red- and white-fruited forms (*Actaea spicata* ssp. *rubra* and *A. pachypoda* respectively). I spent much of that next summer weeding them out.

Clearly something had to be done to improve matters. I knew very little about woodland plants in general and my dealings with primulas to this point had been restricted to alpine varieties. I clearly had a strong reaction against certain color combinations and was making slow progress in mixing colors in general. I concluded it would be best to start over again.

Rose and mauve astilbes in the Shade Borders seen over plantings of Hosta sieboldiana *and* Primula florindae *in early August.*

The first step was to get rid of the polyantha hybrids and banish their garish displays once and for all. After this expulsion I felt much the same elation I had experienced when I gave up golf. The juliana and vulgaris hybrids were a different matter; at least their behavior was restrained and a few of each were allowed to remain.

Then, one day, while extricating a young actaea seedling from a clump of astilbes, I noticed that the foliage of the two genera was very similar and, what's more, so was the foliage of the goatsbeard and the snakeroot that were fighting it out with the Solomon's seal and ostrich fern. The next step was an easy one. Why not think of the shade borders as a mass of interrelated but varied foliage, interplanted in such a way that when color was added it would result in a harmonious and complementary effect?

The baneberries dictated the design of the beds. While their small white blossoms are inconspicuous and fugacious, their fruits are large and showy and last from midseason well into autumn.

In quick order most of the ostrich fern and Solomon's seal, other than those encircling the trunks of mature birches at the Woodland's edge (where nothing else

Tulips in the Shade Borders in mid-June

could compete with the birch roots) were moved back into the Woodland. The cimicifuga were divided once again and planted to fill the background gaps between the aruncus, which were becoming more majestic with each year. Interplantings of astilbe and actaea filled the rest of two of the beds.

The first bed combined the white-fruited *Actaea pachypoda* with the dark red *Astilbe* 'Fanal' while the second bed was just the reverse, the red-fruited *Actaea spicata* ssp. *rubra* with white-flowered astilbe of intermediate height in the front of the bed, grading up to taller-flowering varieties in the center backed by snakeroot and goatsbeard.

The results were wildly successful although, without the primulas, the two beds were a sea of green until the aruncus bloomed in early July. By the first of August the contrasting reds and whites were a show-stopper for a good three weeks, while the fruiting actaea carried on well into September.

Michael Dodge, the English plantsman and horticulturist at White Flower Farm, visited us late one June and was kind enough to help me weed among the interplantings while they were a sea of green. It wasn't long before he observed, "What you need is some color in these beds!" He did not subscribe to my view that living with the monotony of green for most of the season was justified by the explosion of red and white in late July and early August. Ever since we have been adding bulbs to extend the panels of color throughout the season. Again, in the first two shade beds, the primary colors are repeated: white lilies with the white-fruited actaea and red lilies with its red-fruited counterpart. Plantings of early, mid-season and late forms of these lilies bloom in succession. In recent years we have done the obvious and filled the panels with tulips which show to great advantage against their leafy green foil. Now there is color from late May into September and it is hard to decide which is the best moment.

Two large panels of interplanted astilbe and actaea are more than enough. There is no actaea in the third panel. Instead there are only astilbes in the front two-thirds of the bed. This time they are in softer shades of mauve and rose with the soft pink of 'Mariette' tulips contrasting with a mass of showy, dark blue *Camassia leichtlinii* in June, followed by a succession of duff and apricot lilies (*Lilium martagon* x *L. hansonii*), yellow tiger lilies, and other yellow lilies whose tones are not too strident, something that is difficult to judge from the catalogues. *Campanula persicifolia* has escaped from the perennial beds into the woodland; it is one of those territorial plants that can soon dominate a habitat if one doesn't cut the stalk before it sets seed. We move intruders regularly to flesh out the shade borders; the blue-flowering form into the panel with yellow lilies and the white into the bed where it can reinforce the white-fruited actaea.

The last panel is more complicated and has undergone more transformations than the others. It is at the far end of the shade borders where they narrow to border one side of the grass path that separates them from the rear corner of the perennial allée. At one point this panel was shaded by an aging crabapple and dominated by a mature

ABOVE

A form of Lilium martagon *that we have dubbed 'Midnight'.*

OPPOSITE

Red lilies highlight a patch of pale-flowering astilbe.

THE GREATER PERFECTION

OPPOSITE

Lily-flowered 'West Point' tulips emerge through a mass of variegated hostas including Hosta *'Frances Williams'.*

BELOW

Tropaeolum peregrinum *scrambles up the backdrop of thuja and frames a view over the Shade Borders.*

OVERLEAF

White lilies emerge through white-fruited actaea and the dark red plumes of Astilbe *'Fanal'.*

spruce which, inevitably, succumbed to the spruce budworm. The hostas had been moved to this corner. With the demise of the spruce, the increased light permitted a more adventurous planting, and a felicitous mixture of white martagon lilies, *Meconopsis betonicifolia*, the pale yellow *Primula alpicola* var. *luna* and *Allium christophii* replaced the hostas which, for the most part, were moved deeper into the woodland. Then the crabapple gave up the ghost and now there was *too* much light for the meconopsis which, along with the alpicola primula, had followed those itinerant hostas into a shaded habitat. This time I planted astrantia in their red- and white-flowered forms and tall mauve delphinium were gathered in the background, interspersed with *Angelica gigas* for late color and with 'Mariette' tulips and *Allium aflatunense* in June, offset by the palest cream blossoms of *Trollius* 'Alabaster'. The pink *Lilium martagon* now fills the bed. A mauve curtain of *Clematis macropetala* 'Markham's Pink' has climbed the screen of thuja that serves as a backdrop for the bed, intermingling with the tendrils of *Tropaeolum peregrinum*, whose yellow flowers show to advantage against the dark green wall from midseason on. Occasionally for its shock value (and to show some progress on the color tolerance front), I try the gray and magenta of *Lychnis coronaria* in the foreground, forgetting that the last time it happened it proved to be a bit much.

This discrete corner of the garden is the "hot" corner where I experiment with wild colors. It is just visible at a distance, as one turns into the shade border realm from the dam of the little lake, and then is forgotten as one becomes preoccupied with the plantings in the nearby shade borders.

The corner area benefits from Pat Morgan's placement of a *Viburnum trilobum*. Our most successful hosta plantings line the corner surrounding the base of the viburnum, and *Hosta* 'Frances Williams' is the star. Given the plethora of hosta varieties, I have given up trying to remember all their names and rely on the appearance and texture of their leaves. I am addicted to those with large, gray/blue "seersucker" leaves and those with partial to complete yellow variegations, planted *en masse* rather than dotted about. I'm afraid I belong to the no-flower school of hosta cultivation and, with the exception of the fragrant *Hosta plantaginea* and a tiny, thin-leaved hosta with delicate blue flowers that I find appealing, I derive great satisfaction from chopping off the flower stalks so they won't divert attention from the textural attributes of the genus.

Those hostas that *pass* muster provide the ideal foil for the experimental corner where the red-hot flowers of *Crocosmia* 'Lucifer' mingle with *Euphorbia polychroma* (the only species hardy enough for Zone 4), and *Origanum vulgare* 'Aureum' against a backdrop of *Berberis juliana* and *Prunus cistena*, both neighbors of the viburnum. Recently, and inadvertently (the best plant combinations at Les Quatre Vents invariably seem to be unwitting), 'Frances Williams' showed her worth when a planting of the lily-flowered tulip 'West Point' spread their perfectly matched yellow petals above her.

AN INDIRECT APPROACH

The back side of the perennial border is massed with ancient clumps of delphinium, the pale yellow *Hemerocallis* 'Hyperion' along with a look-alike that blooms at a different moment, *Thalictrum flavum, Eremurus himalaicus,* and *Crambe cordifolia*. It terminates with some unkempt but serviceable caraganas underplanted with a host (I suppose that's the correct collective term) of miscellaneous, textured, flower-free hostas.

A pair of welcome seats under an ancient crabapple, abutting the lilacs and thuja that frame the Rose Garden, invite a pause. After resting for a while in the seats and taking in the peonies and birches, it is time to move into the Woodland, as yet an unexplored and unknown element in Les Quatre Vents series of gardens.

THE ROPE BRIDGES

THE PATH INTO THE WOODLAND FROM THE SHADE BORDERS PASSES through a dense thuja thicket that leads to a shaded junction, between beds massed with martagon lilies and hybrids underplanted with a groundcover of *Aruncus aethusifolius*, that marvelous species introduced by Dick Lighty after one of his trips to Korea. As delicate as a dwarf astilbe and quite similar to that genre, it is tough as nails, has a long blooming season, a good autumn color and can be divided *ad infinitum*, although it will be perfectly happy if left to its own devices. We use it extensively, massing it in parts of the Woodland Garden. For a number of years it had the added cachet of being a plant the British were unaware of, a rare opportunity for plant one-upmanship on our part.

Directly in front is a surprise – a rope bridge extending one hundred feet to the lip of the far side of the Ravine. Through the Ravine the stream spills from Lac Libellule and courses in a descending arc some four hundred feet downstream to a small pond that can just be glimpsed if one ventures out on to the floorboards of the bridge. The bridge originates between clumps of aruncus and cimicifuga that bracket the entrance frame.

The idea for the swinging bridge came during a 1983 visit to Wakehurst Place, the Sussex extension of the Royal Botanical Gardens at Kew and the former home and great garden of Sir William Price. Tony Schilling, the Director of Wakehurst Place and a Deputy Curator of Kew,[22] had invited us to see *his* gardens before jointly embarking on a spring trek to the Rupina-La in the Gurkha Himal of Central Nepal. While leading us down his beautifully planted Himalayan Glen at Wakehurst, Tony pointed to the top of the surmounting ravine and said that he had always hoped to span it with a swinging rope bridge. Given the public nature of the garden, he had been unable to secure permission from the local planning authority. I thanked Tony for giving us an idea and, after returning to Quebec that summer, showed Jean-Claude Bernier a sketch of the Nepalese bridge depicted in Roy Lancaster's *Plant Hunting in Nepal*. Could we throw something similar across our ravine?

OPPOSITE

The sight of the upper rope bridge, in a deceptively immobile state, that confronts the intrepid visitor.

Two weeks later four oil drums filled with cement in which serious iron rings had been embedded were entombed on opposite sides of the Ravine. Door frames of thick thuja logs served as a support for the two-inch nylon ropes from which the bridge was to be suspended. A smaller, second set of ropes was suspended from the larger set with spaced thuja floorboards threaded across them.

In Nepal the rope bridges are suitably unsettling, in large measure because of the height of the span over the raging, rocky torrent below. Gaping holes in the floorboards reinforce the sense of unease. The new bridge at Les Quatre Vents looked like a piece of cake by comparison as I ventured to cross it. By the time I was halfway across, however, I was convinced that I had made a terrible mistake. The bridge swung in *three* directions at once — at least two more than I'd bargained for. It not only swayed from side to side but the floorboards undulated along the axis of the bridge as well as wobbling alarmingly. It was terrifying and I found it impossible to look down into the ravine at the masses of large-leaved species, which was a principal reason for the exercise. Despite misgivings, once past the center of the span, the traverse became easier and the terror subsided. It was a real challenge, but a surmountable one, and in the best romantic tradition terror might as well be included in the range of emotions to be evoked by a journey through the elements in the garden at Les Quatre Vents.

Each subsequent traverse became more manageable. In a short while I could cross without touching the ropes, so long as no one else was on the bridge. First-time users are urged to free both hands so they can grasp the guard ropes, to place one foot directly in front of the other in the center of the floorboards, and to bend their knees to achieve flexibility and a lower center of gravity. Most visitors traverse without any real problem. Children race across the bridge and some dogs take it in their stride. There are those who grit their teeth and struggle slowly across, vowing never to repeat the exercise.

I find that women, in general, have an easier time than men, especially tall, big-chested men whose center of gravity can be a bit high for comfort, even with bent knees. In the first years of the bridge we moved a small rustic kiosk from the Stream Garden to be used as a bar for the occasional cocktail party given on the far side of the bridge, so that one *had* to cross it for nourishment or, shamefully, choose to come around to the kiosk by a less challenging route (climbing down one of the several stairways leading to the floor of the Ravine, and then climbing back up the single stairway that leads up the other side). Here again, women showed far greater determination to achieve their goal, I presume because they really needed their martini.

In the beginning there was nothing on the other side but a field surrounded by a snake fence with a narrow strip of open land between the fence and the aspens clothing the lip of the ravine. There was just room for the little kiosk and one had to either recross the bridge or clamber back down and then up the stairways in the Ravine. Another way to return to home base was called for.

The lower of the two rope bridges high above the plantings that sweep down to the floor of the Ravine.

The Greater Perfection

Fortunately, it was possible to throw a second rope bridge, from the general area of the kiosk, back to the other side of the Ravine at a point near its end. The new rope bridge could terminate near the old Gazebo that had been banished from the original house and then been hidden deep in the woodland by my mother.

As it turned out, the two bridges are sufficiently far apart so that when the trees are in leaf, one is not conscious of a second bridge. The lower bridge is less of a challenge than the first, since the guard rail ropes were deliberately raised. However, it wobbles reassuringly in just as diverting a manner as its predecessor. To enhance the view of the lower end of the Ravine, the dam of the old reservoir was raised three and a half feet so that the pool of water behind it soon became a small pond, winding its way up the Ravine to a point just short of the new bridge.

The second bridge made crossing the Ravine into a more interesting circuit, but the kiosk, which was inaccessible from any other part of the garden, was not in itself a sufficiently interesting goal for such a dramatic traverse. The undefined space in which it was set had to be transformed into something more interesting.

OPPOSITE

Looking up the Ravine below the second rope bridge. Ligularia and petasites line the stream bed and the upper bridge is barely discernible.

BELOW

The cedar planks of the rope bridges have accumulated lichens over the years and are beginning to crack, adding a typically Himalayan quality to the bridge and to the air of imminent peril associated with the traverse.

CHAPTER VIII
THE PIGEONNIER GARDENS

THE SANDY FIELD BEHIND THE KIOSK SLOPED GENTLY DOWN FROM the level of Lac Libellule. As children, we would play and scramble in the small, steep sandbanks at the field's edge, digging holes and facilitating erosion in general. In 1985 when considering how to make the area a worthier destination for the rope-bridge traverse that could be tied into the rest of the garden, I remembered a photograph from a National Trust picture book of the Pin Mill at Bodnant in North Wales. A large rectangular pool, centered on a terrace, led to a handsome building at one end of the terrace, an appealing combination of elements that was also inherent in the approach to India's Taj Mahal.

From the ravine's edge the field opens to the west and is skirted for about three hundred feet by a woodland on its south side, before also opening to the south and sloping down towards the village and the bay. With a modest amount of leveling, a plateau of some three hundred by eighty feet could be created without interfering with the axis running across Lac Libellule from the house to the hills.

Adapting elements of the Pin Mill and the Taj Mahal to the site, I came up with a rough sketch of a ground plan and elevation. On axis there was room for a long, narrow pool, centered on an appropriate structure and with a small lake beyond. The space was also wide enough to contain matching allées on either side of the pool to channel the eye and frame the view. I started with a framework of the ubiquitous thuja hedge, lining the strip of lawn on either side of the pool. It then ocurred to me that here was a chance to create something akin to the bulb walk at Sissinghurst which I had seen one April, carpeted with primula and dwarf bulbs. It would be somewhat tight, but we could install a double row of little-leaf lindens, spaced eight feet apart (in both directions), on either side, adjacent to the thuja hedges. They could be clipped as a raised hedge. In the spring before the leaves were out there would be ample light for bulbs. Later on, shade tolerant plants could take over. These bulb walks could extend

OPPOSITE

The Pigeonnier's reflection pool is just large enough to do the job. The vista of fields and hills beyond Lac des Cygnes is framed in the archways.

ABOVE, RIGHT

One of Charles Smith's talented musical frogs.

The pigeonnier *on the farm at Gourdon, Lot.*

beyond the structure and attain significant length, up to one hundred and sixty feet.

Once the basic concept was developed it appeared to make sense to enclose the outside of the bulb walks with a matching thuja hedge and next to each hedge, as an outside frame, to plant an allée of Lombardy poplars which would match the scale of the structure and further underline the linearity of the space. There could be a transverse axis terminating the linden allées, then a bosquet and a lake flanked by a rock garden (at long last, a proper rock garden) and a heather garden.

The Pin Mill at Bodnant is a handsome, rectangular, eighteenth-century, two-story structure. The Taj Mahal is in another league. Neither would look appropriate in rural Quebec. In the library at Les Quatre Vents there was a copy of *Small French Buildings*, published in 1926, by Coffin, Polhemus and Worthington, architects of New York. It consisted of a series of sketches and photographs of cottages, farmhouses, and minor *manoirs* with their *bassecours* and the like, around France. There was a section on *pigeonniers* and one, attached to a barn on a farm in Gourdon, Lot, appealed to me. I had first been shown this delightful book by George Hickey, the architect who designed our house in Cold Spring. He used the book for many of his buildings, including all of those at Stonecrop. Later I found a copy in the library of an uncle, whose furnished summer house we had acquired to protect the seigneurie property, and I periodically looked through it for ideas.

THE GREATER PERFECTION

The Gourdon *pigeonnier* looked to be about twenty feet square and just right for the space. Messrs. Polhemus and Coffin must have liked it, for they included several photographs and sketches of it in their book. *Pigeonniers* in France are hollow, with the pigeons nesting in roosts around the periphery of the interior, obligingly filling the central cavity with organic matter and providing the household with squabs, which Quebeckers refer to as *"les innocents."* In feudal France, only the seigneur had the right to build a *pigeonnier* and his pigeons had the right to seek nourishment from his tenants' crops, a lesser known exercise of his *droits de seigneur*. At Les Quatre Vents the Pigeonnier was destined to be in the garden rather than the barnyard and to serve other functions than the gathering of organic matter.

But first the land had to be leveled and prepared, and the sketch was staked out on the ground to see whether it made sense. It was at this point that Benoit Bégin, a retired professor of landscape architecture, took an interest in my scheme and volunteered to help. Together we established the levels and discussed the elements of the new garden and their relationship to one another. There needed to be a transition from the edge of the ravine to the linden allées and, given the slope of the land, there had to be steps to get down from the level of Lac Libellule to the level of the new garden. Benoit's help was invaluable and I learned a lot from him. He prepared a series of plans of a formal and rather imposing layout, at one point with a baroque rendition of a

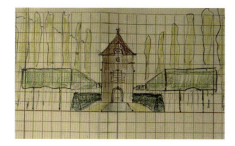

ABOVE

The author's first sketch of the Pigeonnier and its plantings.

BELOW

The Pigeonnier goes up after the reflection pool and the initial plantings are in place.

THE PIGEONNIER GARDENS   175

pigeonnier. While adopting one of his ideas in its entirety (a frame of a narrow water channel around a landing that divided the steps into two staircases and created the illusion of a squarish, floating island of lawn) I felt compelled to pursue my own less imposing plan, as I saw it in my mind's eye, and one that I felt comfortable with.

I had somewhat the same experience with the design of the Pigeonnier. I had sent a copy of the Gourdon sketch to Roger Bartels, the architect who has helped us these many years in both Stonecrop and La Malbaie, and had asked him to come up with the right proportions for the setting, which I felt unable to conjure up without professional help. Roger, in turn, came back with his modernized version of what the Pigeonnier should look like and had to be nudged back towards the Gourdon role-model. The end result was similar to Gourdon, in scale and spirit, with the inspired addition by Roger of a ground floor pierced by four arches through which, from whatever direction, the eye flows to what lies beyond.[23]

Creating the Pigeonnier Gardens took fifteen years. The leveled plateau was so sandy that the soil had to be heavily improved, especially where the allées of trees were to be planted. For two long years all we did was plow successive crops of oats under as soon as they had grown to a height of twelve inches. Where there were to be trees, copious amounts of rotted cow manure were incorporated twice a year.

In the third year the little-leaf lindens (*Tilia cordata*) were planted. There were eighty of them and they were planted bare-root in early spring. The young one-inch-caliper trees cost $10 Canadian apiece and grew beautifully. As soon as they were in place they imbued the space with the promise of what was to come. The next spring the Lombardies and the thuja hedges were begun and there continued to be regular dressings with rotted cow manure where the bulbs were to be. While the area was unkempt at first and filled with weeds (which kept being plowed under), once the reflection pool (100 x 10 feet) was in place and filled with water it unified the elements and made sense out of what had been a mess. The full dramatic effect was realized when the framing of the Pigeonnier was completed, towering over the new plantings.

At the same time, the area near the ravine was being furnished with pools and hardscape, as well as being shaped with thuja into three spaces. The Oval, now sans kiosk, lies where the rope bridges terminated. The long, rectangular Pool Room with two reflecting pools on either side of the central axis leads out of the Oval. The Water Staircases and intermediate, floating Antechamber/landing lead up to a circular Cylinder, providing a view back towards the Oval.

OPPOSITE

The Pigeonnier as viewed from a bank in the Ravine in early June.

BELOW

Polhemus and Coffin's sketch of the Gourdon *pigeonnier.*

THE GREATER PERFECTION

THE WATER GARDENS

Having mastered the first rope bridge, the visitor is no longer forced to return on the second one and is drawn naturally to a central opening that leads to the Pool Room, with the Water Staircase beyond. This central axis terminates within the Oval with Walter Matia's bronze of two otters chasing trout. We have placed the otters in the middle of a small, circular, mossy pool. Water courses down the otters' backs, over the trout and into the pool with the statue providing an effective, and needed, vertical accent. The pool and the bronze are placed in a niche in the Oval's thuja hedge which we have dubbed a "diverticulum," for want of a better name, feeling sure that the Romans must have had such a space.

The Oval's hedges are thick and tall and geometrical and proclaim the return to formality after the exuberant Douanier Rousseau effect in the Ravine that one has just crossed and presumably glimpsed, albeit nervously.

THE POOL ROOM

From the opening in the Oval, we look into an intensely formal space: a rectangle hedged by thuja with three additional entrances. To the right and left are openings that lead out of the rectangle, and straight ahead lies an opening leading up the Water Staircase to the Cylinder, in which one can just discern a low stone bench.

The pool surfaces are flush with the lawn, with no apparent edge, and the water within them is continually being recycled to minimize the build-up of algae.[24] By periodically adding one ounce of Pylam powder to their recirculating system, they miraculously become black mirrors that have been placed on the grass.

In typically Louis XIV fashion I insist visitors walk along the left side of the pools and go directly to the water staircases, looking to their left (if they must) while they pass the opening in the hedge. With the mature thick thuja hedge surrounding the Pool Room, visitors are not aware that the linden allées and the Pigeonnier are there until they pass the opening and catch a first glimpse of the long reflection pool and the mirror-image of the Pigeonnier within it. At this point, after the gasps and exclamations (often occasioned by the swans on the little lake beyond the Pigeonnier, seen through its arches, who have a habit of appearing on axis right on cue), visitors generally need reminding that their destination is the Cylinder, along with the assurance that they may return to look at the Pigeonnier in a bit.

There is a third flush pool in the Pool Room crossing the extent of its far end below the staircases and spanned by a large stone slab that leads from the central part of the bottom step to the lawn. This pool is fed by the runnels of the water staircase and empties subterraneously into the other pools which, in turn, empty into a barrel hidden on the slopes of the ravine, where a pump propels the water back to the top of the staircase.

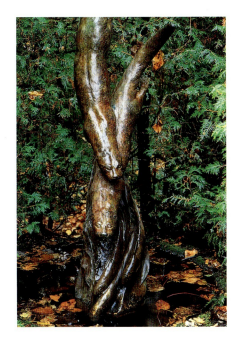

ABOVE

Walter Matia's bronze of otters chasing trout in the Oval's "diverticulum."

OPPOSITE

The Pool Room and Water Staircase have their own recirculating system.

179

THE GREATER PERFECTION

THE WATER STAIRCASES AND ANTECHAMBER

THE STONE STEPS are five feet wide and have runnels cut near each end down which the small streams of water cascade, step by step, until they reach the Pool Room pool. On either side masses of thuja fill the end of the Pool Room, their surfaces sloping up to the next level at the same angle as the steps.

After walking up this first set of steps you find a landing some sixteen feet square, again surrounded by thuja, known as the Antechamber. With the exception of the steps leading in and out of it, it is surrounded by a fourteen-inch-wide canal of black water, flush with the apparently floating lawn. Where the canal edges face north, moss has become established on its outside edge under the thuja. A second set of stone steps with identical runnels, flanked again by masses of sloping thuja, leads up to the level of the Cylinder, where two stone pools on either side of the topmost step, nourished by the recirculating pump, feed the runnel cascades.

The Cylinder evolved from a space that was originally the upper access to the steps from a path through a grove of thuja that extended from Lac Libellule to the Water Staircase. It is now an enclosed circle. The only access, other than by the steps, is through a hidden chicane or zigzag path that leads out to a meadow that borders the

RIGHT

The vista from the Cylinder across the Pool Room to the Oval.

OPPOSITE, ABOVE

The runnels on each side of the Water Staircase were inspired by the Generalife in Granada.

OPPOSITE, BELOW

The Water Staircase is divided into two sections and leads through the Antechamber, surrounded by a water canal, to a curved stone bench within the Cylinder.

Pigeonnier Garden. A curved stone bench stands where the old path entrance used to be and we are encouraging the thuja around the circle to grow ever higher, trimming the interior to form the highest cylinder possible.

In the middle of the space, a slowly revolving pool of water fills the open center of a small mill wheel, the apparent *Urquelle* for the series of pools in the Water Garden. In the real world it is yet another scam, with a pail under the millstone and a pump and barrel hidden in the bushes.

Sitting on the bench one looks over the slowly rotating pool and Water Staircases to the two large pools below (the third pool is hidden by the mass of thuja) and the Oval, with its otters on axis and a backdrop of tall aspen. It's a peaceful sight: shades of green and the sound of splashing water.

The ideas for these spaces followed from a trip to the Generalife in Granada. While we had no space to emulate the delightful water railing in which one can dip one's fingers as one descends a staircase, we tried to depict the three forms of water represented in Arab gardens; the *falling* water of the staircases, the *flat* water of the pools and (stretching it a bit), the *rising* water represented by the otters. The usual *jet d'eau* was considered and abandoned once we acquired the otters.

When the thuja that form the Cylinder reach their maximum height, they will provide a needed vertical accent to balance the aspens behind the otters across the way, the Lombardy allée on their flank and the Pigeonnier, which awaits our closer inspection.

THE PIGEONNIER SURROUND
THE REFLECTION POOL

AFTER A PAUSE for rest and contemplation on the bench in the Cylinder, the visitor walks down the staircases to the Pool Room and, keeping to the left of the first rectangular pool, stops on axis in front of the opening that leads to a path and to steps descending into the Ravine. This is one of the best vantage points to view the Pigeonnier, framed by the shaped opening of the Pool Room's thuja hedge.

In fact, as an alternative to crossing a rope bridge, it is also rewarding to walk up the path and steps from the Ravine to view the Pigeonnier because, as one's head rises to ground level, one has an unimpeded worm's-eye view of the structure in all its glory. As one steps up to the level of the Pool Room, the reflection pool comes into view. At first it is an empty sheet of water but, as one walks towards it, the Pigeonnier's reflection gradually comes into view until one can see the full reflection immediately below the structure.

By this time the swans often can be seen through the arches on their small Lac des Cygnes. The lake is flush with the reflection pool and encourages the eye to sweep over it, and the ha-ha and fields beyond, to the blue hills and western sky in the distance. Occasionally there are Highland cows in the view as well. Russell Page would approve, and I suspect Mary McCarthy would not consider this part of the garden naive.

Now that the population of semi-wild mallards has grown, the reflection pool is occasionally appropriated by them and it is a touching sight to see a hen, with her flotilla of tiny ducklings, enjoying that very structured environment. The mallards have a proprietary air towards the place and it is no longer uncommon to be standing near the reflection pool, or even in the ground floor of the Pigeonnier, and have a duck come whistling through, at what seems to be sixty miles an hour, to land at high speed on its chosen landing strip. Conversely, when D'whinnie, our cairn terrier, badgers the poor birds in his unsuccessful efforts to enjoy a duck dinner, they get fed up with the aggravation and leave their formal surroundings by taking off down the pool, flying straight through the arches to the open sky. The action is startling, but a not unpleasant surprise in a tranquil setting.

OPPOSITE

The dark water of the reflection pool works its magic on a calm, windless day.

ABOVE

Puddle ducks on the reflection pool, avoiding the swans on Lac des Cygnes.

THE PALISSADES

When Penelope Hobhouse saw the double row of lindens in their early stages, she exclaimed: "Ah! You've put in *palissades à l'italienne*." That is what we have called them ever since.

Once the trees were established in enriched beds, stone paths were run down the middle of the allées with short transverse sections extending to openings in the thuja hedges and into the ground floor of the Pigeonnier, across a set of pools flanking the structure. Since Penelope had named the feature, it seemed appropriate to copy the stone path in the garden at Tintinhull,[25] using squares, and half-squares cut diagonally, set within a framing coping.

The autumn after both of the 160-foot long "Tintinhull" walks were installed, the first planting of bulbs went in and the next spring we had the joy of watching the display unfold. The length of the bulb walk, which is a good deal narrower than its role model at Sissinghurst, gave us scope for a great variety of bulbs in waves of bloom during the six to seven weeks from the earliest crocus to the last of the tulips, by which

ABOVE

The Palissades in mid-May. Mirrors at either end of each allée convey the illusion that they lead to infinity.

OPPOSITE

The leaves of Rodgersia podophylla *form a muted backdrop for an exuberance of bulbs in the Palissades in early June.*

ABOVE

A mélange of the Kaufmanniana tulip 'Ancilla and *Tulipa turkestanica.*

OPPOSITE

The "Tintinhull" walkway in a corner of the Palissades. The mirror extends the view and epimedium join the blossoming fray.

time the linden leaves are fully out. Over some six years, through trial and error, we have encouraged the good color combinations and slowly enlarged the plantings of the reliable repeat bloomers. The tulips, while more reliable repeaters in Zone 4 than they would be further south, need to be supplemented at least every two years, if not annually. The tulip species that are reliable, such as the Greigii hybrids, or *tarda*, *turkestanica*, or *urumiensis*, appear to be irresistible to our voracious and well-nourished population of chipmunks. They wait until the species tulip blooms are spent and systematically exhume the lot. We no longer despair and have learned to expect the loss, taking pains to make sure we know what needs to be replaced. The varieties they fancy tend to be the least expensive ones and, if they get their fill, they appear to leave the important bulbs in place. It is a reasonable trade-off.[26]

The plantings reflect our color preferences with lots of white and paler, softer tones at the beginnings of the walks, building to richer colors near the center, and then softening again towards the far end where there is a final strident flourish. To appreciate the ever-changing bulb walks, we try to visit them every day and see them both morning and evening, on sunny or cloudy days or in the rain. They are a sight that almost no one sees, an early-season pleasure reserved for those who live and work in the garden.

The view down the length of the walk becomes more and more colorful as the season evolves, especially as the young leaves on the lindens emerge. To enhance this long allée of color, we have added mirrors at either end of the walks to give the illusion that they stretch to infinity. They work pretty well at first glance, but may need some fine tuning as they can reflect a warped view, from a distance, of the figures walking towards them, lending an unintentional Coney Island flavor to the scene.

Adding shade-loving plants to the long beds is a slow, but cost-effective, process due to our practice of starting with one plant of a species and then dividing it every year. Slowly but surely, bits of garden auriculas are spreading into masses, along with *Tiarella wherryi* and choice epimediums whose labels invariably seem to disappear. It is a tricky business because the shade-loving plants have to share the space with the bulbs, rather than dominate it. The invariable transitional moment when the bulk of the bulb foliage is spent and messy soon vanishes to be replaced by the likes of rodgersia, cimicifuga, thalictrum, and kirengeshoma, whose yellow blossoms animate the long green borders in September.

The Palissades require some maintenance. The lindens need an annual clipping and topping and we have found it effective to keep a one-foot-wide swath open between the double rows over the "Tintinhull" walks. These channels in the greenery let much-needed light into the Palissades, which have such a tendency to become overly shady that we regularly resort to thinning the canopy radically, within each row. The lindens do not appear to resent being kept within bounds.

THE REZ-DE-CHAUSSÉE

The ground floor of the Pigeonnier is covered with large concrete/pebble squares and is reached from the Palissades by turning at right angles on to the walkways that cross the rectangular pools flanking the structure. These pools share the main reflection pool's recirculating system and its periodic Pylam powder treatment, ensuring they will be suitably black. From the center of the Rez-de-chaussée, each of the four arches offers a distinct prospect to north, south, east, or west.

A bench occupies each of three interior corners. The fourth corner is filled with a cylinder which encloses a circular staircase. Four wall panels are each carved with a line of an encouraging homily of unknown provenance, from a sampler in the living room of Les Quatre Vents:

> The Time that's past
> > Thou never canst recall
> Of Time to Come
> > Thou art not Sure at all
> The Present Time alone
> > is in Thy Power
> Therefore, see Thou improve
> > the Present Hour

A further admonishment is carved into the surface of the cylinder and helps conceal the barely distinguishable curved door. It is from Alexander Pope's 1731 essay *Of the Uses of Riches*, in Epistle IV to Richard Boyle, Earl of Burlington:

> Let not each beauty
> Everywhere be spyed,
> Where half the skill
> Is decently to hide.
> He gains all points who
> pleasingly confounds,
> Surprizes, varies and
> Conceals the bounds.

Such is the philosophy of the garden at Les Quatre Vents, reiterated in its most prominent feature from which, once again, the main western view has been channeled and, for the most part, concealed. To discover it, one must leave the Pigeonnier, cross the Patio and head towards the swans and ducks on Lac des Cygnes.

TOP, RIGHT

West Prospect *Out to Lac des Cygnes over a mosaic patio through a grassed opening in yet another thuja hedge. The vista carries on beyond the lake over a textured and patterned lawn confined within a thuja "frame," the ha-ha, the cow pasture and on to the hills.*

TOP, FAR RIGHT

South Prospect *Across a flanking pool and walkway, bracketed by clumps of Astilboides tabularis, to a period statue of a hunter with his dog and gun, set against a semicircular thuja backdrop.*

BOTTOM, RIGHT

North Prospect *Across the opposite flanking pool to the hunter's mate, or at least significant other, with several dead birds cradled in her arms.*

BOTTOM, FAR RIGHT

East Prospect *Back down the reflection pool, through the shaped openings in the Pool Room thuja hedge, to the far bank of the Ravine, where the bole of a large paper birch serves as a distant focal point.*

THE GREATER PERFECTION

THE PIGEONNIER GARDENS 189

THE ROTUNDA

A visit to Thomas Jefferson's Academical Village at the University of Virginia was the catalyst for this feature. The interior of Jefferson's Rotunda in that imposing "Village" consists of a circular perimeter in which are placed three oval rooms around a smaller, circular central hall, the entrance to the Rotunda precluding a fourth oval.[27]

I had always planned to have a transverse axis between the Palissades/Pigeonnier/Patio complex and the area around the little lake. Why not use Jefferson's design of the ovals incorporated in a circle, the whole transected by grassy paths at right angles? Les Quatre Vents' Rotunda would anchor the termination of the intensely formal part of the garden, separating it at the same time from the less formal lake surround.

Developed only once the Pigeonnier itself was complete, this area is taking shape more slowly than its counterpart around the reflection pool, not least because fierce winter winds sweeping over the open pastures retard plant growth. When the forms were first outlined in spindly field-dug thuja, it took an elaborate leap of faith to envision the Rotunda that was to be. Gradually, however, the design is becoming evident, especially when you look down upon it from the *Nid d'Amour*.

ABOVE

Weeping mulberries intertwined with Eccremocarpus scaber frame the vista over a five-pointed star mosaic designed by Anne, through the Pigeonnier's archways, and over the reflection pool to the far bank of the Ravine.

OPPOSITE

A view of the western vista from the Pigeonnier's top story as it runs through the patio with Anne's mosaic and surrounding canals, through the geometry of the Rotunda, across Lac des Cygnes and the center of a textured lawn, towards the distant view.

The Greater Perfection

THE FROG MUSICIANS

The Patio with its mosaic leads into the Rotunda through one of the oval "rooms." Directly ahead, through a matching oval "room" and a hedged corridor, lies a small bay off Lac des Cygnes where, more often than not, the resident swans are lurking. I suspect it is their innate curiosity and desire for company that motivates them rather than the hope of a handout.

The transverse axis runs through openings in the oval "rooms," to one's right and left, into larger rectangular "rooms" that lead to matching "theaters," flanked by benches, on which anthropomorphic copper frogs cavort, making music on raised stages, against a backdrop of dark green thuja. The frogs are the creation of Charles Smith, a retired physician of Johns Island, South Carolina, who, in the company of his two sons, is gradually peopling (or should it be frogging), North America with his engaging and whimsical charges. We first met a Charles Smith frog group — a golfer and his caddy — one afternoon in a Charleston shop. Later that evening we were introduced to a musical trio of frogs (violin, cello, and flute) on Charles Duell's spectacular rooftop patio overlooking the Charleston Battery.

Charles Smith's anthropomorphic frogs play excerpts from Mozart's Flute and Harp Concerto.

Penelope Hobhouse and the philosopher frog.

The sight of Charles Duell's musical trio immediately suggested the presentation of a similar group at the end of the transverse axis to the left of the Rotunda and we commissioned Charles Smith to produce a chamber-music quartet of violin, cello, flute, and harp (the last because Anne is a practicing harpist). My mother had purchased an eighteenth-century harp in the 1920s while on a trip to Sicily. This harp became a decorative feature of her living room and she was just barely able to play the instrument, a feat I never achieved. When I first met Anne and found that she could actually play the harp, it made a strong impression. The moral of this story is twofold: one should realize there may be consequences to one's descendants from the way the house is decorated, and, if you choose to marry a musical spouse, the smaller the instrument the easier it will be on your back.[28]

A charming, seated philosopher frog reading a book was added to the order. It would be almost a year before the frogs were ready. Charles Smith drove up from Charleston, with the commissioned frogs in his pickup, entertaining (or, occasionally, irritating) his fellow travelers on the thruway with the sight of these genial anthropomorphs leering at them as they sped by. To enjoy his engaging creatures, we invited friends and neighbors over to a frog party.[29]

That summer the first frog theater was built and surrounded with the ubiquitous thuja hedge. A log bench, enclosed by thuja, was built on either side, the log frame of the stage was concealed with a low thuja hedge, and sod was laid on the stage floor awaiting the arrival of the performers. By the next year, the quartet and the literary frog were in place, the thuja was growing and thickening, and a second, Dixieland, quartet consisting of a double bass, trombone, saxophone, and what looks suspiciously like Dizzie Gillespie's battered trumpet, had been commissioned.

The Dixieland four were duly installed on a matching stage at the right-hand terminus of the transverse axis. While the classical frogs enjoy a woodland backdrop, the Dixieland frogs' stage was next to a field and required a mass of conifers behind it to balance the backdrop of the classicists.

Visitors enjoy discovering and confronting the frogs and many are the photographs of carefree enthusiasts sitting on the edge of the stage and enjoying their company and imaginary music. I wondered if it would be possible to create a sound accompaniment for them and, thanks to our son Colin's involvement in the performing arts, was led to John Huntington, at the time a consultant for the Metropolitan Opera and the New York Philharmonic. John installed a sound system, complete with control panels under the circular stairs in the cylinder on the ground floor of the Pigeonnier, with loudspeakers concealed behind the quartets and infrared sensors in the hedges of the ovals which trip the music as a visitor walks towards the musicians. The effect is magical.

Each quartet plays a number of musical excerpts, lasting for a few minutes. The chamber-music frogs play excerpts from Mozart's Flute and Harp Concerto and

Andante in C, which tie in beautifully with their instruments, along with a bit of the second movement of Schubert's "Trout" Quintet where the different instrumentation is not too apparent. The "Trout" was added to encourage the otters in the Oval and to celebrate the trout that abound throughout Charlevoix. The Dixieland four "play" thirteen bouncy excerpts from the repertoire of the Preservation Hall Dixieland Jazz Band. Confronting the musical frogs gives range to the emotions – from tears to uninhibited joy.

From each musical "room" a gap in the hedge provides a vista looking back between the allée of Lombardy poplars and the outside thuja hedge of the Palissades. The perceptive visitor to the Dixieland group notices sculptures of a snail and a turtle well down into the vista. In the matching allée on the woodland side a six-foot-long grasshopper invites closer inspection. These creatures are the commissioned work of William Wessel of Pittsburgh and, along with the frogs, illustrate some French couplets:

> *Il pleut, il mouille,*
> *C'est la Fête à la Grenouille.*
>
> *Il pleut, il ne pleut plus,*
> *C'est la Fête à la Tortue.*
>
> *Il pleut, il fait beau,*
> *C'est la Fête aux Escargots.*

and, for good measure, so as not to exclude the grasshopper:

> *Il pleut, il grêle,*
> *C'est la Fête aux Sauterelles.*

OPPOSITE

This frog quartet belts out the best of Preservation Hall Dixieland Jazz.

BELOW

William Wessel's grasshopper, turtle, and snail sculptures confront the visitor in the Lombardy allées.

LAC DES CYGNES

ONCE THE TRANSVERSE AXIS was hedged and in place, I abandoned the idea of high-maintenance rock and heather gardens on either side of the little lake and opted for the Stream Garden approach of using indigenous species that would fit in with their surroundings and provide interest in the spring and fall. Four crabapples were planted in the corners of the square frame surrounding the Rotunda and mountain ash and shadbush were liberally mixed with the conifers and birches and maples. The circuit around Lac des Cygnes was completed in 1999 with the placement of the Pont des Quatre Vents, or Bridge of the Four Winds.

A landscaped walk is slowly encircling the pond. There are openings where you can glimpse the village and the nearby hills. From the shaped, hedged opening on the axis of the central vista, by the ha-ha, you look back over Lac des Cygnes to and through the Pigeonnier, down the long, distant Reflection Pool and through the Pool Room to the bole of the mature paper birch on the far bank of the Ravine. From this direction the vista comes to an end. Reginald Arkell, the gardener's poet and author of *Green Fingers*, said it all:

> THE VISTA
> A vista is a thing which shows
> How far your garden really goes:
> A slightly arrogant affair
> To make the simple stand and stare.
> It doesn't twist or turn about,
> It leaves you in no sort of doubt:
> Solemn and stiff, without a bend
> It goes to its appointed end.
>
> People with vistas, you will find,
> Have often got the vista mind:
> The sort of folk who love to show
> How far their gardens *really* go.

The Bridge of the Four Winds, designed by David Birn, newly installed over the stream that feeds Lac des Cygnes. Once the plantings mature, the surrounding landscape will be visible only through the arches of the bridge.

The swans and the Pigeonnier reflection in Lac des Cygnes.

The Greater Perfection

THE PIGEONNIER INTERIOR

To open the door set into the cylinder corner of the Pigeonnier's Rez-de-chaussée, there are times when one has to know the password. There are other times when pressing a switch hidden in one of the quoins will do the trick. It helps if either the Patron or Patronne is present.

The Quebeckers call a circular staircase *un escalier en colimaçon*, a snailshell staircase. The Pigeonnier's *colimaçon* rises to the floor of the topmost room. When Roger Bartels designed the structure, he created a square room above the ground floor with a cathedral ceiling, a sloping home for pigeons above the ceiling, to be accessed through the pigeon holes, and a top-floor space with dormer windows looking out over the main axis. Making new gardens was one thing; creating and decorating rooms another.

After puzzling over the challenge, the solution appeared in the form of David Birn, a theatrical designer and teacher of design at New York University and Vassar. David had just completed the design and execution of a masterful *trompe-l'oeil* for a new, small, "baroque" opera theater in Milwaukee's third ward. The theater was conceived and promoted by our son, Colin, on behalf of the Skylight Comic Opera, where he had been the Managing Director.

For the theater David had taken a concrete structure and, solely through *trompe-l'oeil* decoration, had converted it into a festooned and swagged Tiepolesque illusion that is now a thriving and intimate setting for the performing arts. Designing the interior of the Pigeonnier was very much down his alley and he soon created a *"Salon"* above the Rez-de-chaussée and a bedroom in the attic.

ABOVE

A glimpse of the Pigeonnier's cathedral ceiling with its cartouches by David Zinn of mythological figures who have lent their names to genera - in this instance Adonis, and Daphne.

LEFT

Part of the collection of botanical prints and paintings set off a Meissen tea set that is painted with scenes of the garden.

OPPOSITE

The circular staircase in the Pigeonnier's salon. Reginald Farrer's sketch lies directly behind it for viewing on the way up to the Nid d'Amour. An autumnal Flora is depicted in the cartouche.

Before David arrived we had installed a tall, cylindrical Swedish porcelain stove, adding a chimney to the roofline of the Pigeonnier, something I had resisted initially for fear of spoiling the structure's outline but which Anne insisted was necessary. The tile stove heats the interior spaces in the spring, fall, and mild midwinter days, so that one can use and enjoy the rooms year-round. Anne's conviction proved right, and the chimney serves its function without harming the structure's overall appearance. The Swedish motif was a natural choice, given the eighteenth-century "feel" of the building and its northern setting.

The Salon was the logical place to display a small collection of botanical prints and watercolors we had gathered over the years. The paintings and prints are primarily of plants that have special meaning for us, such as species primulas and choice alpines and bulbs. Some are eighteenth-century prints from Curtis' magazines, others are watercolors by the late Lawrence Greenwood (petiolarid primulas from the Himalayas) or by Jane Watkins, who painted some of the more interesting alpines, bulbs, and woodland plants in the alpine and pit houses at Stonecrop and in the woodland gardens of both Stonecrop and Les Quatre Vents. One painting is by Annie Farrer, the talented botanical illustrator affiliated with RBG Kew. We had come upon its subject, *Primula boothii* 'Alba', the first white form of that particular petiolarid to be introduced into cultivation, while jointly trekking to the Rupina-La in the Gurkha Himal in 1983 with Tony Schilling. Thanks to Annie's kind generosity there is also a page from her Great Uncle Reginald's[30] sketchbook of *Primula sibirica* and *Corydalis curviflora* painted near Chebson Abbey in the Da Tung Alps of Kansu Province, China, in late May and early June, 1915, a treasure that any alpine enthusiast would die for. (While many visitors find the general effect of these precious paintings charming, I am always particularly pleased by those few kindred spirits who can identify the subjects and appreciate the elements of the collection for what they are.) David's principal constraint was the need to incorporate this collection into the decorative scheme, and his principal challenge was what to do with the sharply-vaulted cathedral ceiling.

David's solution was to create a series of *trompe-l'oeil* panels on both walls and ceiling. The wall panels frame the prints and paintings while the ceiling panels frame cartouches of classical figures whose names have been appropriated by the great Linnaeus for various genera: Adonis, Daphne, Narcissus, Hyacinthus, and Hebe. In the triangular spaces formed by the north and south walls abutting the cathedral ceiling and pierced by oval windows, there are cartouches of Flora in the spring and fall. The *trompe-l'oeil* paneling, in turn, is festooned with the tendrils and blossoms of *Rhodochiton volubile*, that showy denizen of the cloud forests of Oaxaca, where it climbs as high as thirty feet up the trunk of a tree before cascading back to the ground in a shower of blossoms.[31] The outside edge of the circular staircase is decorated with a twining garland of *Tropaeolum peregrinum*. David's design was executed masterfully by Philip

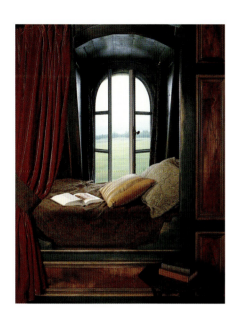

ABOVE

The Nid d'Amour *with Philip Creech's murals of the countryside and an early nineteenth-century Swedish clock.*

OPPOSITE

The bed alcove in the Nid d'Amour *with its bird's-eye-view window.*

Creech (panels and vines) and David Zinn (cartouches) and is complemented by period furniture and pieces designed by David.

The attic loft – dubbed *le Nid d'Amour* – was converted by David into a replica of a tower room in a Swedish castle, replete with cove ceiling, elaborate moldings, an alcove bed, and murals above a paneled wainscoting. The paneling and woodwork were painted by Philip Creech in a "stressed" fashion so as to appear ancient. Philip also designed a highly sympathetic mural, depicting vignettes of Les Quatre Vents' landscape. From the *Nid d'Amour* the axial view is one above it all with an unobstructed panorama to the west, a bird's-eye view from a most appropriate setting.[39]

UN JARDIN EXTRAORDINAIRE

UPON RETURNING TO THE GROUND FLOOR, WE ENCOUNTER A THIRD musical experience, this time precipitated by walking through the eastern archway towards the reflection pool.

On a Friday in August 1996, a visitor with two guests pulled into the garage court unannounced. While visitors with appointments are welcomed enthusiastically on Wednesdays and Saturdays early in the season, to appear unannounced when the garden is invariably closed at this time of year invites a hostile response. So when a tousled figure, with a three-day growth of beard and Giorgio Armani pants cut off below the knees, appeared and asked if he and his guests could visit the garden, the icy response was that he could come back the next day. The visitor, who looked vaguely familiar, appeared crushed and responded that his guest was a very important person and wouldn't be able to come the next day. This elicited an even icier response to the effect that were it the Pope himself, there would be no exception to the rule.

I then asked the visitor if he had made a contribution to the local nature center – a prerequisite for a visit to the garden – and was told that yes indeed he had, with the mention of a sum that reminded me that he was, in fact, the largest contributor to date to the project. Less icily I asked who his guests were and was told they were a French singer, Charles Trenet, with a young companion.

In 1948, when I had been courting Anne in Paris, Charles Trenet's *"La Mer"* was the hit of the moment and became "our song." Clearly, the Pope notwithstanding, Charles Trenet had to be the exception!

There followed a three-hour tour of the garden with Charles Trenet, aged eighty-four, his young camera-wielding companion, and Gilbert Rozon, his tousled host and, as I later learned, his manager. Gilbert had reinvigorated Trenet's career after he retired in his late sixties and had brought him to new heights of success.

Charles Trenet is an extraordinary man. He writes, paints, and, since 1937, has composed the words and music of over four hundred songs, many of which are deeply

Charles Trenet is accompanied by the Jazz Quartet.

woven into the fabric of France and French culture worldwide. He also loves gardens.

It was a wonderful tour and whenever Trenet came upon a vista or a setting that he liked he would say "*une photo, une photo*," often inviting me to stand next to him. The second time this happened, I noticed that he wasn't just standing there, but was "on stage," wreathed in smiles, hands set expressively and eyes atwinkle.

The high point came when he discovered the frog quartets. It was recorded in a hilarious set of photographs taken with Trenet mouthing songs to the Dixieland quartet's imagined accompaniment, and fondly peeking over the philosopher frog's shoulder at his reading matter.

At one point Trenet slipped on a stone staircase, banging himself up a bit and cutting himself slightly in the process. Once he'd recovered his *sangfroid* we sat down on a sheltered seat so that he could have a rest. After a while he asked if I knew his song "*Un Jardin Extraordinaire?*" I pleaded ignorance and he proceeded to sing it to me. It was a revelation! The song was composed in 1957, but the words could have been written about Les Quatre Vents; virtually all the elements in the song are in the garden — the ducks, singing frogs, dancing statues, a love nest, primulas having a ball: the works.[33]

When we returned to the house I gave him the garden guest book to sign. Again it was a different experience. He took the book, tore out a full page and drew his own characteristic cartoon of "*Le Fou Chantant*" with the exhortation, "*Vivre votre Jardin Extraordinaire!*" Later I wrote asking permission to play his "*Jardin Extraordinaire*" in the Pigeonnier. Now, whoever goes through the eastern archway — whether human, large dog, or speeding duck on the wing (at just the right level) — sets Charles Trenet off, singing his song in its entirety to the bemusement of the swans and the Highland cattle.[34]

ABOVE

The author with an animated Charles Trenet.

OPPOSITE

A pigeon's-eye view of the Pigeonnier in its completed setting. The textured lawn along which the vista flows, and the adjoining ha-ha, are clearly visible, as is the relationship between the Bridge of the Four Winds and the Pigeonnier.

LEFT

The Nid d'Amour *was inaugurated on David Birn and Felicity Campbell's wedding night. They arrived by carriage from the reception. David's rendering of the occasion captures the moment.*

A magical moment on a foggy day.

CHAPTER IX
A JAPANESE INTERLUDE

OPPOSITE

The Kan Son Tei consists of an Azumaya and, in the background, a Hoōgyo, a pair of pavilions that contemplate one another across a courtyard.

ABOVE, RIGHT

A carp from a scroll acquired in Shingo, Wakayama Prefecture, that hangs in the Azumaya's tokunoma.

To the east of the Pigeonnier and the Palissades along the Lombardy allée bordering the woodland near William Wessel's six-foot grasshopper sculpture, a staircase leads steeply down into the woodland. The stones are rough and rounded and set in cement, and there are bamboo railings at either hand, underplanted with *Adiantum pedatum* mixed with *Tsuga canadensis* 'Cole's Prostrate'.

At the foot of the staircase a stone path leads through a thick and shaded grove of spruce between ground-covering panels of the dwarf tsuga, on one of which sits a large Mosquito sculpture. These are followed by panels of *Shortia galacifolia*, thriving in the deep shade. From a T-junction, stepping stones to the right lead to a *shi-shi-otoshi*, a bamboo seesaw that fills regularly with water, then tips, empties, and falls back on a stone with a resounding clack. Its repetitious sound has registered subconsciously from a distance, serving one of its principal purposes, namely, to draw one towards it for closer examination. It seems to be saying: "Come and look over here, this may interest you!" At the same time it is serving the broader purpose of keeping unwelcome fauna, demons, or evil spirits at a safe distance.

On the left the T-junction leads through a Nakamon, or ceremonial gate, towards the edge of the Ravine. The stone path is flanked by thick panels of *Galax urceolata*. Beyond the Nakamon there are flanking panels of *Adiantum pedatum* backed at first with bracken (*Pteridium aquilinum*) and then further down the path with thuja hedges overhung with *Amelanchier canadensis*. Near its thuja-hedged terminus there are thick panels of *Diphylleia cymosa*, the umbrella leaf of Appalachian gulleys, an underused showy native plant whose large leaves and bright blue fruits on tall red stalks lend interest to the Woodland Garden. Here the rough stone path ends. To the left, a dirt path leads up through conifers to the entrance to the lower of the two rope bridges. *Rhododendron yakushimanum*, underplanted with *Shortia galacifolia*, is abundant throughout this part of

OPPOSITE

Looking back towards the Nakamon, or entrance gate, over plantings of umbrella leaf (Diphylleia cymosa) *and maidenhair fern* (Adiantum pedatum) *with a* shi-shi-otoshi *in the background.*

BELOW

Another shi-shi-otoshi *beyond the pavilions. These regularly tipping and clacking devices catch one's ear from a distance and draw one to the spot. They also serve to ward off animals and evil spirits.*

the woodland. While the rhododendron are healthy and growing slowly, they have been loath to bloom. Perhaps we are too far north for success or maybe it's a question of adequate light or the right exposure. I'm comforted by the fact that the late, great David Leach[35] couldn't explain their reluctance either.

The narrow staircase that descends gently on the right hand is composed of flatter stones of a different color. The steps slope slightly forward and are edged with small, roughly-hewn, hexagonal logs. They are flanked by short cedar pilings and the ubiquitous thuja corridor, and lead down to a platform. To the left is the top of a waterfall tumbling into the Ravine. Directly ahead there is a steep, twisting staircase made of small boulders leading down to the edge of a pond. To the right is a series of wide, broadly extended step platforms, paved with yet another pattern of smaller, smooth, flat stones. These steps flow gently between thuja hedges surmounting low, moss-covered flanking stone walls down to a final platform from which one descends a steep, handsome staircase of cut limestone. It is in turn flanked by sloping, pebbled gutters, and leads to where one emerges, between tall, elegant retaining walls with a curving batter, into a graveled courtyard. Here you discover two fifteenth-century-style Japanese contemplation pavilions: an Azumaya and a Hoõgyo. The ensemble is known as the Kan Son Tei, a name suggested by the noted sculptor Satoshi Saito, meaning "a beautiful place in which to stop and view trout deeply."

At the end of World War Two I was stationed in Japan[36] and had occasion to visit the teahouse at Mino in the Roko mountains (then a blissfully isolated spot) as well as some of the temples at Nara and Kyoto. In 1980 we returned on one of Harold Epstein's tours to Japan, systematically visiting public and private gardens of note. One that I found particularly appealing was the Sambo-In on the outskirts of Kyoto. Its scale and plantings struck a resonant note. Another consequence of Harold's tour was the realization that the surroundings and setting at the lower end of the Ravine, with its tall curving thujas, was quite similar to many landscapes in Japan and that, given its discreet site and discrete location in relation to the rest of the garden, it was a logical spot in which to create an oriental setting.

I am a firm believer in the principle that Japanese gardens don't travel well and are best situated around a temple in Japan. They are intensely complex, full of symbolism and meaning that only experts understand and, almost invariably, are poorly executed or overdone in the west.

My plan was to re-create an authentic Japanese structure in a setting that was peaceful and Asiatic in spirit, and not try to re-create a Japanese garden as such. It took ten years to achieve and three years before the master carpenter who could build it was found. Through friends of our daughter, Marianne, who were architectural students, I was led, after a year of looking, to Tadoshi Hashimoto, a sculptor/Japanese carpenter who was working in New York City. He listened to my thoughts but had no suggestions

Primula kisoana 'Alba', a Japanese stoloniferous primula, near the outlet of the pond.

and shook his head gloomily. Nothing happened and I more or less gave up on the project. Two years later the phone rang one evening and an unknown voice said: "the man you are looking for to build your Japanese structure is in this room and I am putting his American wife on the line."

Ann Gerber, the daughter of a professor at the University of Iowa, explained that while in Japan she had met and married Hiroshi Sakaguchi, a master carpenter from Wakayama prefecture who, as an apprentice, had had experience in the construction of classic Japanese structures. They were living in Occidental, California, and he was doing Japanese carpentry work in and around San Francisco. It was decided that he and Tadoshi would fly to Quebec at our expense to inspect the site.

It was a successful visit. Not only was the site deemed appropriate but both Tadoshi and Hiroshi were captivated by the countryside and the abundance of burdock and Japanese butter burr (petasites) which are delicacies regularly consumed in Japan but not available in most western settings. Yes, something like the Sambo-In could be achieved and I would be hearing from Hiroshi.

Two weeks later a set of working drawings for not one, but two structures was received from Hiroshi. The smaller structure was needed to enclose the graveled courtyard and balance and complement the Azumaya. The plan was to spread the work over seven years. Specimens of Port Orford cedar (Chamaecyparis lawsoniana) would be chosen in northern California and southern Oregon, then cut and dried in Hiroshi's back yard for two years. The next two years would be needed to complete the joinery, and it would take another three summers to erect the structures and complete the pavilion surround.

Patience is an important attribute for those who choose to make new gardens. The best long-term results often spring from the elements of a garden growing together over a number of years and being tinkered with and amended as needed. Those who want an immediate effect miss out on the anticipation and joy to be derived from the maturing of the landscape. In this instance, the long wait gave ample time to mold the surroundings and had the added benefit of spreading the project's cost over a number of years.

THE BUILDINGS

THE AZUMAYA HAS A CLASSIC IRIMOYA ROOF TOPPED WITH TWO TONS of clay tiles. It is set on posts that rest in part on rounded river stones and in part on concrete pilings set below the surface of the pond. It is said to be the kind of structure a retired Samurai would build, in which to contemplate during his remaining years. Steps lead from the graveled courtyard to a gallery which encircles the building. Gallery railings, punctuated by Giboshi finials, cross one another at right angles at the corners and curve upward with a terminal lilt. Shoji panels slide open on the two walls that front the pond to reveal a view over the water and up the Ravine with its rope bridge suspended high above. You hear the sound of the Waterfall, which is just out of sight, and take in the massed plantings that sweep down the slopes of the Ravine to the water's edge. The posts that support the Azumaya's roof are hand-planed to a satin finish. The scent of the cypress from which they are made, combined with the soft tatami under one's stockinged feet, transport one directly to Japan.

Except for the nails in the rows of shingles and a very few hidden bolts tying the roof framing together, there are no nails in the structure. All wood joints are mortise and tenon, with many of incredible complexity. The posts that rest on the smooth, curved river stones set just above the surface of the ground fit each stone exactly. This is achieved in much the same way that a crown filling is designed to fit with its companion teeth.

The Hoōgyo is smaller; it has a square roof surmounted by a ceramic Roban. It is without railings, but similar in other respects to the Azumaya. It houses an hibachi, and from its interior the view is over a small, graveled court towards a grassy corridor, rolling fields and a part of the Laurentian chain. It represents the kind of teahouse that was used in Japan before the tea ceremony became so stylized in the sixteenth century.

Between the two structures large and varied stepping stones are embedded in moss. There are trees as well; *Pinus sylvestris* doing its Scottish best to look oriental, a

weeping willow, a ginkgo and a three-trunked paper birch, all within circles of *Cornus canadensis* or moss. A number of shaped clumps of thuja were planted to emulate the shaped azaleas of Japan. The courtyard is contained by parallel walls of trimmed thuja. On the slope of the Ravine above the thuja on the Pigeonnier side the autumn colors of *Rhus typhina*, *Amelanchier canadensis*, *Acer ginnala*, and *Betula papyrifera* blend and spill over the dark green wall.

A stream, framed with rocks, winds its way from the little pond around a mossy hummock and spills out of the courtyard and back to the mother stream bed below, obscured by the vegetation surrounding it. A bridge made from a flat ledge crosses the stream leading to steps that mount the far bank.

THE PAVILION SURROUND
THE WATERFALL

THE RESERVOIR POND HAD BEEN ENLARGED, BUT THE SLOPES AROUND IT WERE a jumble of tangled thickets of *Cornus stolonifera* and alders. A wagon trail from an earlier time led down the steep slope on the Pigeonnier side of the Ravine to the water's edge, providing access for a horse and tumbril to drag away the silt that built up regularly in the reservoir. Tadoshi and Hiroshi agreed that the wagon trail slope was a logical and appropriate place for a waterfall. The long lead time before the erection of the structures gave us the opportunity to build the waterfall and plant it. By the time the pavilions were installed it would be properly upholstered and softened by vegetation.

By the summer of 1989, Cono — our live-in master mason — had finished the rehabilitation of the walls and terraces surrounding the Tapis Vert and was looking for new challenges. We decided that his August "vacation" would be entirely devoted to the new waterfall. In preparation, I pored over books and sketched my idea of what a Japanese waterfall should look like.

When Cono arrived I showed him the site and my sketches. We discussed the logistics and mechanics and the need to have some means of bridging the stream in order to walk *around* the pond. The next morning we set out looking for rocks with a large backhoe and truck.

In the 1960s the pristine mountain hinterland of Charlevoix was forever marred by rows of giant transmission towers, bringing the hydroelectric power generated by the massive dams of northern Quebec and Labrador down to the populated south. The power was cheap, efficient, non-polluting, and extremely important to the citizens and industries of the Province. The transmission lines, however, created multiple scars for thousands of miles through virgin wilderness and secondary forests alike; a terrible and permanent disfigurement of what had been limitless and majestic nature.

TOP, LEFT

A backhoe in the stream bed, digging holes for stepping stones.

TOP, RIGHT

Making the forms for the basins within the Waterfall.

BELOW

Pouring cement into the Waterfall forms.

A Japanese Interlude 217

The Waterfall, rocky and bare but complete after a month's herculean effort, with Cono and his cohorts celebrating the event.

The good news for us turned out to be that the pylons were built on concrete footings, which required blasting of the Cambrian shield before the footings were poured. As a consequence, masses of large boulders and slabs of ledge had been created around each pylon. Obligingly weathered over the thirty years they had lain on the surface, some even had the beginnings of moss on their shaded flanks. They were there for the asking and we trundled the equipment to the base of a pylon near a public road and began to pick and choose.

I soon learned that my choice of rocks was not necessarily Cono's; only occasionally would we agree. I would point proudly at what I considered a prime candidate only to have Cono shake his head discouragingly. It was not until the truck had dumped its first load of rocks near the site and the backhoe had gingerly slid down to the edge of what was now a drained pond that I realized that Cono had devised his own vision of how the waterfall would look and how it would blend into its surroundings. After a few blustery recriminations, and knowing that on similar work on rock ledges in Cold

Spring Cono had invariably been right, I acquiesced and settled back to watch what was destined to be a Sicilian's version of how a Japanese waterfall should look in that particular Canadian setting.

Cono's vision turned out to be complete in every detail, with an ingenious and perfect solution for how the small pond was to be bridged. I had worried that the pond was too small for a classical arched or zigzag Japanese bridge and that a bridge, in whatever form, would detract from the open water that should surround the water side of the Azumaya. It would also look out of place if it was too close to the point where the stream entered the pond from the Ravine and where there was already a simple plank-bridge crossing between banks that were several feet higher than the edge of the pond.

Cono's solution was first to block the stream with a boulder so that the water would spill uniformly over the boulder's curved and rounded edge and fall about twelve inches to the surface of the pond. This involved bringing the backhoe precariously down the slope and making a dirt ramp so that it could get far enough into the pond to *just* place the boulder in its designated site with the backhoe bucket at its fullest extension. Then, working from this farthest point back towards the proposed waterfall, large boulders were slowly but surely placed on either side of the upper end of the pond to shore up its banks to a height of about four feet, the natural level of a plateau where we had already planted rodgersia and bergenia and the like.

Then, to my surprise and delight, I watched giant boulders being placed in the pond itself with their one flat surface uppermost, almost flush with the water level-to-be, and leading from the lower level of what we shall call the Gazebo side of the pond, where a rough path at the water's edge had been shaped at the foot of a steep slope. These giant stepping stones ran in a circle from this new path in front of the newly-splashing fall at the mouth of the stream over to a soon-built flight of steps up to a terrace. It then skirted the edge of the newly-shored terrace and curved in front of the prospective waterfall so as to join in due course another rough path at the edge of the slope on the Pigeonnier side of the pond.

Cono's solution then had been to skirt the banks of the pond with large flat stepping-stone boulders, providing alternate routes across and around it. The beauty of the solution was that the maximum amount of open water was left to enhance the future Azumaya. Furthermore, the stones would complement rather than detract from the Azumaya; they were oriental in spirit and provided a series of marvelous vantage points to view the surroundings. What's more Cono had chosen *each* stone knowing exactly where it was to be placed. It was a *tour de force*.

This endeavor was not without its moments of excitement. At one point the backhoe, struggling under the weight of a boulder weighing several tons, slid ignominiously into the muddy bottom of the pond and had to be laboriously rescued and winched out by an even larger machine. The beginning placements took time as well. The levels had to be just right and the boulders had to be carefully underpinned and solidified with painstaking care. The large boulders used for shoring the banks had to be carefully backfilled and partially covered so that they appeared to be natural to their setting. After a week's work the lower tier was in place and it was time to return to the transmission pylons and gather more rocks for the waterfall itself.

There are few more satisfactory, if costly, ways to spend one's time than to direct giant machines to do one's bidding by means of hand signals. This is particularly the case when choosing giant boulders and slabs of ledge and carefully wrapping them with chains while a backhoe hoists them out of a jumbled pile where they are serving no purpose and then, in due course, carefully places them in a spot where they will be admired by all and sundry. The placing of the chain, with burlap to protect important surfaces; the hand signals, invariably given by those involved in the exercise to the backhoe driver who can almost certainly do it all without any help; the lifting of the great weight high in the air and the positioning as it is lowered so that it will be best presented and fit exactly where desired — all of these steps make for an exciting spectator sport, empowering those involved and yielding wonderfully constructive results when directed by one who understands and knows how to work with rocks.

Guided by the topography of the site and by Cono's master vision, the Waterfall became a combination of nine different falls, tumbling in three tiers of basins from the top of the slope and returning to the lake from both the lower and an intermediate tier in two falls, one with a drop of five feet. By the end of August it was finished, three cement basins had been incorporated in the rockwork and endless pebbles of decreasing size had been packed into the interstices between the boulders. Soil was then added and hosed and packed in, cycle after cycle, until there was some confidence that it would not easily erode. A pump was installed and, the evening before Cono returned to his regular work back in Putnam County, it was turned on, finely tuned so that the water was divided between the nine splashing falls. The event was celebrated with champagne, with Cono beaming and standing on an intermediate tier as his own rustic version of the Villa d'Este splashed around him, a counterpoint to the stream across the way now coursing into a dramatically enhanced pond.

I was thrilled, but those nearest and dearest to me were horrified by what they considered to be the totally unnatural imposition of a pile of enormous rocks on a perfectly nice woodland pond. Cono had envisaged his rock formations from the start and I had had little idea of how it was going to look. I did, however, have a very clear idea of what the planting was going to be and how, in time, it would soften, if not hide most of the boulders. I pleaded for time, and for trust in my judgment, to a very skeptical audience.

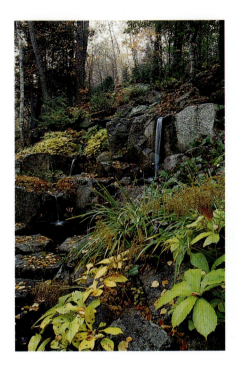

ABOVE AND OPPOSITE

Plants now soften the Waterfall's rockwork, and autumn leaves make random patterns on stones and water.

The matured plantings fill the interstices in the Waterfall rocks. Layers of plants mount the falls with Aruncus aethusifolius, Bergenia cordifolia, Primula japonica *and* P. marginata *and* Thalictrum kiusianum *at the base — then a layer of* Kirengeshoma palmata *and* Darmera peltata *topped with* Anemonopsis macrophylla, *underplanted with* Iris gracilipes 'Alba', *against a background of* Petasites japonicus var. giganteus *— surmounted in turn by a sweep of* Rodgersia podophylla.

THE GREATER PERFECTION

Today there are no complaints. The plantings fill the interstices and have spilled out over the rocks. They match the plants on the opposite bank and are almost entirely of an Asiatic provenance. They can be admired from across the way from vantage points at a number of different levels, as well as up close, from the stepping stones. I enjoy weeding the tiers with the water splashing on all sides, watching the cracks fill with *Primula marginata* and *Thalictrum kiusianum* or discovering the masses of *Iris gracilipes* 'Alba' that I had forgotten about, underplanted among the *Anemonopsis macrophylla*; or admiring the *Gentiana asclepiadea* 'Alba' planted at the very top of the complex, so as to spill over in emulation of the Waterfall, and now in danger of being smothered by the branches of *Tsuga sargentii* as they begin to trail over the upper escarpment. Today, with the Pavilions in place and the pond surround filled with plants, the waterfalls appear to be their thoroughly natural companion.

THE PAVILIONS

THE PAVILIONS ARRIVED four years after Hiroshi's first visit. They were shipped as a truckload of wood, each piece individually wrapped and ready to be assembled and joined with its respective mate in the new structure. Hiroshi arrived soon after and the work began. Concrete pilings were poured in cylindrical forms that reached seven feet below ground level and in forms placed on bedrock footings at the bottom of the pond. (At this point Hiroshi decreed that the level of the pond had to be raised several inches, which meant that not only the dam but all of those carefully placed stepping stones had to be adjusted.) Posts were set on the footings, beams were mortised to the posts and the core of the Azumaya began to take form. Hiroshi then built a two-story scaffold around the core with fresh-cut poplar trunks lashed together and planking obscuring what was taking place within. Large square posts to support the roof were mortised on to the foundation beams with ceiling-level beams then mortised to them. Day by day the structure grew.

With the exception of the pouring of the pilings and the manhandling of the very largest beams, Hiroshi handled and placed every piece of wood himself, working up to twelve hours a day entirely by himself, ignoring curious spectators and focusing solely on his mission. He worked and shaped the wood, as needed, with his set of Japanese tools, not one of which looked familiar to a western eye. All measurements were based on a Japanese scale. I tried to keep a thorough photographic record of the steps involved in the creation of this classic Japanese structure. I took pictures almost every day when I was there but there were stretches of up to two weeks when I was absent and missed vital steps in the construction. Ann Sakaguchi, with their children, Morio and Kaya, spent the central part of each summer with Hiroshi and often kept him company at the site.

ABOVE

Hiroshi Sakaguchi building the stream bed running through the Kan Son Tei's courtyard.

OPPOSITE

Top: Hiroshi at work on the Azumaya's complex roof.
Below, left: A corner of the Azumaya's gallery.
Below, right: Detail of the complex joinery.

THE GREATER PERFECTION

A JAPANESE INTERLUDE

THE GREATER PERFECTION

OPPOSITE

The pond side of the Azumaya. The untapered shingles at the roof's edge are twelve thick.

ABOVE, LEFT

View of the plantings in the pavilion surround from the interior of the Azumaya.

ABOVE, RIGHT

Brushes for calligraphy. The table was made by Hiroshi Sakaguchi.

It took two summers to complete the Azumaya and much of the time was spent on its complex and intricate roof. Japanese shingles have no taper and were made to order out of British Columbia red cedar. Their placement on the curving roof is a conundrum in itself and there is an inordinate number of layers of them, reaching up to twelve on the Azumaya's Irimoya roof and up to eight at the edge of the Hoõgyo's roof. Heavy tiles acquired in Japan were then placed on the ridge of the roof, with decorative tiles at each end. Towards the end of the second summer the Azumaya's scaffold came down and the gallery was added with its characteristic railings and supporting posts shaped to fit on the surface of large rounded stones selected from the river's edge.

During the third summer the Hoõgyo went up, tatami mats were installed and both Pavilions were finished inside and out. The courtyard stepping stones, collected both on the beach and under the transmission lines, were placed. Finishing touches were made to the stream as it flowed through the courtyard, to the curbing surrounding the structure and to the plantings, in time to have the area roughly finished for an opening ceremony that took place on August 23, 1994.

Hiroshi was honored; Tadoshi came up to help him celebrate; a barrel of sake was consumed along with a sashimi dinner and everyone was a bit bleary-eyed the next

A JAPANESE INTERLUDE   227

morning. Later that autumn the Nakamon entrance gate was constructed, and work began on the series of stone steps leading down and back and forth and every which way from the level of the Pigeonnier. Hiroshi returned the next spring for several months to finish these projects and to build a Machiai on the Gazebo side slope, a small structure made of local thuja that would serve a waiting, resting, and reflection stop for visitors who come down to the Kan Son Tei from this side of the Ravine.

THE PAVILION COURTYARD AND ITS ROCKS

WHEN WE STARTED I had no idea of Hiroshi's capabilities or interest in creating the hardscape and rockwork for the stream and plantings between the two pavilions. I expected that I would design the garden and toyed with various plans using Japanese iris and a meandering stream. But, once the pilings were in and the stepping stones in the pond lifted the requisite few inches, Hiroshi announced that we should make the stream *before* beginning the construction of the Azumaya. It was *déjà vu*, only this time it was Hiroshi who toured the countryside and chose the stones, dutifully followed by a bucket loader. He knew *exactly* where they would be placed in the stream that was already completely formed in *his* mind's eye. Forms were built and rocks wrestled into place, often standing on end. Smallish flat stones interspersed with an occasional boulder were set in the base cement rendering the stream bed convincingly natural. The pond entered part way into the new stream around a larger boulder before the water spilled over a long rounded slab that served as a small dam. A ten-inch-square plug was installed just above the little dam, that could be removed in the event of a heavy downpour which might overrun the sides of the inlet. The plug itself has an inch-square opening to enable the stream to flow when the level of the pond is below dam level. This hole is normally covered by a small stone. A very thin slab, found as an isolated specimen at the foot of a cliff along a newly enlarged highway, served as a most elegant bridge over the stream between the courtyard and the foot of the staircases made out of thuja logs that mount the Gazebo slope.

The rockwork of the stream, the first such work ever executed by Hiroshi, is consummate. Clearly he is an intuitive master mason and landscape designer in the Japanese tradition, as well as a master carpenter. Hiroshi's talents with the rockwork in the courtyard were as much responsible for the authenticity of the setting as the buildings themselves. Among his achievements are the sizing and placement of the stepping stones that lead from a giant central stone in three directions, and the mixing of types of stone for variety. Two notable stones that he found on the beach are the large stone that serves as a bench and the *Meotoiwa* or marriage stone that had been split into two halves by the ice floes and that he reformed as a unit to serve as the largest element in the traditional grouping of three stones near the center of the courtyard. Hiroshi used to sit for long periods looking at his *Meotoiwa*, whose surface

ABOVE

The drainage channel for water dripping off the Azumaya's roof.

OPPOSITE

Stepping stones, collected in the countryside, lead to the Hoōgyo.

was filled with striations and swirls. He claimed that this particular stone, for him, reflected all the history of the world since its formation. All these stones, in their different ways, add importantly to the ensemble. Cobble stones line the base of the thuja hedges and encircle the pine, willow, ginkgo, and birch, separating the cornus groundcover that surrounds them from the courtyard gravel. Somewhat larger cobbles line a foot-wide drip-line trench, under the eaves of the pavilions, that is filled with rounded two-inch pebbles collected patiently on the beach by Ann, Morio, and Kaya in their own bucket brigade. All these stones were collected on or near the property and enhance its Asiatic corner.

I am responsible for placing a single stone in the small courtyard that lies between the Hoõgyo and the distant view. Hiroshi had left for good before this area was finished. Having watched him in action for several years, I was hopeful that some of his methodology in selecting a stone might have rubbed off. While on a picnic in nearby St. Irénée I came upon an interesting outcrop of metamorphic stone that was distinctly different and full of interesting facets and textures. Despite its friability we were able to move a stone of the required size to the site, only to have it split cleanly in two as it was being partially buried in its setting. Lacking the gumption and talents of Hiroshi to fuse it as another *Meotoiwa*, and concerned that it would only crumble further if I touched it again, I filled the crack with gritty, humusy soil and chinked it with moss that has happily flourished ever since, showing that there is more than one way to handle a *Meotoiwa*!

THE PLANTINGS

HIROSHI WAS NOT CONCERNED with plants other than to specify that moss be used as much as possible. For days we collected moss along wood roads in deep forest where it had become established on north-facing sandy banks. We placed it in small humus-filled trenches around most of the stepping stones, watered by leaky pipe and separated from the gravel by a narrow strip of sheet metal. We also covered a mounded hillock with moss on the Gazebo side of the stream where Hiroshi had placed a large, squarish, lichen-covered boulder. The boulder was surrounded on two sides with a mass of thuja, trimmed as a backdrop to set off the rock. Along the courtyard edge of the stream, low clumps of thuja simulate the azaleas in a Japanese garden (which would not tolerate Zone 4). They are linked by a long ribbon of *Hakonechloa macra* 'Aureola', the dwarf Japanese grass that obligingly grows so that its long variegated pendent leaves appear to be combed in a single direction. Opposite the hakonechloa and near the mossy bank we planted *Petasites japonicus* 'Variegatus'. Its white variegations balance the yellow-green sweep of the hakonechloa. Completing the corner plantings behind the stream are *Osmunda japonica* and a pale white and blue form of *Primula sieboldii*, the *Sakurasoh* of Japan.

The golden tones of Kirengeshoma palmata *are a bright note in this October view of the Waterfall.*

A swath of Hakonechloa macra 'Aureola' along the courtyard stream with Petasites japonicus 'Variegatus' on the far bank.

The circles at the base of the deciduous trees are filled with *Cornus canadensis* and *Maianthemum canadensis* (which sneaks in wherever it can and has to be periodically expunged from the mossy border around the stepping stones). The thuja masses are shaped to evoke the shapes in a Japanese garden and are underplanted with sphagnum moss. On the shady side of the Hoōgyo, an area of soil that was left bare is now covered with its own spontaneous moss. A Tsukubai drips water into its stone basin nearby.

A second Tsukubai functions at the base of the rustic thuja staircase that mounts the Gazebo side of the Ravine once you have crossed the stream. On this slope in August the delicate blossoms of *Anemonopsis macrophylla* can be seen from below as one ascends the stairs. On the left, by the water's edge, a large mass of *Primula kisoana* 'Alba' encircles the trunk of a large thuja. It fills the bank between the pond and a large stone ledge placed there by Cono. You can step down on to this ledge from a staircase landing and skirt the edge of the bank until you reach the flat path, at the foot of a heavily planted slope, that leads to the stepping stones around the pond. Two other staircases step down the slope to this path.

The stone ledge is the perch where D'whinnie, our cairn terrier, driven to complete frenzy, watches the large trout rising from the depths of the pond to wolf their allotment of trout chow thrown to them from the landing above. Given the meaning

A golden streak of Kirengeshoma palmata *spills down the Ravine bank, contrasting with the lush green sweeps of* Bergenia cordifolia *and the autumnal rustiness of* Aruncus aethusifolius.

of Kan Son Tei, the traditional koi or carp were eschewed for Charlevoix' native fish (*Salvelinus fontinalis*), the elusive and noble brook trout. By summer's end some of the trout have grown to several pounds and can be seen from the Azumaya's gallery darting among the pilings and around the water lilies floating in frames of bamboo. They are there for the pleasure one derives from watching them and not for the catching and eating, although, mysteriously, the population needs to be supplemented from a nearby hatchery each spring. Perhaps some enterprising local Izaak Walton, as yet unapprehended, visits the premises and fishes them out with worms in the dead of an early winter night.

The Ravine slope opposite the Waterfall is sufficiently steep to have been shored up with thuja logs, as well as thuja pickets that line the thuja staircases. The staircases were built before the plans for the Kan Son Tei came into focus. Laurent Lapointe, a woodsman who, in keeping with his compatriots, can fashion almost anything out of wood with his ax and saw, has carpeted the Ravine with a labyrinth of thuja boardwalks and staircases. Those near the Kan Son Tei fit the oriental flavor of the setting and underline the fact that this approach to the Pavilions is very different from the formal zigzagging series of varied stone pathways and staircases that lead to it from the Pigeonnier.

THE GREATER PERFECTION

CHAPTER IX

ABOVE

Rodgersia aesculifolia *enjoys its riparian site at the entrance to the ravine, beneath the lower of the two rope bridges.*

OPPOSITE

Top, left: Rodgersia podophylla, *a Japanese species, flanks a staircase near the pond.*
Top, right: Primula kisoana *'Alba's stoloniferous habit makes it a useful groundcover.*
Below, left: Aruncus aethusifolius, *and* Waldsteinia ternata.
Below, right: Sambucus canadensis *'Aurea'.*

Hiroshi built the Machiai near the top of the slope out of local thuja. It is a crude, simple shelter; traditionally a place for the common people to sit, discard their everyday concerns and collect their thoughts before they descend for their spiritual encounter with the Kan Son Tei; something apparently not required of the Nobs who are to use the grander staircase across the way. It is a relaxing setting, looking out over the top of the steep slope to the pond and the waterfalls and on up the Ravine with its rope bridges. It is a good place to rest and talk, as well as to think. The slope itself is so steep that we have had to peg logs across it at intervals to have something to stand on while weeding. The logs soon disappeared under groundcovers which, for much of the area, consist of *Tsuga canadensis* 'Cole's Prostrate', acquired as twice-transplanted, rooted cuttings and planted about fourteen inches apart.

The idea for this came from watching the feathery, procumbent branches of a single specimen gradually flowing down the slope at the rate of a half-inch a year. We now use it extensively in the Waterfall and pavilion surround. In time the slow-growing plants will merge to form a soft, billowy, dark green comforter, masking the abruptness

The ensemble in a late June fog with Bergenia cordifolia *in the foreground and* Aruncus aethusifolius *softening the lower tier of boulders as it prepares to bloom.*

of the slope; a counterpoint to the thuja canopy overhead. Where the slope is less pronounced, the dwarf tsuga are interplanted with shortia or anemonopsis, which thrive in the setting. The tsuga is one of the few non-Asian plants on the slope, hailing from the hills of New Hampshire where Mr. Cole happened to come upon it.

The masses of Asian plants consist of panels of the dwarf *Thalictrum coreanum* (or *ichangense*) and the even smaller *Thalictrum kiusianum*, presented at chest height for close inspection on top of the wall that shores up the slope above an intermediate path, both a froth of dainty white blossoms as they succeed one another in July and August. A third choice species, *Thalictrum diffusiflorum*, tumbles over the wall a bit further on where its large, campanulate, pale blue, pendent blossoms can be seen from below as one mounts the furthest staircase. Behind it the easy *Symphyandra hoffmannii* flourishes, seeding itself freely and indiscriminately, but nonetheless pleasantly, among the other plants on the slope. They are easily weeded out but have the gratifying habit of growing in tiny cracks and corners where one would least expect a plant to take hold.

My favorite woodland plant is *Anemonopsis macrophylla*, which is used copiously on the slope of the pavilion surround. A native of Japan, it is the one of the last of the woodland flowers to bloom, sending airy sprays up to three feet with spheres of green buds. These unfurl in August into exquisite, long-lasting, violet-mauve umbrellas over two inches in diameter with a dark purple cup centered beneath them. It is something to look forward to, the more welcome since its flowering companions are few and far between.

Below the mid-slope there are more ordered plantings; long sweeps of *Rodgersia podophylla* flanking a curving staircase; *Cimicifuga japonica* var. *acerina* displaying its broad leaves and decorative spikes after the sheet of *Hylomecon japonicum* that surrounds it is spent and done with. Beside them is a large mass of the indispensable *Aruncus aethusifolius* that fills much of the space flowing down the center of the slope on either side of a large triangle of *Jeffersonia dubia*, that most desirable cousin of our native *Jeffersonia diphylla* and one of the harbingers of spring.

A plant left to its own devices on a slope will colonize the area below it, much as paint will run down a tilted palette. The balance of the planting simulates this principle. Sweeps of bergenia bracket a steep staircase starting from the base of the wall above it. A fifty-foot swath of *Kirengeshoma palmata* starting above a distant path high on the slope flows down over the wall to the pond's edge. Below the rope bridge in the Ravine proper, the slope is covered with a mass of ostrich fern.

Autumn is the best time to see these sweeps of plants, despite the fact that the hylomecon and jeffersonia are dormant. The aruncus and rodgersia are burnished bronze with orange and purple overtones respectively, the bergenia is the darkest crimson and the foliage of the kirengeshoma forms a luminous, golden swath that tumbles down the slope — echoing the tiers of the Waterfall across the way.

OPPOSITE

An autumnal view of the Azumaya from the floor of the Ravine, over plantings of rodgersia. The leaves of Rodgersia aesculifolia *are still green while those of* R. podophylla *have turned.*

BELOW

Anemonopsis macrophylla *opens its enchanting parasols in mid-August.*

CHAPTER X
DEEP SHADE AND SUNNIER BORDERS

OPPOSITE

The floor of the Ravine is filled with ostrich fern and rodgersia. Staircases and bridges help the visitor navigate the area.

ABOVE

Astrantia and geranium in the Perennial Allée.

I REDISCOVERED THE RAVINE DURING THE LONG, TEDIOUS CLEANUP of the woodland as a consequence of the ravages of the spruce budworm. This feature of the property, forgotten since my childhood experience of being run over by the horse-drawn tumbril, opened up an entirely new form of gardening on a scale much larger than anything I had tackled before. In the Ravine there was at least an acre to clear and plant. The far slope (below the Pigeonnier garden) was almost vertical, precluding any cultivation. In retrospect it was just as well, since one slope is quite enough to worry about. The drama afforded by the precipitous facing bank is sufficient for the setting.

The scale and dimensions of the Ravine pandered to my taste for using large-leaved plants, to cover the surface and make an impact from a distance. This became even more important once the rope bridges were in place, since large-scale, massed plantings of a given species would be viewed from a distant height.

Not long after clearing the Ravine, I was introduced to the genus rodgersia in the Savill Garden at Windsor where a number of different species of these woodland perennials, all with large, textured leaves and tall spirea-like blossoms, were planted in groups of four or five. They were ideal architectonic subjects for the Ravine. As they were not then available in the U.S. I imported a specimen of each variety offered by Alan Bloom's Bressingham Nurseries and planted them to see how they would behave in our Zone 4 site.

The rodgersia species, with their tuberous roots, reveled in the Ravine's rich soil and sheltered setting to such an extent that each spring or autumn they could be lifted and divided tenfold. In no time the desired drifts of these easy and important colonizers were established, with surplus tubers proferred annually for plantings in other parts of the Woodland Garden and the Palissades.

Wooden steps, boardwalks, decks, and staircases of varying sizes made out of thuja

OPPOSITE

A mass of Athyrium goeringianum *'Pictum' underplanted with* Waldsteinia ternata.

BELOW

The author collecting seeds of Paraquilegia anemonoides *in a high valley near Sigunian-Shan in Western Szechuan.*

logs were built to provide access from the edge of the Woodland Garden, down the Ravine slope to the stream level, as well as to access intermediate levels along its curving length. Rodgersias are effective in covering up and softening the exposed sides of the walkways and decks and are of particular interest in July when their tall white and pink plumes wave above their bold and striking foliage. It wasn't long before there was a staircase that led through a mass of *Rodgersia pinnata*, and another flanked by *Rodgersia podophylla* from Japan.

The most decorative of these rodgersias was what was then known as *Rodgersia tabularis* (now called *Astilboides tabularis*) from China, with its large circular leaves held up to three feet off the ground, forming a particularly striking mass. Since rodgersias took a while to get going in the spring, I interplanted the astilboides with the double form of the native bloodroot, *Sanguinaria canadensis* forma *multiplex* which increases in a similar tuberous way. The choice, long-lived, pristine, peony-like bloodroot flowers — so much more effective than the fugacious single form — enlivened the astilboides area until the latter's leaves began to unveil and thrust upward like unfurling cobra heads. Furthermore, once the astilboides were fully in leaf, the round, indented sanguinaria leaves provided an echoing counterpoint as an underplanting below its larger companion. This serendipitous result has now been repeated under rodgersia plantings throughout the garden. There is no reason why tier upon tier of compatible plants should not be mixed together for effect, although one has to face a major separating, dividing, and replanting every five years or so.

In October 1988 we had occasion to visit the Wolong Valley in Western Szechuan, site of a panda reserve and home of the richest temperate forests in the world, *en route* to a trek to the base of Sigunian-Shan on the edge of the Sino-Tibetan massif. Here we hoped to collect seeds of *Primula cernua* and *Paraquilegia anemonoides*, that choicest of alpines. We spent only one night in the valley and had only the briefest chance to investigate its incredibly rich flora. Little did we know that the valley floor was carpeted with the then-dormant *Corydalis flexuosa*. The path along the valley floor winds through a myriad of perennials and shrubs that are now used regularly in western gardens. It seemed implausible that it was a natural setting filled with indigenous plants. When we came to the river's edge, the far bank, under a tangle of *Davidia involucrata* and *Acer davidii*, was carpeted with *Rodgersia aesculifolia* growing happily right down to the water's edge. It wasn't long before this effect was created (this time underplanted with sanguinaria) in the Ravine, where the stream empties into the pond next to the Waterfall. To this day, for me, it evokes that brief moment in Wolong.

Rodgersia is just one of the large-leaved genera used in the Ravine. *Petasites japonicus* var. *giganteus* increasingly fills the stream bed and inches higher up the precipitous far bank each year in gingerly fashion. A large heracleum grown from seed — labeled *Heracleum antasiaticum* and collected in the Caucasus, presumably a form of *Heracleum mantegazzianum* — is colonizing part of the Ravine slope, as is a regularly divided clump of *Rheum palmatum* 'Atrosanguineum' acquired originally from Beth Chatto. The drama of its unfolding, thrusting, red-sheathed flower stalk warrants at least a daily inspection as it emerges from its bed of giant gray-blue leaves with purple undersides. It is infinitely happier in the moist, shaded Ravine than it is in full sun, no matter how carefully it is coddled. It is one of those plants, along with anemonopsis and kirengeshoma, that one must remember to divide *just* after the snow has melted and the ground has thawed. The lovely green form of *Rheum palmatum* revels in the same conditions along the floor of the Ravine, whereas it is clearly unhappy in a sunny garden setting, lacking the chutzpah of the coarser, common rhubarb that is indestructible in any setting but not choice enough to mingle with its more elegant kinfolk.[37]

The large-leaved masses are echoed in somewhat smaller-leaved species such as *Darmera peltata*, *Podophyllum hexandrum*, and *Caltha palustris* var. *alba* from the western U.S. (and much easier on the eye than the vivid yellow of its indigenous cousin) as it follows a wet seep down the slope from one of the small woodland streams above. The tableau

OPPOSITE

A staircase runs through large-leaved plantings of Rheum palmatum 'Atrosanguineum', Darmera peltata, *and* Rodgersia pinnata. Primula japonica *intermingles with* Myosotis sylvestris, *and* Tricyrtis latifolia.

BELOW

A vertiginous view looking down at the stream bed from the upper rope bridge.

LEFT

Rodgersia aesculifolia *enjoys its riparian site.*

BELOW, LEFT

Bergenia cordifolia, Athyrium goeringianum *'Pictum',* Rodgersia pinnata, *and* Waldsteinia ternata *infiltrate a Ravine staircase.*

BELOW

Matteuccia struthiopteris *and* Myosotis sylvestris *claim any open space for themselves.*

ABOVE

The incomparable, long-lasting blossoms of Sanguinaria canadensis *forma* multiplex.

is completed with masses of the perennial, ever-blooming forget-me-not *Myosotis sylvestris*, and part of a hillside filled with *Matteuccia struthiopteris,* the indomitable ostrich fern. Other ferns abound as well: osmundas, adiantums, dryopteris, and, my favorite, *Polystichum braunii*, which I "rescued" from the middle of a footpath while making the four-hour climb up to the 4,000-foot plateau in the Shickshocks of the Gaspé Peninsula with Fred Case. Fred's knowledge of every plant on that twelve-acre mountaintop was encyclopedic although it was his first exposure to the site. *Polystichum braunii* has class and is statelier than its sister species. Would that it were quicker to increase!

Groundcovers and underplantings carpet different portions of the slope: *Waldsteinia ternata*, epimediums in variety, *Hylomecon japonicum* whose bright yellow flowers are the perfect foil for the dark blue of *Pulmonaria angustifolia* ssp. *azurea*, and a mass of the native *Pyrola rotundifolia*. There are also pockets where choice and tiny plants such as *Ranunculus crenatus* can flourish by a mossy stump.

Another unforgettable sight among the forested slopes of Western Szechuan were the drifts of the massive *Ligularia wilsoniana* growing out of a stream bed in a shady gully. On the slopes of the Ravine I had tried the usual forms of ligularia with spires, such as *przewalskii*, 'The Rocket', and others, only to find them rather inadequate and insignificant among the masses of the other large-scale plants. I had also tried planting the coarse *Ligularia veitchii*, which was closer to the scale required but not particularly effective. After seedlings of *wilsoniana* were planted in the stream bed itself, and thrust up their stately three-foot spires to achieve an overall height of eight feet, filling the space around them with sprays of large circular leaves, it was clear that nature had once again shown the way to use a given plant in a particular setting.

In fact nature always does us one better. After the initial clearing of the Ravine *Impatiens biflora*, the ubiquitous jewelweed, colonized almost every inch of cleared soil and I despaired at the prospect of coping with it and weeding it every year. Now that the Ravine is fully planted, the impatiens restricts its colonizing to the banks of the stream bed and produces a delicate, apricot swath along the floor of the Ravine in August. Who would have intentionally tried to achieve such an effect?[38]

A large metal crayfish by William Wessel stretches a menacing claw towards visitors as they cross the bridge that separates the rodgersias from the ligularias, while a bronze beaver contentedly munches on a bronze sapling nearby. A bench encircles the trunk of one of the ancient balsam poplars that provide the light, upper-level shade canopy for the Ravine and account for much of its success as an ecosystem. From the bench you can look out over the little pond past the Waterfall to the Azumaya, where a trout may rise to the occasional fly and where gentians bloom in early autumn in the interstices of the stone steps leading down to the stepping stones. The relentless signal of a second *shi-shi-otoshi* clacks to attract those who may come down to the Kan Son Tei from higher up in the Ravine.

In the autumn the gold of the paper birch and the orange of the mountain maples (*Acer spicatum*) illuminate the length of the Ravine as the western sun sets on axis. The ferns and the rodgersias are returning to dormancy, the trout rarely surface and the Kan Son Tei is boarded and locked for a long winter sleep under its thick mantle of snow.

LEAVING THE RAVINE

SEVERAL THUJA LOG STAIRCASES lead from the floor of the Ravine to the level of the Woodland Garden on the planted side of the Ravine. There is also a pathway that crosses a bridge at the head of the Ravine — below the Lac Libellule dam — that leads back up to the Pigeonnier Garden, emerging on axis with the Pigeonnier and its reflection pool. Each of the staircases is bracketed by particular plantings. One mounts through different species of iris, ranunculus, and primula; another through banks of *Petasites japonicus*, *Heracleum antasiaticum*, and *Rheum palmatum* 'Atrosanguineum'. One staircase is gradually being swallowed by *Rodgersia pinnata*, whose unreachable tubers poke their stalks between the chinks in the log boardwalks. On either side of the stream bed a mass of *Petasites japonicus* var. *giganteus* is doing its best to spread in every direction. It is allowed free rein on the precipitous Pigeonnier side of the stream, which it is slowly climbing, but is kept within bounds on the planted side by large and equally competitive plantings of *Rheum palmatum*, *Rodgersia podophylla*, and *Polygonatum biflorum*. Where the staircases reach the valley floor *Polystichum braunii* and *Darmera peltata* intermingle with *Myosotis sylvestris*, *Primula japonica*, and a mass of *Tricyrtis latifolia*. Above the thicket of rodgersias surrounding the staircases, *Patrinia gibbosa*, *Pachysandra procumbens*, and a mantle of the beautiful native *Pyrola rotundifolia* hold sway. *Lysichiton camschaticum* grow happily on a wet terrace among the myosotis, while *Diphylleia cymosa* line the banks of the steep gulley above. The route visitors most often take leads past a mass of *Athyrium goeringianum* 'Pictum', their silver-gray fronds contrasting dramatically with a dark green hillside of *Waldsteinia ternata* that turns a rich yellow in June. It was here that the serendipitous combination of *Hylomecon japonicum* and *Pulmonaria angustifolia* ssp. *azurea* was chanced upon. Here also occurred the failed effort to provide a north-facing slope for the *Rhododendron yakushimanum* that are now lodged in the woodland near the Nakamon.

The narrow path at the top of the stairs emerges into a corner of the woodland opposite a mass of interplanted astilboides and sanguinaria. Here a group of gray-leaved hostas provides a foil for a galaxy of orange-red *Lilium tenuifolium* blossoms that hover over them in early July.

Eschewing the temptation to explore the partially obscured woodland plantings that lie to the right along the rim of the Ravine, visitors are urged to turn to the left, passing near the marhan and martagon lilies they glimpsed before crossing the rope bridge. Then, turning sharply to their right through a thuja thicket underplanted with ostrich fern, they emerge in a sunlit, grassy clearing, a total contrast to the Ravine.

Charles Smith's Gardener Frog, replete with trowel and knee pads, is seen over the large leaves of Astilboides tabularis, *which grow through the complementary foliage of* Sanguinaria canadensis *forma* multiplex.

THE PERENNIAL ALLÉE

IF THE EAST-WEST AXIS ALONG THE TAPIS VERT IS THE SPINE OF THE GARDEN, we are now at its heart. When you find the right spot in the circular patch of lawn at the foot of the Perennial Allée, you can look back up the transverse axis that divides it, through the Rose Garden, up the White Garden steps and across the oval pool to the statue of Pan. At the same time, to the left, you can see the sweep of the Shade Borders leading away to a corner of Lac Libellule. On the right the façade of the house is glimpsed through a frame of mature paper birch trunks. At their base chanterelles obligingly proffer themselves for harvest a good month before they make their appearance in the boreal forest.

Visitors who were deflected from a close inspection of the Perennial Allée when they started their tour are now encouraged to examine it in detail. It is the permutations of both the Perennial Allée and the Shade Borders over the course of the summer that makes the exercise so exciting. Since the beds step up from the circular patch of lawn

OPPOSITE

Campanula lactiflora, *backed by the foliage of* Gentiana asclepiadea, *begins the view up the stepped Perennial Allée through the Rose Garden to the White Garden in July.*

BELOW

A form of Iris sibirica *against the mauve haze of* Thalictrum aquilegifolium.

The Greater Perfection

through several terraces, the best view of the ensemble is from a tall ladder which we provide for professional photographers, and which enables one to see the flowers in all four gardens at once.

Every autumn all the beds are heavily mulched with rotted manure and compost. In early May the Perennial Allée beds are a swath of dark brown, except for two ancient *Potentilla fruticosa*, which were planted by Pat Morgan in the late 1950s to buttress the lower shrub corner of the ensemble.

By mid-May the new green shoots of perennial clumps have reappeared through their heavy mulch, and an ephemeral light blue edging of *Myosotis alpestris* frames the central path. The clumps seem much too far apart and each year, as in the case of the Goose Allée, I wonder if there will be enough annuals to fill the empty spaces. By early June, however, there is *just barely* enough room to fit in the supplementary annuals, biennials, and replacement perennials. By the end of the month, a succession of blossoms begins that extends into September and is punctuated by moments of glory as the season progresses.

First there is the conjunction of oriental poppies, Siberian iris, *Thalictrum aquilegifolium* in variety, species peonies, true geraniums, and dictamnus. The showy hybrid peonies then appear along with the early aconites, followed by an extended wave of delphinium as the different hybrid strains peak in turn. Filipendula, cimicifuga, ligularia, and the later aconitum, all in variety, take the place of the delphinium, with sprays of willow gentian cascading over the steps between the terraces. By late August the endearing blossoms of *Anemone hupehensis* proclaim that the end is near.

One of the consequences of a Zone 4 summer is that the perennials tend to bloom in a more concentrated fashion than would be the case further south, as if to make up for the late spring and early fall. The effect is stunning and gives the impression that the gardener has pulled off an accomplished coup. In fact, it is Mother Nature's biological clock and the extended northern twilights and dawns of early summer, combined with the cool evenings and foggy mornings of a maritime climate, that account for the effect. In my view there is no easier place to garden in eastern North America than Charlevoix County.

The Perennial Allée was created by Pat Morgan in the late 1950s and some of his plantings are still in place, a testimony to the fifty years of nourishment they have received. The central path passes between two majestic clumps of *Dictamnus fraxinella*, planted in the corners next to the steps leading from the uppermost terrace. Cut limestone retaining walls separate the terraces from the surrounding sloping ground — resulting in level beds. By late June they are obscured by the mass of plants that appear to flow down an uninterrupted slope on either side of the stepped, level central path. The Allée, which is twenty-five feet wide, can be seen from both sides, as well as from the central path and the grassy circle below. My favorite vantage point is from the front

The Perennial Allée from early May through June to early July. The different levels and beds become obliterated as the season progresses.

RIGHT

The spring to summer progress of the Perennial Allée approaching its climax in late July when delphinium varieties take center stage.

OVERLEAF

A classic Charlevoix combination: long-lived clumps of delphinium seen through the branches of a paper birch.

254   CHAPTER X

lawn, looking at the outside of the Allée through the birch tree trunks. This flanking view is quite different, both in an overall sense — as one sees the border in its entirety — and in the constantly changing details; when one is in the central path, for example, the veronicastrum obscures the appealing display of *Daphne mezereum*'s scarlet berries presented against a background of white cimicifuga spires.

At both ends of the Allée the bright blue of *Clematis integrifolia* flowers spill over retaining walls. At the upper end it provides a transition from the rose bushes underplanted with a sea of pinks in the Rose Garden. At the lower end, as one steps from the central path into the grassy circle, it is followed by *Clematis heracleifolia*, extending the theme into early autumn.

Pat Morgan's 1950s fountain — a small dolphin, applied to a graceful limestone wall, that drips water into a low, moss-covered, ferny basin — terminates the axis and is set into a semicircle of maturing thuja. The thujas serve as foils for climbers such as *Tropaeolum peregrinum* and *speciosum* and for *Clematis macropetala* 'Markham's Pink' behind the mauve shade border.

The success of the Perennial Allée follows in part from its configuration — the different levels, the extended width of the plantings, the hidden walls that frame the beds. Another contributing factor is the way shrubs and small trees have been placed to anchor and balance the beds as they step down the slopes. This inherited structure and upholstery, again the legacy of Pat Morgan, has made the job of furnishing and maintaining the planted beds far simpler than it would otherwise have been; a blessing, since this central feature of the gardens at Les Quatre Vents, at once its most visible and conventional horticultural expression, has been a never-ending worry and preoccupation.

The Perennial Allée would be far more tolerable if it were the only feature in the garden. All available time and energy could then be devoted to it with weekly, if not daily, notations of what works and what needs to be moved or introduced to improve or sustain the orchestration of the bloom cycle. The changes needed, in turn, would mean growing appropriate replacements in a nursery bed and being willing to wade in and tear the beds apart in late August to prepare for the next season. While some plantings have endured, thanks to the appropriateness of their original placement, most have changed. At first there was an excess of *Phlox paniculata* and shasta daisies. Later oriental poppies spread to the detriment of their neighbors, geranium species seeded themselves with abandon, and ancient Siberian iris clumps became sparse bloomers. Slowly the quality of the plantings was upgraded with a more diverse and longer season of bloom. Early blooming varieties of trollius and aconitum were introduced, along with some species peonies and a number of filipendula varieties. An *Inula magnifica* was added to the anchor corner so that its mass could replace the aruncus and thalictrums once they were spent.

There seemed little point in including the Pacific Hybrid delphiniums once they became the dominant feature of the Goose Allée. The other hybrid forms which, for the most part, were there to begin with (the Blackmore & Langdon, and Connecticut Yankee strains, along with some thoroughly different and unidentified varieties), are concentrated in the upper reaches of the Perennial Allée. Their large, forty-year-old clumps are not seriously bothered by being moved around and divided when a major reworking of the beds is undertaken. This happened in the early 1990s when *everything* was removed one August and the beds were redug and reinvigorated. The recovery of the whole, however, takes several years and when the plants finally regain their natural vigor one has to start the whole process of editing and repositioning once again to correct the inevitable clashes that arise. The wonderful filipendula that looked well against a planting of cimicifuga turns out to be the wrong shade now that it is close to a shell-pink astilbe. The problem can be solved in the short term by cutting off the offending blossoms. The trick is to remember to move the plant to an alternative spot when the autumn comes. Often I find that I am "gardened out" by this time, so the jarring element is left in place and becomes all too apparent the next year.

Nothing induces prevarication for me the way a perennial border does, and I will go to extreme lengths to avoid grasping the nettle and making the changes required. I do my best to divert visitors from examining the beds at close range and rationalize my lack of heart on the grounds that there are more important chores to be taken care of.

Fortunately for me, when Pat Morgan created the Allée and its grassy terminus, he also put in the smallest of woodland gardens at the edge of the tongue of woodland that crept up its far side towards the mature birches.

BELOW

The delphiniums in the Perennial Allée include varieties other than Pacific Hybrids. The pale yellow of Thalictrum flavum *provides a counterpoint to the shades of blue.*

OPPOSITE

A view of the house from the center of the Perennial Allée, framed by dictamnus, astrantia, geranium, Aconitum 'Ivorine' *and* Thalictrum aquilegifolium, *with* Hieracium pilosella *blooming throughout the front lawn.*

CHAPTER XI
THE WOODLAND GARDEN

OPPOSITE

Drifts of Primula *'Peter Klein' (*P. clarkei *x* P. rosea*) and* P. *'Johanna' (*P. clarkei *x* P. warshenewskyana*) cover opposite banks of a small pond in a corner of the Woodland.*

ABOVE, RIGHT

This hybrid of Primula florindae *and* P. alpicola *var.* luna *appeared for the first time in 1999.*

P AT MORGAN'S BIT OF WOODLAND GARDEN WAS ABOUT TWENTY-FIVE FEET long and several feet wide and included a stream — originating in a hidden, dripping faucet — that wound its way down to a minuscule pond, fashioned out of a shallow tin tub encased in sphagnum moss, by the edge of the grassy circle. The garden was filled with transplants from the boreal forest — *Linnaea borealis*, *Maianthemum canadense*, *Cornus canadensis*, and two species of pyrola.

When I began to deal with this tiny woodland garden, considerable effort was required to bring it back from its neglected state. During the 1960s and '70s the spruce budworm had decimated the woodland copse at the end of the Perennial Allée. Ancient spruce had fallen every which way, and deciduous trees were sprouting through the debris. It had become an impenetrable thicket.

In keeping with the configuration of the Shade Borders, I elected to clear a bed that curved down to the fountain, between the edge of the woodland copse and the grassy circle. This bed was shaded throughout the day and faced due north — a spot tailor-made for alpine woodlanders.

The next spring several individual specimens of alpine primulas were planted, as well as several soldanella species, some mossy saxifrages, and Asiatic gentians. The plants originated in Stonecrop and their pleasure at being moved into this shady bed was almost audible. Gone were the high heat and humidity, the muggs of summer that plague the Hudson River Valley. Instead there were cool, foggy nights, copious moisture, and a sandy woodland duff filled with organic matter. The primulas waxed so enthusiastically that they could be divided several times that summer, with one plant turning into ten by season's end. The soldanellas not only bloomed — something they had never done in Cold Spring — but increased tenfold, becoming thick clumps that required division. The site was not only suitable, it was ideal. It has served as an "incubator" and nursery for choice plants ever since.

The native plants, however, appeared to resent their new neighbors and the preferential treatment accorded them and resorted to their own form of ethnic cleansing. *Cornus canadensis* and *Pyrola rotundifolia* roots raced through the bed and did their very best to strangle the introduced plants.

At the time, native plant gardens were quite the rage in the U.S., to the point where they had become as much an expression of attitude as a horticultural exercise. Purists supported their cause with almost religious fervor. While I am as fond of native plants as the next enthusiast, I am ambivalent about the idea of a native-plant garden outside of the bounds of a botanical garden in a major city, whose inhabitants may not have much of a chance to walk in the woodlands of their region. It seems an unnecessary horticultural limitation, given the fact that all species are native somewhere. When it came to a choice between ubiquitous and aggressive groundcovers engulfing treasures from the Maritime Alps, there was no question about who should be suppressed.

The success of the north-facing "incubator" bed indicated that, if the woodland thicket could be cleaned out, the plantings could be moved into it and become more extensive. The cleaning process took seven years to complete. First the fallen trees were removed, leaving massive stumps. Most deciduous seedling trees were cleared with only a few *Acer spicatum*, *Betula papyrifera*, and *Amelanchier canadensis* left to provide shade. A few thuja were added to make up for the loss of the spruce. Once Pat Morgan's mini-woodland garden was removed, an entrance path was introduced from the grassy circle.

OPPOSITE

Lilium pyrenaicum, *a gift from Pat Morgan, adapts well to the Woodland.*

BELOW

Les Quatre Vents' *small collection of* Trillium grandiflorum *'Flore Pleno'. It is hard to come by and slow to increase, particularly if one gives pips to needy friends.*

THE GREATER PERFECTION

WATER IN THE WOODS

Over the seven years, five artificial streams were threaded throughout the acre-sized woodland. A two-inch pipe brought water from the main stream to the uphill edge of the woodland. The first stream used a plastic liner covered with pebbles and led into two small ponds in the center of the woodland. The second, thanks to Cono, was lined with concrete and ran from the rear of Pat Morgan's fountain. It included a deep, dark pool. The three remaining streams run on the ground without benefit of liner and have proved the best solution. Once the sandy subsoil becomes saturated, the water courses down the stream bed, provided one is careful to remove roots running underneath it that often create alternate channels for the water to follow. An unlined stream also has the merit of soaking the soil on either side, to the enhancement of moisture-loving plants. The water from all the streams ultimately returns to the mother stream.

As each stream bed was cleared, a system of paths followed, leaving room for stream-side plantings on the one hand and woodland plantings on the other. In time an intricate network of paths, streams, and planting areas was developed, the latter with varied exposures and conditions. We soon found that the roots of the deciduous trees made a beeline for the moisture along the stream beds so that a sweep of introduced plants that flourished the first year would reflect the competition the second year, and start to give up in the third year. The solution has been to create a wide corridor along each stream bed. The roots at the edge of the corridor are cut as close to the tree trunks as is feasible. An eighteen-inch strip of sheet metal is then buried as far away from the stream as possible. The plants in the corridor enjoy the best of horticultural worlds with periods of direct sunlight and constant moisture, an Asiatic primula's dream! Between the corridors, among the indigenous trees, the native flora flourishes, content within its restricted bounds.

Over the years the plants have been moved again and again as the woodland has gradually been converted to a Woodland Garden, and the logic of planting a given species in a specific site has become apparent. For the first few years, as an area was cleared, it would be invaded by all the persistent weeds, requiring endless weeding and the removal of what seemed like tons of dandelions and raspberries that found the newly cleared site irresistible. The process was repeated year after year until, finally, the increasing shade from the deciduous trees and a dearth of weeds reaching the seeding stage turned the tide. It is still a significant chore, but one that is quite manageable.

Some fifteen years after the clearing was begun, the woodland has become a settled garden, the success of a given planting dictating its layout. New species are added each year, often in several locations at once. There is an experimental bed along the rim of the Ravine where the moisture content and quality of soil can best be monitored for rarities such as *Diphylleia greyii* from Japan, and questionably hardy specimens.

ABOVE

Primula anisodora, *a native of high meadows in Yunnan and Szechuan in western China, blooms in late July and early August.*

OPPOSITE

A slab of limestone, surrounded by Saxifraga x urbium *and a mossy saxifrage, serves as a bridge over the first stream to be created in the Woodland. In the background are* Erythronium revolutum *'White Beauty' and* Primula x pruhonicensis *'Lady Greer'.*

OVERLEAF

The first woodland stream runs through a twenty-foot-wide clearing filled with primulas, saxifrages, and dwarf iris. In the foreground, in addition to Anemone blanda *'White Splendour' and* Erythronium *'Pagoda', there is a mass of* Cardamine enneaphyllos.

The Greater Perfection

OPPOSITE

A drift of Erythronium 'Pagoda' near the lip of the Ravine.

THIS PAGE

Top, left: Tulipa batalinii.
Top, right: Scilla mischtschenkoana.
Middle, left: Anemone blanda *'White Splendour' and* Erythronium *'Pagoda'.*
Middle, right: Scilla siberica *and* Anemone ranunculoides.
Left: Anemone nemorosa *'Alba Plena'.*

THE WOODLAND GARDEN   269

IMITATING ASIA

There are years when heavy snow falls in November, before there is significant frost in the ground, and builds to several feet before it finally melts in mid-April. These insulated conditions, comparable to those above 10,000 feet in the mountains of Asia, permit herbaceous plants normally restricted to Zone 7 to come through the -30° F winters unscathed and give the horticulturist a dangerously smug sense of omnipotence. While the deep early snowfall is quite a regular occurrence, in occasional years either a dearth of early snow or a devastating thaw occurs. If the frost sinks deeply into the ground, a humbler horticultural outlook prevails. (One year we measured the frost as deep as eight feet!)

It is always worth a try to see whether Asiatic species will enjoy the Zone 4 conditions in the Woodland. So often it is the torrid, humid North American summers that do in these plants rather than the frigid winters. Meconopsis is a case in point, their perennial species reveling in the Charlevoix climate year after year, while struggling unhappily in most habitats to the south. As a consequence, we generally ignore the hardiness designations of most nursery catalogues until we have given the species a try. Not all experiments are successful, of course, but there are enough surprises to justify continuing the practice. Shrubs and trees are another matter; there is little point in growing specimens that are killed back to the snow line every winter.

To simulate the rain forests of the Himalayas and the Sino-Tibetan massif, we have resorted to an elaborate irrigation program for the woodland as a whole. In the beginning

ABOVE, LEFT

Meconopsis napaulensis 'Rosea' is monocarpic.

ABOVE, RIGHT

The choice perennial "lampshade" poppy, Meconopsis grandis, *displays the darkest of blue flowers two weeks earlier than other Tibetan poppies.*

OPPOSITE

Meconopsis betonicifolia *is at home in northern Quebec and is easily propagated. This view illustrates three stages, from bud to incipient seed pod.*

OPPOSITE

Glaucidium palmatum, *a woodland jewel from Japan, is a slow but constant grower. Its white form has proved less vigorous.*

BELOW

Russet shades of Primula florindae *border the lower part of the first woodland stream.*

we emulated the late Harold Epstein's practice of mounting "rainbird" sprinkler heads well up the trunks of trees so that they could cover a radius of at least fifty feet. These sprinklers are used religiously whenever a day passes without rain from the beginning of May to early October. As a consequence both the Woodland and the Ravine are kept constantly moist. In recent years, as we have upgraded, enriched, and screened the Woodland plantings from competition, we have buried "leaky pipe" at fifteen-inch intervals throughout the beds and have been able to reduce the need for overhead irrigation during periods of drought when the reservoirs for the garden are taxed to the limit. When the reservoirs are full we can run as many as twenty sprinklers at once throughout the gardens. When water is in short supply, we rotate two or three sprinklers at a time, especially in the Woodland. The flow of the artificial streams can also be reduced, reluctantly, if needs be. Droughts require the constant monitoring and management of sprinklers — the gardens are too widespread and diverse for a computerized system — and are stressful times for those emotionally linked to the health and happiness of their plants. When a drought is ended by a soaking rain I know no greater pleasure or more comforting satisfaction. Generally the Woodland is fresh and moist and the planted slopes of the Ravine dripping moisture.

DEGREES OF SHADE

THE RAVINE ENJOYS THE HIGH SHADE OF MATURE BALSAM POPLARS (*Populus balsamifera*). These statuesque old trees grew through their coarse and scruffy immaturity, which makes them so undesirable in a garden, decades before the Ravine was developed horticulturally. They are also a static element with virtually no change in the shade cover from year to year.

The Woodland Garden's shade, however, has been anything but static and has required far more manipulation and adaptation than was ever foreseen at the outset. In the beginning it seemed doubtful that the young deciduous trees would ever give enough shade. Shortly afterwards their shade became too much for the plantings and required drastic thinning. Some specimens, especially the short-lived mountain maple, *Acer spicatum*, would inexplicably die, presumably due to an excess of moisture, leaving gaping holes where sunlight streamed in. The fifteen or so mature spruce that survived the spruce budworm slowly succumbed to senility, their absence causing a sea change in the way light reaches the ground below. The paper birches, which now form the chief element of the shade cover, tend to thicken their canopy from year to year. What seems just fine in June becomes intolerable in August, requiring judicious, and sometimes major, thinning.

One unexpected and delightful consequence of the constant moisture applied to the Woodland Garden is that the fifty or so spruce stumps that were left in place have become enchanting moss gardens on their own. Delicate volunteer seedlings of choice woodlanders such as *Moneses uniflora* and *Chiogenes hispidula* have established themselves

ABOVE, LEFT

Shortia galacifolia.

ABOVE, CENTER

Corydalis solida *'George Baker'*.

ABOVE, RIGHT

Sanguinaria canadensis *forma* multiplex *and* Anemone ranunculoides.

OPPOSITE

Soldanella carpatica.

in the nooks and crannies of the stumps. The small protected bays between the major roots at the base of the stumps also provide sheltered sites for fragile treasures. They are virtually maintenance-free, requiring only that birch and maple seedlings be removed once a year.

PLANTS FOR THE WOODLAND

We try to grow just about every woodland perennial we can lay our hands upon. There are well over a hundred varieties and species of primula. At one point there were seven different species of meconopsis — four monocarpic species, as well as three perennial species (the well-known *M. betonicifolia*; the glorious lampshade poppy, *M. grandis*, rarely seen in North America, and the harebell poppy, *M. quintuplinervia*). There are six varieties of soldanella, the enchanting tiny harbinger of spring that enlivens the wooded fringes of alpine meadows throughout Europe and which would never bloom for us in the alpine house in Cold Spring.

Corydalis are well represented, along with cypripedium, including the rare, diminutive *Cypripedium pubescens* var. *planipetalum*. This northernmost ladyslipper was collected on Mingan Island in the northern St. Lawrence and given to Les Quatre Vents by the Montreal Botanic Garden. Horticultural generosity is also highlighted by a thirty-

TOP

Cypripedium pubescens var. planipetalum *from the Mingan Islands on the north shore of the Gulf of St. Lawrence.*

ABOVE

Cypripedium pubescens var. parviflorum, *which is indigenous to central Quebec.*

LEFT

Cypripedium reginae.

OPPOSITE

Cypripedium pubescens var. pubescens, *the yellow ladyslipper found throughout eastern North America.*

blossom clump of *C. reginae* originating from a single root, a gift from Pat Morgan who, in turn, had been given a piece by a friend in the Thousand Islands. We learned early on not to try and transplant the indigenous and fickle *C. acaule* and look forward all the more to seeing it romp and spread about in its perfect, sandy pine-woods habitat on Ladyslipper Slope.

Lilium species enjoy the Woodland. One of the serendipitous consequences of a garden of some age filled with a variety of species of a given genus is that new hybrid forms emerge from the critical mass of plants. Several somewhat different martagon hybrids have appeared at Les Quatre Vents. One is such a dark purple that we have named it "Midnight." Another splendid and large white form has been called "Alabaster." A third is wonderfully and uniquely spotted and awaits a name (Polka Dot? Dalmatian?). We are getting these forms to the nursery trade so that others can enjoy them.

There are woodland gems, such as *Shortia galacifolia*, happily spreading around the base of conifers as they do in their limited North Carolina habitat. *Glaucidium palmatum, Pteridophyllum racemosum, Arisaema sikkokianum*, and other natives of Japan enjoy the setting.

OPPOSITE

Primula vulgaris *ssp.* sibthorpii *intermingled with* P. 'Wanda', Scilla siberica, *and* Anemone ranunculoides.

BELOW

Primula farinosa *and* Anemone ranunculoides.

Primula *'Johanna'* and Caltha palustris var. alba *by a woodland pond with the reflection of Primula 'Peter Klein' in the background.*

The Greater Perfection

A PLETHORA OF PRIMULAS

Most of all there are primulas — so many of them that the Woodland Garden could really almost be called a Primula Garden. The different species bloom in waves from the first of May, just as the snow is melting and *P. whitei* and *P. sonchifolia* (the two petiolarid species from the Himalayas that have survived to date in Charlevoix) shyly show their delicate blue blossoms, to September when the monocarpic *P. capitata* and *P. glomerata* display their round whirls of attractive dark blue florets. While most of the species are thoroughly perennial, a few, in Charlevoix at least, vanish after they have flowered. As a matter of course we sow these short-lived species every year. In fact it is a good idea to sow many of the perennial species as well, to be sure that the colonies and drifts are kept well upholstered.

Working out the bloom cycle of the primulas in the Woodland to achieve continuous and harmonious color has been an agreeable and challenging pastime. For the most part we've chosen to separate the color variations within a species and to mass a given color for effect, in the belief that the visual impact will be more satisfying. At the same time we have planted each of the five streams with its own distinctive group of primulas that follow in succession.

Primula species are divided into a number of sections. The blossoms of the oreophlomis section follow close on the heels of the petiolarids. Up until recently the oreophlomis section was known as *farinosa* subsection *auriculata*, which helped a lot

Candelabra primulas are a promiscuous lot, as evidenced by this collection of Quatre Vents hybrids.

ABOVE

Madder, yellow, and red forms of Primula waltoni *hybrids.*

since *P. auriculata* is indigenous to the Caucasus and our few plants came from a specimen collected on the slopes of Mount Elbruz, the highest of those dramatic mountains. What's more, the flowers of *auriculata*'s kindred Asiatic species, *rosea*, *clarkei*, and the tongue-twisting *warshenewskyana* are very similar. These, along with their vigorous and wonderfully easy hybrids, 'Peter Klein', and 'Johanna', cheerily illuminate the Woodland with sheets of pink shading to red for several weeks in May, sharing the stage with the drumstick primula, *P. denticulata*.

While trekking in Central Nepal with Tony Schilling in 1983, we walked for two days up and down alpine meadows at the 10,000 foot level which were covered with *P. denticulata*, in every color from white to the darkest purple. There were thousands of them and they looked like a sea of lollipops, with small globular heads, at the most six inches high. In cultivation in Charlevoix this amenable species grows into great multi-stalked, cabbagy clumps with drumheads that could serve only for the largest of base drums. They couldn't be showier or easier but that charming elfin quality, so evident in the wild, is nowhere in evidence. Also, unless they are dead-headed before they set seed, they will spread throughout the garden with a vengeance.

The southernmost of the five streams in the Woodland flows from a little pond flanked by drifts of 'Johanna' and 'Peter Klein' through a narrow, fifty-foot swath of *denticulata*, occasionally intermingled with *rosea*. The *denticulata* are segregated by color, the whites at the upper end, then the good blues, shading through lavender and mauve to the darkest forms.

The last of the oreophlomis section to bloom is *P. luteola*, from the wet alpine meadows of Daghestan. Its configuration shows little kinship to its smaller pink-flowered cousins, as far as those of us who are not taxonomists can determine. Its yellow blossoms coincide with the emergence of the fresh green leaves of the deciduous trees bringing

shade to the Woodland, and conclude the first wave of bloom. By mid-May the Woodland is filled with the blossoms of anemone, cardamine, and erythronium. Low blue carpets of *Primula frondosa* and its section mates (*darialica, modesta*, the choice *farinosa*, and the diminutive, indigenous *laurentaiana* and *mistassinica*) appear just in time to complement the tail end of *warshenewskyana*'s extended blossoming. The pale yellow blossoms of *P. elatior*, the oxlip, follow. The easiest of the genus, like *P. denticulata* it has to be dead-headed to prevent indiscriminate seeding. Being a fan of *pale* yellow, as opposed to the richer variety, in the garden, I've chosen to suppress *P. veris*, the cowslip. Not one to be put down, a specimen has chosen to establish itself in the front lawn where, surrounded by a sea of green, it fits in well with the dandelions and doesn't clash with its neighbors. Carefully nurtured and avoided by the boy who cuts the lawn, it grows into a larger clump year by year.

QUESTIONS OF COLOR

BACK IN THE WOODLAND, *P. chionantha*, now including species that used to be known as *sinopurpurea* and *melanops* (recently relegated to sub-speciesdom by John Richards), takes over the bloom cycle in conjunction with the wonderful jumble of *ioessa* and *waltoni* hybrids. *Ioessa* has a distinctive cowbell-shaped blossom and its hybrids come in a wide range of colors. I tend to separate a primula genus by color rather than letting the colony become a random mix, in this case favoring the light duff and pale madder *ioessa* hybrids. *P. waltoni* hybrids display an even wider color range and I am slowly endeavoring to build masses of the yellow, red, and dark madder forms.

In June there is an explosion of primulas as the month unfolds — *bulleyana*,

ABOVE, LEFT

Primula alpicola *var.* violacea, *a native of the Tsangpo river basin in southeastern Tibet.*

ABOVE, RIGHT

A dun-colored hybrid of Primula ioessa, *a native of wet alpine meadows in southeastern Tibet.*

OPPOSITE

A corner of the Woodland with Primula japonica, burmanica *and* alpicola *var.* luna. Rodgersia podophylla *and* Astilboides tabularis *can be seen in the background.*

cockburniana, and *alpicola* in its violet, pale yellow, and white forms. *P. cernua*'s delicate blue spires complement the scented *alpicola* blossoms. Our plants originated from seeds collected in the valley at 12,500 feet below the great 21,000 foot pyramid of Sigunian-Shan in Western Szechuan. It doesn't persist, once it has bloomed, and has to be germinated regularly — but there are worse chores, given the results. *P. flaccida*, another charmer, and the diminutive *P. reidii* var. *williamsii* behave in much the same manner.

Then comes the stately, if scentless, *P. prolifera* (*helodoxa*) along with *P. secundiflora* and *sikkimensis* followed by the candelabras: *japonica, aurantiaca, burmanica, poissonii,* and *pulverulenta* (including its Bartley Hybrids).

The easy *japonica* tends to self-sow as readily as *denticulata* and, if not watched, a clump of a solid color such as 'Postford White' or 'Miller's Crimson', or a good clear pink or brick red, will turn into a kaleidoscope of color. *P. sieboldii* is even worse. While it can become a useful groundcover with persistent division, it is one of the most variable plants extant, with hundreds of variations in flower size, shape, petal form, and color. The Japanese, who grow most of their plants in pots given their limited space for gardens, have a society for this species, the *Sakurasoh*. So far they have risen to the challenge of naming the constantly increasing number of forms that appear. I use massed plantings of white and pale pink varieties in the Woodland and, since the species has a tendency towards magenta, have planted the rest in the magenta corner.

The two flower colors that I find indigestible are magenta and orange, which many good and vigorous plants flaunt shamelessly — I suppose they attract the pollinating insects more effectively, much as the lurid and ubiquitous MacDonald's arches lure us to try their fastest of foods — but, to date, I've been unable to accept these colors in association with anything other than green or white. The solution has been to reserve corners of the Woodland to which plants sporting the offending colors can be relegated, and where they are surrounded entirely by green and accompanied, occasionally, by white. There is an area near the Gazebo by the second rope bridge, as one approaches the Machiai, that is filled with the orange blossoms of *Trollius ledebourii, Lilium hansonii,* tiger lilies, and all those lilies that were supposed to be red when ordered but turned out to be orange.[39] There is a corresponding area in a southeast corner of the Woodland which is the repository for all the magenta primulas, not only the myriad forms of *sieboldii*, but *P. cortusoides, gemmifera, heucherifolia, kisoana,* the lurid *polyneura,* and *saxatilis* as well, along with *Cortusa matthioli* and its ssp. *pekinensis*. I have no problem with magenta *en masse* as long as it is isolated. The white forms of some of these species, such as *P. kisoana* 'Alba' and *Cortusa matthioli* 'Alba', are used elsewhere in the Woodland.

There are a few exceptions. The delicate, tiered, pale orange whirls of *P. cockburniana*, following closely on the heels of the yellow blossoms of *P. bulleyana*, seem to know their place and blend readily with the rest of the clan, as do the light orange-duff candelabras of *P. aurantiaca*, the purplish candelabras of *poissonii*, and the small purplish

ABOVE

Primula sieboldii *from Japan.*

BELOW

Primula luteola *from the Caucasus.*

OPPOSITE

The magenta corner with Primula heucherifolia and forms of P. sieboldii to the rear and Iris 'Roy Elliott' in the left middle foreground.

blossoms of *secundiflora*, whose name signifies that the flowers are clustered on one side of the stalk.

Slowly the preferred colors — where there is a variation within a species — are being encouraged. This involves hours of crawling about and marking the different color forms so that the rearrangement can proceed once the bloom is finished and they can be divided. The different scents of *alpicola*, *ioessa*, and *waltoni* make this a pleasant chore.

Interspecific hybrids that have resulted from the assemblage of so many species of this promiscuous genus, many of them self-sterile, appear regularly. This natural consequence of cohabitation (does it account for the derivation of the "Primrose Path?") adds a kaleidoscope of color to corners of the Woodland as in the finale of a fireworks display. It isn't the finale, however, because there is the dark red of the choice *anisodora* to follow and the emergence on the scene of *P. florindae*, the most durable of all the primulas in the Woodland.

This stately primula was discovered by Kingdon Ward in the Tsangpo Basin of southeastern Tibet in 1926, where it grew and hybridized with its sikkimensis section cousins, *alpicola*, and *waltoni*. He named it after his wife, Florence. In Charlevoix, *florindae* is in bloom in July and August and appears to be indestructable. It has a tendency to colonize and naturalize, hybridizing readily with its section mates and appearing in a color range from pale yellow through russet to darkest red. We separate the three categories of colors so that the pale yellow form, the true *florindae*, follows one stream to the lip of the Ravine, the variants encompassing the russet shades surround a pool in the middle of the Woodland and follow the stream that flows from it, while the handsome, dark red variants line the banks of a third stream.

In the early 1990s a sterile hybrid, almost certainly a cross with *alpicola*, appeared in an entirely new color, a pinkish maroon with a dusky fawn interior. After frequent division it is now spread along a fourth stream, in this instance the *denticulata/rosea* stream which also features clusters of the very pale yellow *P. alpicola* var. *luna* that are over by the time the new hybrid begins to flower. The hybrid is being registered with the Nomenclature Authorities as *Primula* 'Raynald' after Raynald Bergeron who works with me in the garden and who first noticed that the single specimen was different.

The Woodland during the *florindae* season is filled with scent, especially at twilight on a still, damp evening. It is the apotheosis of the primula year. Long, narrow sweeps of color run through the garden as summer turns the corner. The clear days, golden evenings and cool nights of August follow. The tall, handsome, dark purple blossoms of *P. capitata* and *glomerata* complete the primula tableau into September, blooming so late that we never seem to be able to gather ripe seed before the winter sets in.

The primulas are divided in August, the Woodland soil amended where necessary and the vision of what the next season will bring, *if* the winter snow cover comes early and stays late, is filed away in the memory bank to sustain us until the following May.

OPPOSITE

Primula 'Raynald', a sterile hybrid that originated in the Woodland at Les Quatre Vents, should soon be available in the nursery trade.

BELOW

Primula burmanica, a native of the wet forests and lower-altitude meadows of Yunnan and Upper Burma.

CHAPTER XII
POTAGER, PRAIRIE, AND PISCINE

OPPOSITE

A transitional moment in May when daffodils take over from the smaller bulbs, including Scilla siberica.

ABOVE, RIGHT

Dandelions are welcome when they blend with muscari, myosotis and the occasional late daffodil.

UPON RETURNING TO THE FRONT LAWN, THE VIEW OF POINTE-au-Pic across the bay dispels the Asiatic ambience of the Woodland. We are back on the North Shore of the St. Lawrence with the village of Kamouraska just barely visible on the South Shore, some fourteen miles distant. We are also back in the more cultivated world of the domestic garden with its tended lawns, crops, and amenities, and have borrowed the alliterative labels for this chapter from the local French usage.

As opposed to the Tapis Vert, which has been turned into a relatively luxuriant turf over the years, little effort has been expended on the front lawn, with the exception of the terraces next to the house. The grassy slope from the front terrace down to the swimming-pool staircase reveals its sandy underpinnings in the slightest of droughts. The encouragement of this lawn and the soil supporting it was one of my rehabilitation projects when we first began to improve the garden. It took a year or so before I realized that the years of neglect had turned this scruffy lawn into a flowery mead. After the hopeless groundcover of dandelions goes to seed in mid-June there is a delightful moment in early July when much of the lawn is taken over by an enchanting, diminutive pale yellow hawkweed (*Hieracium pilosella*), an Eurasian species that has become naturalized throughout Central Quebec. Its delicate, solitary, pale yellow blossoms, some seven inches high, turn the area into a fairy meadow for several weeks. During this period the lawn is left unmown until the hawkweed seeds have become dispersed, and each year the display becomes more extensive. In addition to the hawkweed, seedlings of creeping thyme have aggressively established themselves so that parts of the slope become sheets of light purple in August, as well as fragrant ground cover for the rest of the season. (It is only when they lose their leaves that large brown patches appear in what should be a green surface.) The grassy terrace surrounding the swimming pool has, in turn, become entirely a thyme lawn.

THE POTAGER

A GRASSY CARRIAGE ROAD RUNS PARALLEL TO AND BELOW THE EMBANKMENT that incorporates the swimming-pool terrace, adding further diversion for the observant swimmer when a group of riders or a driving pair and carriage pass by. The carriage road comes up from below the woodland edge of the field, passes beside the pool terrace and then continues its curving route along the contour of the hill until it passes diagonally through the lower part of the vegetable garden, ultimately rejoining the entrance drive. As one follows the curve along the contour, the barn complex down by the road, also created by Eddie Mathews in 1936, comes into view. Large berms, newly planted with young conifers and deciduous trees, and molded so as to make them appear as naturalistic as possible, have been built to obscure the disconcerting sight of the tops of trucks flashing by as one looks over the forested berms to the broad expanse of the St. Lawrence.

On its way to the vegetable garden the carriage road – also a mass of hawkweed and creeping thyme – passes below a decorative, but neglected, apple orchard. On its other side it is bordered by a mass of more or less volunteer shrubs – *Rosa rugosa, Cornus sibirica, Lonicera tatarica*, and the like – which line the way, leaving the distant view free and clear until the road enters a thicket composed of larger shrubs and trees (where one *might* build some secret walled garden) and emerges into an area of terraced vegetable gardens.

The Potager has a double slope, down from the house towards the barns as well as down from the entrance driveway towards the field below the swimming pool. A row of apple trees running along one side of the raised terraces brackets the carriage road. On the right a meadow garden is filled with a succession of lupine, oriental poppies, filipendula, and the ubiquitous *Campanula rapunculoides*, a persistent weed in every other part of the garden but here allowed to carry out its rapunculacious mission to colonize the world.

The ease and exuberance with which lupines take over a meadow in Charlevoix has led us to fence a curving strip of the field below the carriage road and swimming pool and turn it gradually into a wide arc of lupine blossoms – a lupine *prairie* – in late June and early July. In mid-August, once the lupine seeds have ripened in other parts of the garden and the stalks have been gathered, we lay them six feet apart in the cleanly cut strip of pasture and let nature take its course.

To the left of the carriage road, as it crosses the garden, is a row of plum trees that produce small yellow and purple fruit. Beneath them lies a majestic long row of the common rhubarb. You can leave the carriage road, which is bordered by a four-tiered cordon of espaliered apples as it curves to join the driveway, by walking up along the row of apple trees or by taking one of the garden paths that intersect with the

THE GREATER PERFECTION

diagonal of the carriage road. The wide central path is the extension of the main axis that runs from the Tapis Vert through the house and slopes down to the greenhouse through the breezeway of the Doodle-Doo. This garden shed was built by my father in the early 30s and, in many ways, is the most charming structure on the property; decorative compost bins flank each end of the building. Stepped paths lead up either side of the central axis through multilevel terraces to the top of the Potager. The highest corner of the garden is a good vantage point for an overview of the terraces, the Doodle-Doo and its meadow garden, against the background of the adjoining field and the Pointe-au-Pic hillside jutting into the St. Lawrence across the bay.

While the distant view and the lilac hedges that border the upper edge of the garden and screen it from the entrance drive have been constants since the vegetable garden was established in the late 20s and early 30s, almost everything else has changed. The original garden, which followed the contours of the slope, suffered from being an area where limestone shale was close to the surface, making it an arduous chore to cultivate vegetables. At one point the path to the side of the garden, now filled with apple trees, was the site of a long pergola that followed the slope down the hill. The exposed site

PREVIOUS

*An upper corner of the Potager. Small-flowered marigolds (*Tagetes tenuifolia*) frame a path leading to a bed planted with perennials for picking. One of Anne's scarecrows protects her crops.*

ABOVE

The stepped beds in their varied configuration are apparent in this view over the central area of the Potager towards the Doodle-Doo. Eremurus x isabellinus *Shelford Hybrids bloom in the foreground next to* Campanula latifolia.

OPPOSITE

A crabapple and nursery beds fill the space below the Doodle-Doo.

and limited soil meant that the structure was never luxuriantly covered with the kinds of vines and climbers my mother had in mind. When the posts rotted the pergola was removed rather than replaced, much to the relief of the summer residents across the bay, who had dubbed the unfortunate structure "The Scenic Railway."

When the mature spruce throughout the property succumbed to the spruce budworm and had to be harvested and sold within three years to generate the funds to cover their removal, we found ourselves well supplied with logs. After impregnating them with a preservative, we used some of them to build raised, terraced beds in an effort to produce a better crop of vegetables. Starting in the highest corner we built the first of what was going to grow to six beds over the next four years. The interesting thing was that it was unnecessary to design the beds since the variations in the two-directional slope did it for us. The lay of the land dictated the configuration of the beds and, since the slopes were varied and uneven, the size of each bed and the terraces within it turned out to be different. The sloped path of the central axis was left intact and two main transverse paths, as well as stepped paths within the beds, were created. As a result the garden is a multilevel series of planted beds of varying sizes and shapes on either side of a strong central axis.

Anne designed and planted the raised terrace beds as they were filled with soil. As the beds proliferated it became clear that there would be enough space for a picking garden of annuals and biennials as well as space for perennials, which I was allowed to plant.

Anne double digs her beds and rotates her vegetable crops in the time-honored fashion of peas and beans followed by greens, and then root crops in subsequent years.

Members of the brassica family have a bed to themselves. Anne mixes decorative with edible species of that nutritious family in a different design each year. As a result, after all the broccoli, Brussels sprouts, and edible cabbages have been harvested, the decorative cabbage and kale form a pattern in the bed.

Single Shirley poppies bloom their heads off for most of the summer and netted circles of sweet peas produce a profusion of fragrant blossoms from mid-July on. Tiny-flowered marigold hybrids form aromatic yellow and orange swaths on either side of the stepped path that runs up the center of the higher set of beds. The asparagus bed improves with age and two scarecrows (*épouvantail* to the French), made and clothed by Anne, do their best to protect the strawberries. All the berries thrive in the northern climate and seem beyond compare. White raspberries are a tradition, as is the making of raspberry vinegar, that most refreshing of familial summer drinks, along with the conversion of part of the black-currant harvest into *vin de cassis*.

I was able to establish various bridgeheads of delphinium before Anne, her vegetables threatened, decreed that I had to stop. Almost every bed has some, with the most dramatic colony being a square of hand-pollinated Pacific Hybrids raised from Delphinium Society seed. It consists of a mass of some forty different hybrids with a few *Eremurus himalaicus* placed in their center, their ten-foot stalks blossoming before the delphinium spires. For my part there is no such thing as too many delphinium.

BELOW

Anne's decorative brassica bed, against a backdrop of delphinium, after many of the early edible species have been devoured.

OPPOSITE

Mauve delphinium and a host of hollyhocks in early August.

Crabapples frame the central axis on both sides of the Doodle-Doo and a majestic Carolina poplar (*Populus canadensis*), planted in 1930 next to a nearby grove of spruce, shows the potential of that useful tree to advantage. The central axis continues through raspberry beds, and then through some nursery and experimental beds that include a collection of *Iris versicolor* x *ensata* hybrids developed by Tony Huber, one of which he kindly named after me.[40]

Once the fruit trees and lilacs have bloomed, the Potager is rather quiet and empty until mid-July when the beds are filled with vegetation. From then until late September it is one of the high points in the garden. The uncertainty of the climate must be reckoned with, and there have been summers when we harvested only green tomatoes and no ears of corn at all. However, on the plus side that summer, the sweet peas and delphinium were spectacular.

ABOVE

The hand-pollinated Delphinium Society hybrids.

OPPOSITE

The Doodle-Doo breezeway and weather-vane flanked by Malus 'Hopa' with a white crabapple screening a foreshortened view of the St. Lawrence and its south shore.

The Piscine

THE SWIMMING POOL AND BATH HOUSES, built in 1936, were Eddie Mathews' creation. The terrace was cut deeply into the slope and the pool dynamited out of a shelf of limestone shale. The cut areas of the slope are shored with limestone walls so that the pool terrace is walled except for the view out over the bay. The singular configuration of the concrete pool (its longer sides curve and are parallel) echoes the configuration of the slope, the curve of the terrace and the curve of the fenced hillside field beyond it. Its shorter sides are straight. Were these to be extended back beneath the stairs and the front lawn they would ultimately join in a triangular point. The pool is also singular in that its water surface is flush with the thyme lawn and its encircling stone coping; one can swim the breast stroke and enjoy the view across the bay at the same time. Fed from the mother stream, the water in the pool is constantly being refreshed, overflowing into a surrounding scupper. This precludes the need

for filtration equipment and keeps its temperature bracingly cool. The color of the water in the pool is dark brown, comparable to that of a local lake.

The two bath houses are cubes topped by a tetrahedron (a low gabled roof of four equilateral triangles). They are joined by a curved wall, pierced by demi-lunes, that incorporates a curved, solid bench. The bench now sports an attractive layer of moss and lichen and inspired the topiary feature that is the centerpiece of the Guest Garden. The stylish bath houses and walls, the dramatic staircase with its landing serving as a diving platform, and the unusually shaped pool, comprise a striking architectural ensemble. Swiss pines (*Pinus cembra*) were planted above the walls on the woodland side of the pool and now lean well out into the space. Two low, thick thuja hedges on the view side of the terrace help frame the panorama. A low hedge of Siberian pea (*Caragana arborescens*) separates the front lawn from the pool complex while the slope flanking the topmost steps is planted with massed mugo pines interspersed with hemerocallis. My mother's practice of planting dahlias in pots in the bath-house niches and on nearby pedestals has been continued.

THE MEADOW

THE CENTRAL PATH OF THE POTAGER LEADS THROUGH A LILAC HEDGE, on axis with the library's French door, into a grassy meadow or *prairie* that is sparsely filled with stunted, neglected apple trees and several mature paper birch and mountain ash. My mother had planted there a very few mixed daffodils which we enjoyed when we were first able to get to Charlevoix in May. They bloomed about a month later than the daffodils in Cold Spring. This welcome reprise, and extension of the joys of spring, encouraged us to plan a bulb meadow in this orchard between the house and the Potager.

The roughly rectangular meadow of about half an acre is bounded by the lilac hedge, a wing of the house, the entrance driveway and a thicket. It is divided into five variously configured large panels by a series of functional paths that give access to the central and peripheral paths of the Potager. A perimeter path runs along the thicket and the lilac hedge, while a strip of lawn separates the meadow from a breakfast

Chionodoxa sardensis *amongst the emerging daffodils in the foreground with* Chionodoxa luciliae *in the rear, seen over* Puschkinia libanotica *and* Crocus chrysanthus *'Snow Bunting'.*

Salmon oriental poppies under an apple tree are a contrasting accent against a mass of lupines.

terrace in front of the wing of the house. The panels and paths lend themselves to large massed plantings. For over twenty-five years we have added quantities of bulbs to the meadow each autumn so that there are now successive, paneled sheets of color as the spring evolves. Swaths of the smaller bulbs fill corners of the panels, or serve as a border on either side of a path. Later on the drifts of daffodils cross a number of panels so that the visitor is led through the midst of a drift.

Les Quatre Vents is on the flyway used by the greater snow geese on their way to and from their breeding grounds on Bylot and Baffin Islands, and their migratory flights in late May and early October more or less bracket the gardening season. After wintering along the coasts of Delaware and North Carolina, the great flock, which is well on its way to approaching a million birds, makes one six-week stop in its 2,500 mile journey to feed on *Scirpus americanus*, a sedge that grows along the brackish marshes of the St. Lawrence to the south of Cap Tourmente. The seven-hundred-mile flight from the Middle Atlantic Coast lasts two hundred hours. No one knows how long the second leg of the flight, from Cap Tourmente to Baffin Island, lasts. Every year the

THE GREATER PERFECTION

ABOVE

Muscari and a mass of daffodils seen against the entrance courtyard wall and trellis.

OPPOSITE

A view of the Pointe-au-Pic headland in June over a meadow verge filled with an unidentified - but none the less pleasing - introduced species.

flight pattern is slightly different although, invariably, the flock turns away from the St. Lawrence and heads inland and due north up the Malbaie River Valley. Quite often the flock is so high that, without the reflected sunlight on their wings, one would be hard put to distinguish the distant skeins. One Memorial Day the entire flock flew low over the house and proceeded up the valley, obscuring the hills. When they banked in unison it was as if a white sheet had been drawn across the view.

We try and arrive in Charlevoix at the end of April just as the *Crocus chrysanthus* emerge. As most of April is melting snow and mud, we have not planted quantities of galanthus or eranthis since we would probably never be there to see them. The bloom season starts with a mosaic of the species crocus varieties 'Snow Bunting', 'Cream Beauty', and 'Blue Pearl', that flank the first half of the central axis path leading from the library window towards the Potager. By early May the vivid blues of *Chionodoxa luciliae* and *C. sardensis* fill the remaining half, while a four foot wide swath of the Lebanese squill, *Puschkinia libanotica*, borders the peripheral path along the lilac hedge and frames both sides of the path leading from the front lawn down to the southern edge of the Potager. As these early bulbs wane, the foliage of the daffodils appears among them along with the buds of two rivers of muscari that border the sides of the main diagonal path. One corner is filled with white muscari. In short order the meadow

POTAGER, PRAIRIE, AND PISCINE

becomes a contrast of the deep blue of the muscari set against a sea of white and pale yellow daffodils. Late into the daffodil cycle comes the sheet of *Scilla siberica* with the rich yellow of dandelions picking up where the daffodils left off, followed by *Fritillaria meleagris* with its more discreet blossoms just high enough to top the lengthening meadow grasses.

It took me a while to enjoy the dandelions and the tall dandelion-like tragopogons that follow them later on. The dandelion moment is overwhelming in Charlevoix and there is no way to eradicate these "weeds" from the meadow. I've gotten rather to like them in seed as well, their delicate seed-heads adding an airy touch to the mass of green.

Thermopsis caroliniana next appears, along with an early salmon/orange oriental poppy. Both are colonizers and need to be kept in bounds so that the lupines can hold sway from mid-June to early July.

The lupine moment is the apotheosis in the Meadow's cycle of bloom and, if the spring is cool, moist, and extended, takes one's breath away. The plants are so well established throughout the Meadow, and so thick, that one forgets that anything else was ever there despite having seen a colorful and constantly evolving display for at least eight weeks before the lupines began.

After that moment of glory the Meadow quiets down, with tangles of *Clematis recta*, filipendulas, and some robust and coarser perennials such as *Campanula latifolia* providing spots of color. Caraway (*Carum carvi*) has seeded throughout the area, adding its delicate white blossoms to the scene and providing seeds to munch in August. The tall blossoms of cow parsley predominate in August and hide the ugly lupine seed-heads until they are gathered and the meadow can be mown and readied for the October planting of even more bulbs.

The mowing of the Meadow signals the end of the season. The neat, green, mown surface is a welcome and peaceful sight after the tangled jumble that preceded it. It is time for encouraging the bulbs with a top dressing of compost and a suitable fertilizer so that the next year, given a wet spring, they will be the best ever.

The Meadow's changing tableau can be viewed from many angles: from the entrance driveway near the house where you catch a tantalizing glimpse of the action; from the front lawn as you walk up to the house from the swimming pool and view a sea of gold and white daffodils framed by the mature birches; and from all the paths leading to and from the Potager. I walk these routes daily in May and early June, taking to heart Reginald Arkell's doggerel:

> In March we long for April.
> In May we long for June.
> Don't be in such a hurry,
> It will all be gone too soon!

OPPOSITE

Tragopogon pratensis *seedheads make their statement in the Meadow in mid-June against a backdrop of an invasive orange poppy and the yellow spires of* Thermopsis caroliniana.

OVERLEAF

The lupine moment lasts for three weeks in late June and early July and is the culmination of the Meadow's bloom cycle.

THE GREATER PERFECTION

POTAGER, PRAIRIE, AND PISCINE 307

The Greater Perfection

AFTERWORD

THERE IS AN ART TO VISITING A GARDEN AND I HAVE LEARNED ITS characteristics by watching those who are good at it. One must take ample time to drink in each element and its relation to the garden as a whole as well as to the surrounding landscape. This approach not only takes considerable extra time, sitting reflectively where benches permit, but it is best done alone, or in silence, with no more than one or two equally introspective companions. I derive great pleasure when I see a visitor sitting quietly on the seat surrounding a trunk at the base of the Ravine, enveloped in a sea of rodgersia, and looking past the Waterfall over the pond to the Azumaya; I identify that person as someone I would like to meet when they get back to the entrance court. The greatest of all compliments is when a visitor responds to the beauty encompassing the garden and its settings by shedding a tear. Now there is a soul mate![41]

Emotions and sensuality are what a garden is all about. We should be transported from our regular preoccupations. With an open heart and soul we can be receptive to the images, scents, sounds, spaces, and views that surround us, as well as to the touch of the wind and the rain, to the peace everlasting of the "genius of the place." Ideally all the nobler emotions should be exercised so that we sense fulfilment and satisfaction and an inner peace when we have finished, a sense of communion with those who are no longer with us and those whom we love.

The intellectual appeal of the garden will vary depending on our bias, on whether we care more for the architectural underpinnings of the ensemble, the decorative use of plants, or the pedigree and characteristics of the individual plants. The gardens at Les Quatre Vents are designed to accommodate all these preferences within the limitations of a Zone 4 climate. One thoughtful friend has suggested that it is a garden of allusion, incorporating a number of garden forms from different parts of the world. But then, plagiarism is the life blood and the principal impetus in the creation of gardens. There is no more agreeable challenge than adapting someone else's good idea to one's own surroundings. In Quebec I'm told that others are doing just that with ideas they have gleaned from Les Quatre Vents. Considering myself a life-long practitioner, I am indeed sincerely flattered.

It is the person who makes a garden, who thinks of little else in his or her spare time, who "sees" the garden as it will be fifteen years hence and for whom it is an overwhelming preoccupation, who perhaps in the end must derive the greatest enjoyment from it. Not only does the exercise of "painting" the picture absorb all your interest and attention, but then you find unexpected rewards in the continuous changes within the picture, and the reaction of the enfolding landscape and its creatures to its existence, all of which add unexpected depth and dimensions to what has been created.

The reflection pool on the terrace fulfils its function.

I am thinking of such surprises as that swath of volunteer jewelweed in the Ravine, the proliferation of chanterelles around the mature birches adjoining the Perennial Allée, and the exquisite sprinkling of diminutive hawkweed blossoms throughout the front "lawn." There are the martens from the stream bed who gambol on the front lawn just as autumn turns to winter, the blue heron waiting patiently near the Waterfall for a trout to come within range, rendering the setting that bit more oriental, and the green-winged teal who are the first birds of passage to use Lac Libellule as a base. These itinerants must tell the young mallards that it is time to get up and go, for soon the flock is wheeling and careening around the property between the different ponds and the bay. One twilight this year, standing and looking at the Tapis Vert and hills through the large bay window, a flight of mallards appeared suddenly at high speed from over the roof, barreled down the Tapis Vert and pitched at right angles to splash into the hidden Lac Libellule. The effect was so startling and so dramatic that my heart skipped a beat. It was only later that I realized that those birds must love the configuration of the place as much as we do.

It is in the autumn that the place seems most attuned to Nature. The first weeks of October are the high point for autumn color, and our favorite moment in the garden year. It is too late to worry about transplanting. The perennial beds and vegetables have been cut down and heaped with rotted manure. The haunting sounds of the Angelus bell and the evocative train whistles drift clearly across the bay in the crisp air. The leaves of *Cornus canadensis* have turned purple on the damp forest floor, *Coprinus comatus*, the inky cap mushroom, appears in the fields, and the fresh scents of the woodlands permeate the countryside. It is the horticultural evensong, when the season is over and our work done. It is a time to enjoy the surroundings to the fullest and to sketch plans and ideas for the future.

One crystal clear October morning, some years ago, I had time to wander at length along the more remote trails in the Forêt and to explore rarely visited byways that had been cleared. Along one such trail, down a gently sloping, moist gully where the forest had been spared the ravages of the spruce budworm, there were still many fine, ancient specimens of red and white pine. Partridge, woodcock, and hare flushed from along the trail and the mosses and mushrooms glistened. As the trail came to a cul-de-sac and I was beginning to explore how it could be blazed on, the unmistakable sound of snow geese calling in flight broke the stillness. I hurriedly struggled out of the thicket and back up the trail to a point where I could look up at the sky. There was only one opening, a small one, and it was framed by the autumn colors of the maples, aspens, shad, and paper birch. Disappointed that I couldn't see the geese through that small baroque window of blue sky, I was nonetheless struck by its beauty, a perfection worthy of Tiepolo. The intensity and combination of colors, backlit by the sun, were breathtaking. I gazed at it for a while and was about to move on when five snow geese, in formation and flying so low I could see the black tips of their wings, bisected the

The Azumaya in October. The pink autumnal tones of Aruncus aethusifolius *in the left foreground echo the evening sky.*

window of blue sky, framed for an instant in that incomparable setting.

Later that afternoon the weather suddenly deteriorated and became threatening. I had been planting the last of the bulbs in the Woodland when it began to snow quite heavily. In a matter of minutes snow covered the ground, and I could imagine what it was like to be a petiolarid primula on the flanks of a Himal. The storm was sufficiently intense to cut visibility; all I could see were large swirling snowflakes. Again I heard snow geese, only this time there were thousands of them, and I rushed out and up to the front lawn beyond the edge of the Woodland to try and see them. The snow had become so thick that a tree twenty feet away was barely visible, and I despaired of catching even a glimpse of them when, suddenly, from all sides, hundreds of geese descended from the clouds of snow above — on to the front lawn, in the Woodland, on the Tapis Vert. I wondered if this indeed was heaven, but then it ended as quickly as it had begun. The snow geese, appropriately wrapped in the swirling cloud of snow, and over their apparent disorientation, lifted off the ground (had they ever touched it?) and disappeared.

What did it mean, I wondered? Was it time to stop gardening for that season, to reflect upon the mysteries of Nature, and gather strength for the coming spring when the snow geese would be heading north, and the gardening cycle would begin again? Or was it a message confirming that we are fortunate in our earthly paradise, that we could do worse than to pursue the purest of pleasures in our northern setting until our day was done?

> Let dreamers dream what worlds they please;
> Those Edens can't be found.
> The sweetest flowers, the fairest trees
> Are grown in solid ground.
> We're neither pure nor wise nor good;
> We'll do the best we know;
> We'll build our house, and chop our wood,
> And make our garden grow.[42]

A peaceful February vignette.

NOTES

1. Edith Amer, a nurse by training, came from Birkenhead, near Liverpool. She was engaged by my father more or less off the boat in New York and placed on a train that evening for the long haul to the end of the line on the north shore of the St. Lawrence. Edith married Robert Desmeules, our chauffeur, whose family had been tenant farmers on a part of Seigneurie de Mont-Murray. They moved to San Francisco after the war where Robert became a skilled ironworker and Edith became the head nurse of a women's hospital.

2. Spruce budworm (*Choristoneura fumiferana*).

3. Incredibly, the family sold what remained of the acreage in the 1950s on the condition that the Nairne Manor House be torn down. Thus was destroyed the only authentic bit of eighteenth-century Anglo-Saxon patrimony north of Quebec. This sounded the death knell of the summer community, beginning an inexorable decline. The village, having now lost virtually all of *its* older buildings, has become a serious contender for the distinction of being one of the least distinguished towns in the Province.

4. Today one side of the river is devoted to industrial and commercial enterprises; the other has changed less, but many farms have been abandoned or "modernized" and the last farmhouse of any distinction has been dismantled to make way for a hideous town hall for a municipality that has been merged into its neighboring communities. Today, no one in their right mind would choose to drive up and down the valley for pleasure.

5. The *arpent* is an archaic French measure used for land measurement in La Nouvelle France. By area it constitutes about four-fifths of an acre and, as a linear measure, some 192 feet.

6. Adjutor Harvey who farmed the property for many years, repeatedly told me, with great conviction, the story of his father meeting a Loup Garou (the werewolf of French Canada) in the Forêt when he was a young man.

7. Small, stoloniferous rooted offshoots can be severed in early spring and it is presumably propagable from root cuttings. Bud wood from branches cut in the autumn has been successfully grafted to scions of *Amelanchier canadensis*.

8. For ease of reference we have slightly shifted the points of the compass. What we call "west" is actually "northwest," and so on.

9. The only item in the house to survive the fire was a small metal rooster paperweight. Appropriately it was the crest of the Currie family, a sign that my mother had survived the loss of both husband and possessions and that the new home was to be hers. (The rooster motif has been echoed on the finial surmounting the tourelle entry of the house, surrounded by a mixed spray of barley and thistles.)

10. Among them The Chase Manhattan Bank Head Office, New York City; The Library for the Performing Arts, Lincoln Center; R.J.Reynolds Head Office, Richmond, Virginia; Connecticut Life Insurance Head Office, West Hartford.

11. The formality of a geometric element made sense near the Potting Shed at Stonecrop as a transition to the more naturalized areas of that garden. The first step was to replace a retaining wall made of rounded boulders.

12. This terminology is that preferred by H.Lincoln Foster, the great plantsman and author of *Rock Gardens*, over the sometimes used 'Alba Plena'.

13. In *Gardens Illustrated* (November 1998) James Compton outlines his compelling rationale for lumping cimicifuga into the genus *Actaea*. While respecting his findings (and being pleased that we capitalized on the similarity of what we thought were two genera) we stick in this book with the more familiar nomenclature.

14. In the mid-1930s, a young man appeared with a watercolor for sale for $10. I led him to my mother who gladly bought it and so launched the career of Robert Cauchon. Encouraged by the family artists, Maud and Pat Morgan, Cauchon developed an agreeably modernist primitive style that led to an exhibition in New York and a profitable, if short-lived, career.

15. I have never stopped being grateful that we were able to acquire sufficient adjoining acreage to create an ample buffer zone around the core of the property. A few years later the Quebec government slapped a $33\frac{1}{3}\%$ tax on real estate acquired by non-Quebeckers, if it was not to be a summer house and grounds. Now the peripheries of the property adjoin housing developments. Had these been closer by it would have lent a very different flavor to the site and we almost certainly would not have created the garden that now exists.

16. In the early 1970s we chose to give up livestock on the farm, selling the herd to our farm manager, Jean-Claude Bernier. In due course Jean-Claude developed a landscape contracting business and garden center/nursery which has become a highly regarded enterprise employing up to one hundred and fifty people at peak season. The expansion of our garden would not have happened without Jean-Claude's staff and expertise. Today his organization provides anything from cabinetry to irrigation systems, from the products of a perennial nursery with an exceptional range of varieties, to complete landscaping and construction capabilities. His success is a

testament to his persistence, ingenuity and extraordinary efforts.

17. John Trexler, the Director of the Tower Botanical Garden in Worcester, Massachusetts, while he was the horticulturist at Skylands in Ringwood, New Jersey, proved that gunnera can easily be grown in Eastern North America, given protection in winter. One at Stonecrop attained full size with six foot wide leaves after some twelve years. At Les Quatre Vents our first planting in the Ravine had insufficient light. After moving it to the edge of Lac Libellule, in full sun and with the discharge from the Watercourse keeping it constantly soaked, its performance has improved. However, the shortness of our Quebec summer limits it to a very slow growth rate, despite regular applications of rotted manure (E.A.Bowles recommended "feeding the brute"!).

18. Formerly *Epilobium angustifolium album*. We started with a single root, a gift from the eagle-eyed plantsman Fred Case, the author of *Trilliums* and *Orchids of the Great Lakes*, who spied it on a trip around the Gaspé Peninsula.

19. The stems are peeled, soaked in salted water for several hours, chopped into pieces, and cooked in broth until tender; at which point they can be marinated in an appropriate sauce or vinaigrette. Almost anything given this treatment might be rendered edible.

20. The inverted thuja arches replaced our original effort, which consisted of posts and panels in the same style as the bridge, but never seemed quite right in their setting.

21. I believe the trio comprises *Betula huteri, B. platyphylla* var. *szechuanensis* and *B. albosinensis septentrionale*. They appear to enjoy their setting and provide an interesting contrast with the nearby large specimens of the indigenous *Betula papyrifera*.

22. Tony Schilling, as well as being a brilliant plantsman, must rank in the top level of trek leaders in the Himalayas. He collected botanical specimens for his herbarium with such speed and efficiency that we were hard put to write down their names as quickly as he picked, identified, and packed them. Despite a Monty Pythonesque bravura, Tony combines his extensive knowledge of plants with administrative savvy and great aesthetic sensibility, a win-win-win combination for a horticultural savant, which he is *par excellence*.

23. I have read in French magazines that the Pigeonnier at Les Quatre Vents was inspired by a structure at Eyrignac in Salignac-Eyrignes. While a great admirer of what I have seen in books and articles on that elegant garden, I must confess that our version is not a case of plagiarism since I was unaware of Eyrignac's existence until after our Pigeonnier was topped with its finial.

24. The effect of a mirror laid on the lawn is achieved by shaping the reinforced concrete walls of the pool so that, beginning six inches below ground, the thickness of the concrete tapers to the narrowest possible rim at the surface. This allows the lawn to grow readily to the water's edge.

25. Penelope Hobhouse had the "living" at Tintinhull, Somerset, a property of the National Trust, from 1979 to 1991, during which period she and her distinguished husband, Professor John Malins, brought that delightful garden, created by Phyllis Reiss, to new heights of beauty and interest.

26. The Quebeckers call chipmunks "Les Suisses" due to their fur's resemblance to the uniform of the Swiss Guards at the Vatican.

27. I am a thorough fan of Thomas Jefferson, love the ideas and the architectural ingenuity and furnishings of Monticello and the serpentine walls of the Pavilion Gardens surrounding the Academical Village. I admire Jefferson's interest in landscape and husbandry and the siting of his house and I find his interest in growing things and writing about his activities both sympathetic and commendable. What mystifies me is his deification as a horticulturist and Monticello as a great garden. In my view he couldn't hold a candle to George Washington, who *really* understood gardens and created one that was truly significant.

28. After seventy years of being moved around North America, my mother's harp serves a decorative and nostalgic function. Anne keeps a modern harp in her living room and has become a devoted recorder player. We listen to harp music on CDs and I have been successfully operated on for a herniated disk!

29. Intrigued, we tracked down Charles Smith in his watery corner of Johns Island and were introduced to a frog holding a lantern, a mother frog with a perambulator, a frog with a garden hose, sitting frogs, dancing frogs, even a business man frog carrying his briefcase. The copper frame of all the frogs had been rendered a blue-green verdigris through the application of muriatic acid.

30. Reginald Farrer, the author of *Among the Alps, The English Rock Garden, The Dolomites*, described his travels and plant explorations in China in the early part of this century in the most compelling, if purple, prose. His passion for plants and his literate and articulate descriptions of them have never been equaled. Apropos of *Corydalis curviflora*'s azure blue blossoms he wrote: "The elusiveness of love is nothing compared to that of Corydalis."

31. *Rhodochiton volubile*, a colorful, luxuriant and charming climber was discovered by Baron Karwinski, a Bavarian who collected in Mexico in 1827-32, growing at 8,000 feet in the cool shade at the edge of the Oaxacan cloud forests. A monotypic genus of the Scrophulariacae, very close to *Lophospermum*, the flowers are

striking and distinctive with reddish-mauve campanulate calyces appearing intermittently in the alternate leaf axils along the twining stems from which extraordinary long, dark purple, phallic corollas emerge, ultimately developing a trumpet shape with four decorative large white anthers highlighted against the five petals forming the bell that surrounds the dark trumpet's mouth.

32. The *Nid* was happily inaugurated on David Birn's and Felicity Campbell's wedding night. This fitting prospect spurred its completion!

33. *Un Jardin Extraordinaire* (excerpts):

> *C'est un jardin extraordinaire:*
> *Il y a des canards qui parlent anglais.*
> *Je leure donne du pain; ils remuent leur derrière,*
> *En m'disant: "Thank you very much monsieur Trenet!"*
>
> *On y voit aussi des statues*
> *Qui se tiennent tranquilles tout le jour, dit-on;*
> *Mais moi je sais que dès la nuit venue*
> *Elles s'en vont danser sur le gazon . . .*
>
> *Y'avait un bal qu'donnaient des primevères*
> *Dans un coin d'verdure deux petites grenouilles chantaient . . .*
>
> *La douceur d'une couchette secrète*
> *Qu'elle me fit decouvrir au fond du bois . . .*

34. I invited him for lunch in hopes that Anne, who had been away that morning, could meet him. He demurred on the basis that his host's chef had been working on a rabbit for their lunch since early that morning. I then invited him to return for another visit when it suited. He drew himself up and replied in a suitably De Gaullesque fashion: "Why? To be wounded a second time?"

35. David Leach wrote the definitive *Rhododendrons of the World*. A noted breeder and hybridizer of magnolias and rhododendrons, his collections and property in North Madison, Ohio were left to the Holden Arboretum.

36. We landed on a beach near Kobe, in Southern Honshu, wading ashore from landing craft just a week after the armistice had been signed. There were Japanese women, beautifully dressed in kimonos waiting for us behind tables on which were bottles of Suntory Scotch Whiskey "specially blended for the US Occupation Forces." If I'd been alert I would have realized that the Japanese recovery was going to be an extraordinary phenomenon.

37. I made the mistake of asking a psychiatrist friend why I should be so drawn to large-leaved plants. He replied on his best clinical notepaper that I must consider myself to be so well endowed that I couldn't resist searching for the ultimate fig-leaf.

38. One year an overzealous helper had not been told to spare the jewelweed and all but eradicated it. The few escapees soon recolonized the stream.

39. Suppliers of lilies can't resist the temptation to slip a few orange lilies into each batch of good honest red. I have set aside a remote corner of the woodland garden where orange lilies, in variety, can bloom without offense against a background of solid green along with clumps of *Trollius ledebourii* from the perennial border.

40. I was thrilled when I first heard that *Iris versicolor* 'West Lake' x 'Popular Demand' 4N (tetraploid) McEwen was to be known as *Iris* 'Francis Cabot' and looked forward to my first glimpse of the blossom. My timidity in the use of bold colors in the garden is generally known. Tony's contribution to correcting this situation was to produce a thoroughly voluptuous and colorful lush of an iris that I would have been tempted to name 'Brazen Hussy'. Clearly, a new garden needs to be created for it.

41. Such ideal visitors, who take time to savour the series of different impressions that Les Quatre Vents has been designed to offer, are a far cry from the herded groups who are more concerned with the social dynamics of their party than with what is around them. We used to provide an eight-page guide indicating the suggested route and describing each element in the garden and the plants within it. Few people followed the route or read the words. We have now reduced the guide to a map with numbers, a key, and a clearly delineated route that no one can miss. Anyone who wants to know more can peruse this tome, or its French counterpart, *Un Jardin Extraordinaire* by Jean des Gagniers.

42. From the finale of Leonard Bernstein's *Candide*. It was sung by descendants and friends at the Mount Murray Masque in celebration of our fiftieth wedding anniversary on June 26, 1999.

ACKNOWLEDGMENTS

My thanks first to Jean des Gagniers whose interest in the garden and talents as an author inspired him to write about Les Quatre Vents. Providing notes for his account in French was the genesis for my deciding to write a book of my own, and his publication, *Un Jardin Extraordinaire*, is an objective and articulate view of the garden.

My thanks to all who, over the years, have taken the trouble to tell me their impressions of the garden and what it has meant to them. They have encouraged my conviction that the effort was worthwhile.

Special thanks are due first to Cynthia Ryan and May Brawley Hill, who took time to slog through the early drafts of the text, pointing out deficiencies and doing their best to curb my Henry Jamesian tendency to use overwrought and interminable sentences. Special thanks also to Tom Armstrong for introducing me to the talented Doris Palca, and for being there while Doris patiently provided invaluable guidance in turning the idea of a book into a finished product.

Susan McClellan's keen eye and artistic talents have been responsible for the design of the book. She has gracefully tolerated the inclusion of some of my own photographs that are germane to the text where no others were available. If the book looks and reads well it is primarily her doing.

The artist Nigel Hughes is endowed with a keen sense of what is appropriate in a garden landscape. His sketches and maps add an extra dimension to the book, just as his suggestions have improved the garden. Good advice is always welcome, and the suggestions of Jean Carlhian and Charles Bartlett have also been gratefully accepted.

Penny David has been that rare combination of an accomplished editor and author in her own right as well as someone who understands the garden at Les Quatre Vents. She has brought a semblance of order to my words, rearranging, excising, and pruning ruthlessly in an attempt to spare the reader as much indigestion as possible.

I must thank the photographers who took the time to come to Central Quebec at various seasons to catch the essence of the landscape and the gardens within it. Good garden photographers can make plants, flowers, and gardens look better than they really are. The photographs of Andrew Lawson, Virginia Weiler, Mick Hales, Jerry Harpur, and especially Richard Brown, are a case in point. I am grateful for their interest in and understanding of what they found at Les Quatre Vents.

Without the help of Raynald Bergeron the garden could never have achieved its considerable scale. In the early years I did all the planting and much of the maintenance. No longer! Raynald has been a quick study and I find that he more often than not has anticipated what I am about to ask him to do. He and his stalwarts, Michel Harvey and Louis Filion, work their hearts out to see that the place is in shape. Jean-Claude Bernier and his staff built all the follies and brought order to the extensive water works. There is nothing they cannot do or create and their love for the property, and what it has become, is as evident as our own.

I am eternally grateful for my wife Anne's tolerance. She not only let me indulge my fancies as the garden grew like a number of Topsies, but also allowed her privacy to be substantially invaded by the enthusiastic and the curious. I think in part she thought my enthusiasm for gardening would keep me close to home and off the streets. Neither of us realized that it would end up attracting the female of the species, in particular, like wasps to a trellis of ripe grapes. Again her tolerance is appreciated — as is her determination not to be lulled to sleep too often — in the task of reading, rereading, and checking the text of this book for errors and inconsistencies. To the garden, too, she has made a most important contribution. In creating the well-stocked and decorative salad garden and potager, in coping with the rose garden, and in designing and nurturing her knot garden, her interest and talents are well displayed.

PHOTOGRAPHY CREDITS

Richard W. Brown: pages 2, 3, 11, 15, 32-33, 34, 36, 38-39, 42-43, 47, 48-49, 52, 57, 58, 59, 61, 70, 71, 73, 81, 83, 84, 85 (bottom), 87, 90-91, 92, 93, 96 (bottom), 97, 101, 102, 103, 104-105, 109, 110-111, 115, 118, 124, 125, 127 (left), 129, 130, 131, 134, 135, 136, 143, 146, 147, 150-151, 154, 160, 161, 164-165, 166, 171, 177, 178, 179, 180 (both), 181, 182, 183, 184, 185, 186, 187, 191, 194 (center), 196-197, 198-199, 200 (left), 207, 211, 220, 221, 222-223, 227 (right), 229, 231, 233, 234 (top, right and bottom, left and right), 235, 236-237, 240, 241, 246 (top and bottom, right), 247, 249, 250, 251, 252 (bottom), 254-255, 256-257, 258, 259, 260, 261, 263, 265, 268, 269 (top, right and center, left and right), 270 (left), 272, 274 (center and right), 278, 279, 280-281, 285, 287, 288, 290, 291, 294, 298, 301, 303, 308-309, 314.

Francis H. Cabot: pages 5, 46, 55 (top), 78 (both), 80, 82, 85 (top), 94, 107, 114, 126 (both), 127 (right), 141, 144 (both), 149, 152, 155, 157 (both), 159, 163, 175 (both), 189 (top, right and bottom, left), 193, 194 (right), 214, 217 (all), 218, 224, 225 (all), 232, 238, 252 (top, left and right), 262, 264, 266-267, 269 (top, left), 270 (right), 274 (left), 275, 276 (top and center), 282, 283 (all), 284 (both), 289, 299, 302, 305, 310.

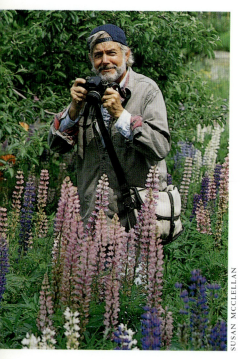

RICHARD W. BROWN

MICK HALES

JERRY HARPUR

Scott Frances: pages 200 (right), 201, 202, 203.

Mick Hales: pages 40, 44, 45, 69, 74, 76 (both), 77, 112, 116-117, 122, 138-139, 142, 156, 162, 169, 170, 190, 210, 212, 226, 227 (left), 242, 243, 244, 269 (bottom, left), 273, 277, 286 (both), 292-293, 296, 297, 304, 307.

Jerry Harpur: pages 9, 53, 62, 65, 67, 68, 95, 128, 140, 153, 172, 189 (top, left and bottom, right), 195, 208-209, 239, 313.

Andrew Lawson: pages 12, 98, 121, 132, 137, 148, 158, 173, 192, 194 (left), 213, 234 (top, left), 328.

Mark Mills: page 35.

Freeman Patterson: page 295.

Virginia Weiler: pages 6, 37, 41, 50, 51, 79 (both), 89, 123, 145, 228, 245, 246 (bottom, left), 271, 276 (bottom).

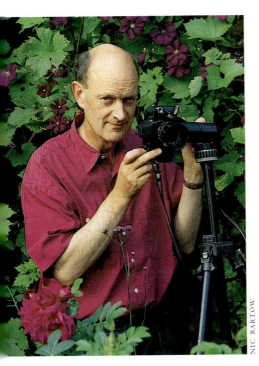

ANDREW LAWSON

VIRGINIA R. WEILER

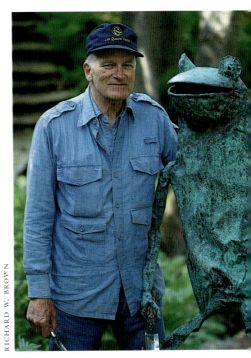

FRANCIS H. CABOT

INDEX

NOTE: Page numbers in *italic* script refer to illustrations and their captions.

A

Aberglasney (Wales) 130
Abies balsamea (balsam fir) 37, *41*
Acer (maple): *A. davidii* 243; *A. ginnala* (Amur maple) *147*, 149, 216; *A. spicatum* (mountain maple) 41, 248, 261, 274
Achillea ptarmica 'Boule de Neige' 81
Aconitum (monkshood) 116, 138; *A.* x *bicolor* 116; *A. carmichaelii* 116; *A.c.* 'Arendsii' 116; *A.c.* var. *wilsonii* 'Kelmscott' 116; *A. compactum* 'Carneum' 116; *A. henryi* 116; *A. septentrionale* 'Ivorine' 99, 116, *258*; *A. tauricum* 'Bressingham Spire' 116
Actaea (baneberry) 157, 159; *A. pachypoda* 158, *160*; *A. spicata* ssp. *rubra* 158, *160*; formerly *Cimicifuga* 316n.13
Adiantum pedatum (maidenhair fern) 211, *213*
Adonis vernalis 76
Alders 216
Allium aflatunense 157, *163*; *A. christophii* *163*
Amelanchier (serviceberry) 37; *A. bartramiana* 50, 316n.7; *A. canadensis* 55, 152, 211, 216, 262
Amer, Edith 18, 315n.1
American Rock Garden Society 75
Amur maple (*Acer ginnala*) 124, *147*, 152
Anderson, E. B. 86
Androsace 86; *A. sempervivoides* 87
Anemone blanda 'White Splendour' *264*, 269; *A. hupehensis* 116; *A. nemorosa* 'Alba Plena' 269; *A. ranunculoides* 269, 274, 278
Anemonopsis macrophylla 223, *224*, 232, 238
Angelica gigas 163
Antechamber 180
Antonia (statue) *123*, 126, *126*, *134*
Aquilegia buergeriana 76; *A. flabellata* var. *pumila* 'Alba' 97; *A. jonesii* 86; aquilegias (dwarf) 75, *87*, 88

Arabis androsacea 80; *A. bryoides olympica* 80; *A.* x *kellereri* 80; *A.* x *sturii* 80
Arch ("Lutyens" arch) 128, 130, 133, *141*, 152
Arisaema sikkokianum 278
Arkell, Reginald 196, 306
Armeria juniperifolia 'Bevan's Variety' 71
Armstrong, Tom 319
Aruncus (goatsbeard) 138; *A. aethusifolius* 149, *167*, *223*, 233, *235*, 237, 238, *312*; *A. dioicus* 116, 157
Aspen (*Populus tremuloides*) 37, 142, 144, 312
Aster x *frikartii* 116
Astilbe 157, 158; *A.* 'Fanal' *160*, *163*
Astilboides tabularis 149, *189*, 243, 246, 284
Astrantia major 114, 241
Athyrium goeringianum 'Pictum' *243*, 246, 248
Auriculas 187
Azaleas 230
Azumaya 213, *215*, 219, 224-7, 229, 247, 311, *312*

B

Balsam fir (*Abies balsamea*) 37, *41*
Balsam poplar (*Populus balsamifera*) 274
Baneberry, see *Actaea*
Banks, Sir Joseph 50
Bartels, Roger 175, *176*, 200
Bartlett, Charles 319
Bartram, John 50
Bassin Bleu 72
Beach Farm 22, *28*
Bégin, Benoit 175
Berberis juliana 163; *B. thunbergii* *106*; *B.t. atropurpurea* 64
Bergenia 238; *B. cordifolia* *223*, *233*, 237, 246; *B.* 'Silberlicht' 97
Bergeron, Raynald 53, 189, 319
Bernier, Jean-Claude 126, 167, 315n.16, 319
Betula / Birch 37, 41, 312; *B. alleghanensis* (yellow birch) 144; *B. papyrifera* (paper birch) 37, 54, 120, 123, 126, 142, 152, 196, 216, *120*, *142*, 254, 262, 274, *312*;

birches at woodland edge 155, 159-60, 167, 251, 317n.21
Birn, David *197*, 200-204, *206*, 318n.32
Black spruce (*Picea mariana*) 37, 41
Bloom, Alan (Bressingham Nurseries) 241
Blue Garden 59, 100
Bodnant (N. Wales): Pin Mill 173, *174*
Bonner, George T. 22, 23, 24, 25, 27
Bonner, Isabel Sewell 25, 27
Bonner, Mabel 25
Bonner, Maud ("Mootzie"), see Cabot
Bourdon, Jean 22
Bracken (*Pteridium aquilinum*) 211
Bread and Knot Garden 64-6, *68*
Bread oven (*four à pain*) 53, 63, *64*, 66
Bridge of the Four Winds (*Pont des Quatre Vents*) 196, *197*
British Columbia fir 152
British Columbia red cedar 152
Brunnera macrophylla 116
Buddha (statue) 147
Bulb walks 184-7
Bunchberry, see *Cornus canadensis*
Burdock 214
Butter burr, Japanese (*Petasites*) 214
Buxus microphylla var. *koreana* 64

C

Cabane (toolhouse) 59, 72, 88, 93, 96, 99
Cabot, Anne Perkins (author's wife) 36, 63, 64, 66, 75, 101, 124, 144, 152, 193, 204, 295-6, 319
Cabot, Currie Mathews (author's mother) 35, 59, 60, 63, 94, *106*, 113, 114, 138, 170, 193, 295, 300, 302
Cabot, F. Colin (author's son) 193, 200
Cabot, Francis Higginson (author's grandfather) 19, 25, 29, 30
Cabot, F. Higginson (Higgie) (author's father) 27, 29, 53, 60, 294
Cabot, George Bonner 27
Cabot, Maud Bonner ("Mootzie") 19, 25, 27 *27*, 29, 30, *30*, 46, 60
Cabot, Quincy Sewell 18
Caltha palustris var. *alba* 244, *281*

Calypso bulbosa (fairy orchid) 23, 39, 46, 47
Camassia leichtlinii 157, 160
Campanula 71, 76, 79, 81, 87, 88, 99, 100; *C. betulifolia* 81; *C. carpatica* 85; *C. cochlearifolia* 71, 79, 87; *C.c.* 'Alba' 81, 95; *C. lactiflora* 116, 251; *C. latifolia* 114, 116, 295, 306; *C.l.* 'Alba' 95; *C. persicifolia* 102, 160; *C. rapunculoides* 293
Campbell, Felicity 206, 318n.32
Cap-aux-Oies 43
Caragana 167; *C. arborescens* 301
Caraway (*Carum carvi*) 306
Cardamine enneaphyllos 264
Carlhian, Jean 131-3, 149, 319
Carolina poplar (*Populus canadensis*) 298
Cartier, Jacques 20
Case, Fred 247, 317n.18
Cauchon, Robert 100, 316n.14
Cedar, British Columbia red 152; Port Orford (*Chamaecyparis lawsoniana*) 214; white (*Thuja occidentalis*) 19, 46, 47, 63, 106
Centaurea dealbata 116; *C. macropetala* 120
Chamaecyparis 94; *C. lawsoniana* (Port Orford cedar) 214; *C. pisifera filifera* 'Nana' 64
Chamaenerion (formerly *Epilobium*) *angustifolium album* 135, 138, 317n.18
Champlain, Samuel de 20, 21
Charlevoix 35, 36, 128, 216, 253; Trust 14
Chatto, Beth 244
Chinese bridge 128
Chiogenes hispidula 274
Chionodoxa luciliae 302, 305; *C. sardensis* 302, 305
Chrysanthemum uliginosum 116
Cimicifuga (snakeroot) 187; *C. japonica* var. *acerina* 238; *C. racemosa* 99, 116; *C. simplex* 116; classed as *Actaea* 316n.13
Clematis 97, *C. heracleifolia* 257; *C. integrifolia* 102, 257; *C. macropetala* 88; *C.m.* 'Markham's Pink' 163, 257; *C. recta* 99, 306
Coffin, Polhemus and Worthington, *Small French Buildings* 174, 175, 176
Colony Club of New York 27

Cornus canadensis (bunchberry) 41, 51, 216, 232, 261, 262, 312; *C. sibirica* 293; *C. stolonifera* 216
Cortusa mathioli 'Alba' 286; *C.m.* ssp. *pekinensis* 286
Corydalis 276; *C. curviflora* 203; *C. flexuosa* 243; *C. solida* 'George Baker' 274
Cow parsley 306
Crabapples 160, 196, 298; *Malus* 'Hopa' 142
Crambe cordifolia 93, 167
Crataegus 'Toba' 142; see also Hawthorn
Creech, Philip 203-4
Crocosmia 'Lucifer' 163
Crocus chrysanthus 305; *C.* 'Blue Pearl' 305; *C.* 'Cream Beauty' 305; *C.* 'Snow Bunting' 302, 305
Cup Garden 68
Curtis' magazines 203
Cylinder 176, 179, 182
Cypripedium (ladyslipper orchid): *C. acaule* 42-3, 46, 278; *C. pubescens* var. *parviflorum* 276; *C.p.* var. *planipetalum* 276 276; *C.p.* var. *pubescens* 276; *C. reginae* 276, 278

D

Daffodils 184, 302, 303, 306
Dandelions 291
Daphne mezereum 116, 257
Darmera peltata 233, 244, 248
Davidia involucrata 243
De Forest, Lockwood 68
Delphiniums 81, 95, 99, 100, 119, 120, 253, 254, 258, 296-8; Blackmore & Langdon strain 258; Connecticut Yankee strain 257; Pacific Hybrids 119, 257, 296
Delphinium Society 119, 296
Des Gagniers, Jean 13, 318n.41, 319
Desmeules, Kelley 114, 123, 141
Desmeules, Robert 316n.1
Dianthus Allwoodii group (pinks) 102; *D.* 'La Bourboule' 75; "old-fashioned" pinks 80, 87
Dicentra peregrina 86; *D. spectabilis* 97

Dictamnus albus 97 97; *D. fraxinella* 253
Diphylleia cymosa (umbrella leaf) 211, 213, 248; *D. greyii* 264
"Diverticulum" 179
Dixieland jazz 193-4, 206
Dodge, Michael 160
Dolphin (statue/fountain) 133, 257
Doodle-Doo 60, 294, 298
Doronicum orientale 114
Dorycnium hirsutum (dogbane) 138
Draba rigida 86
Dryas octopetala 78, 80, 86
Duell, Charles 192-3
D'whinnie (cairn terrier) 7, 56, 182, 232

E

Eccremocarpus scaber 190
Echium vulgare 35
Epilobium, see *Chamaenerion*
Epimediums 187, 247
Epstein, Harold 213, 273
Eremurus himalaicus 167, 296; *E.* x *isabellinus* Shelford Hybrids 295
Erythronium 284; *E.* 'Pagoda' 264, 269; *E. revolutum* 'White Beauty' 264
Euphorbia polychroma 163

F

Fairy Land 41
Fairy orchid (*Calypso bulbosa*) 23, 46, 47
Farrer, Annie 203
Farrer, Reginald 200, 203, 317n.30
Faust, Franklin 152
Ferguson, Barry 147
Filion, Louis 319
Filipendulas 116, 257
Four à pain, see Bread oven
Fraises des bois 66
Fraser, Lt. Malcolm 22, 23
Fraser, William Malcolm 22
Fritillaria meleagris 306; *F.m.* 'Alba' 97
Frog (sculptures): Gardener 248; Musicians 173, 192-5, 206
Fuki, see *Petasites japonicus* var. *giganteus*

G

Galax urceolata 211
Garçonnière 124, 128, 133
Gaspé 24
Gazebo 170, 219, 230
Generalife (Granada) 181
Gentiana / Gentians 261; *G. asclepiadea* 'Alba' 224, *251*
Geranium 102, 241; *G. phaeum* 97; *G. pratense* 97; *G. sylvaticum* 97
Gillespie, Dizzie 193
Ginkgo 216, 230
Glaucidium palmatum 273, 278
Goatsbeard (*Aruncus*) 157, 158, 159, 160
Goddess of Flowers (statue) *127*, 130
Goffinet, François 107
Goodyer, John 50
Goodyera oblongifolia 50; *G. repens* 41, 50; *G. tesselata* 41, 50
Goose Allée 113-20, 124, 127, 138, 141, 253, 258
Gourdon (Lot): pigeonnier 174, 175, 176
Grasshopper (sculpture) 211
Greenwood, Lawrence 203
Guest Garden 67-8, 93, 130, 144, 301
Guilin (Guang Xi Region, China) 147, 148
Gunnera 133, 138, 142, 317n.17
Gypsophila aretioides 'Caucasica' 86; *G. repens* 'Alba' 80; *G. tenuifolia* 80

H

Hadspen (Somerset) 130
Hakonechloa macra 'Aureola' 230, *232*
Hales, Mick 152
Hall, Elizabeth 75
Hart, Moss 152
Harvey, Michel 319
Hashimoto, Tadoshi 213, 214, 216, 227
Hawkweed (*Hieracium pilosella*) 291
Hawthorn hedges (*Crataegus flabellata*) 68, 93, 97, 99, 106, 114, *126*, *127*, 155
Hemerocallis 'Hyperion' 167
Heracleum 138; *H. antasiaticum* 243, 248; *H. mantegazzianum* 243-4
Hickey, George 174

Hidcote (Glos.) 124
Hieracium pilosella (hawkweed) 258, 291; *H. villosum* 87
Hill, May Brawley 319
Hilliers Nursery 155
Hobhouse, Penelope 184, *193*; 317n.25; Foreword 10-11
Hollyhocks 296
Hoōgyo 213, 215, 227, 229, 230, 232
Hosta 157, 158, 167, 248; *H.* 'Frances Williams' 163 *163*; *H. plantaginea* 163; *H. sieboldiana* 158
Huber, Tony 298
Hudson River 21, 261
Hughes, Nigel 130, 319
Hunter & mate (statues) *188*
Huntington, John 193
Hylomecon japonicum 238, 247, 248

I

Iberis saxatilis 80
Impatiens biflora (jewelweed) 247
Inula magnifica 257
Iris 'Francis Cabot' 318n.40; *I. gracilipes* 'Alba' *223*, 224; *I. pseudacorus* 134; *I.* 'Roy Elliott' 286; *I. sibirica* (Siberian iris) 149, *251*; *I.s.* 'Perry's Blue' 134; *I. versicolor* x *ensata* hybrids 298

J

Jack pine (*Pinus banksiana*) 37
Japanese bridge 134, 138, 155
Jardin de la Boulangère 64
Jefferson, Thomas 190, 317n.27
Jeffersonia diphylla 238; *J. dubia* 238
Jellicoe, Geoffrey 67, 133
Jewelweed (*Impatiens biflora*) 247, 312, 318n.38
Juniperus communis 149

K

Kalm, Peter 50
Kalmia (sheep laurel) 50

Kan Son Tei *211*, 213, 229, 233, 235, 247
Kaufman, George 152
King, Frederick Rhinelander (Freddie) 60, 63
Kingdon Ward, Frank & Florence 289
Kirengeshoma palmata 187, *223*, 230, *233*, 238
Knot Garden 64-6
Kwan Ying (statue) 138

L

La Malbaie 21, *20*, 22, 23, 35, *60*, 152
Lac des Cygnes 182, 188, *190*, 196, *197*, 199
Lac Libellule *123*, 134-8, 141, 144, 155, 167, 173, 175, 248, 251, 312
Ladyslipper orchid, see *Cypripedium*
Ladyslipper Slope 42, *46*, 277
Lamium maculatum 102; *L.m.* 'White Nancy' 97
Lancaster, Roy 167
Lapointe, David 114
Lapointe, Laurent 233
Larch / *Larix* 37, 142; *L. leptolepis* (Japanese larch) 152
Larkspur 113
Laurentian Mts. 18, 35, *47*, 50, 53, 56, 59, 149, 152
Lavatera cachemirica 119
Le Barachois 23
Le p'tit bonhomme (statue) *126*
Leach, David 213, 318n.35
Lebanese squill (*Puschkinia libanotica*) 305
Lee, Mary 29-30, 46, *47*
Lighty, Dick 167
Ligularia 170; *L. przewalskii* 247; *L.* 'The Rocket' 247; *L. veitchii* 247; *L. wilsoniana* 247
Lilac (*Syringa*): hedge 302; and thuja screen 155, 167; Preston hybrids (*S. reflexa* x *S. villosa*) 152
Lilies / *Lilium*: 97, 160, 318n.39; *Lilium hansonii* 286; *L. martagon* x *L. hansonii* 160; *L. martagon* 99, 163, *155*, 248; *L.m.* 'Alabaster' 278; *L.m.* 'Midnight' 160, 278; *L. tenuifolium* 248

Lily of the valley (*Convallaria majalis*) 66
Lindens, little-leaf, see *Tilia cordata*
Linnaea borealis (twinflower) 50, 261
Linnaeus (Carl von Linné) 50, 203
Lombardy poplar, see *Populus nigra* 'Italica'
Long, Hallie 75
Lonicera tatarica 293
Louis XIV 21, 179
Lupine 97, 138, *291, 293, 303, 306*
Lutyens, Sir Edwin 152
Lychnis coronaria 163
Lynch, Kenneth 127, 138, *147*
Lysichiton camschaticum 248

M

Machiai 229, 235, 286
Maianthemum canadensis 232, 261
Malbaie River 35, 126, 305
Malus 'Hopa' 142, *298*
Maples 37, 196, 312; red maple 142; sugar maple 141, 142; see also *Acer*
Marigolds *295, 296*
Mathews, Edward J. (Eddie) 54, *56, 56,* 59, 60, 67, 71, 72, 82, 93, 94, 96, 108, 293, 300
Matia, Walter 179
Matteuccia struthiopteris (ostrich fern) 138, *155,* 157, 158, *159, 246,* 247, 248
McCarthy, Mary 101, 108, 182
Meadow, see Prairie
Meconopsis betonicifolia 163, 270; *M. grandis* 270; *M. napaulensis* 'Rosea' *270; M. quintuplinervia* 270, 276
Meotoiwa (marriage stone) 229, 230
Milwaukee (Skylight Comic Opera) 200
Moneses uniflora 41, *274*
Monkshood (*Aconitum*) 116, 138
Monkwearmouth (near Durham) 22
Montreal Botanic Garden 276
Moon Bridge *141,* 147-9
Morgan, Pat 100, *100,* 128, 138, 163, 253, 257, 258, 261, 262, 264, 278
Mosaic (Pigeonnier Patio) *188, 190, 192*
Mosquito (sculpture) 211, *215*
Mountain ash (*Sorbus americana*) 37, 142, 196

Mountain maple (*Acer spicatum*) 41, 248, 261, 274
Mount Murray Manor (seigneurie de Mont-Murray) 17, *18,* 23, 25, 27, *31,* 35, 53
Mozart 14, 193
Mugo pine (*Pinus mugo*) 142, 301
Mulhern, Sarah 28
Murray River 22, 24, 35, 41, 50
Murray (Murray's) Bay 22, *23, 25*
Muscari 305
Music Pavilion 142, 144-7, 152
Myosotis alpestris 253; *M. sylvestris* (forget-me-not) *244, 247,* 247, 248

N

Nairne, Lt. John 22
Nakamon (ceremonial gate) 211, 229, 248
New York Botanical Garden 75
Nicandra physaloides (apple-of-Peru, shoo-fly plant) 120
Nicolson, Harold 94, 124
Nid d'Amour 190, *200,* 203, 204, *206,* 318n.32

O

Olin, Laurie: Foreword 8-10
Orchids 41; see also *Calypso; Cypripedium*
Oriental poppies 257, 293
Origanum vulgare 'Aureum' 163
Osmunda japonica 230, 247
Ostrich fern (*Matteuccia struthiopteris*) 138, 157, 158, 159, *241,* 247, 248
Otters and trout (statue) 179, *181,* 182
Oval 176, 179

P

Pachysandra procumbens 248
Page, Russell 93, 102, 106-8, 182
Palca, Doris 319
Palissades 184, 187, 188, 190, 194, 211, 241
Pan (statue) 94-5, 99, 113, 251

Papaver sendtneri 81
Paper birch, see *Betula papyrifera*
Paraquilegia anemonoides 243
Paterson, Allen 66
Paterson, William 24
Patrinia gibbosa 248
Penstemon campanulatus (*pulchellus*) 87
Peonies 99, 116, 155, 167, 257
Perennial Allée 95, *97,* 99, *102,* 155, 251-8, 261, 312
Perenyi, Eleanor 101, 108
Petasites 170; *P. japonicus* var. *giganteus* (Fuki) 142-4, *233,* 243, 248; *P.j.* 'Variegatus' 230, *232,*
Philadelphus 95, 97
Phlox 99; *P. paniculata* 257; *P. subulata* 'Ellie B' 80; *P.s.* 'Schneewittchen' 80
Phoebe (statue) 130, 133
Phyllodoce and Plucky-Lucky (cats) 64
Picea (spruce) 134, 142; *P. glauca* (white spruce) 37; *P. mariana* (black spruce) 37, 41
Pigeonnier 130, *131,*137, 147, 176, 179, 182, 184, 196, 211, 233, 317n.23; Gardens 173-209, 248; interior 200, 241
Pine / *Pinus* 142; *P. banksiana* (jack pine) 41, 50; *P. cembra* (Swiss pine) 301; *P. mugo* (mugo pine) *134,* 142, 301; *P. resinosa* (red pine) 37, 42, 134; *P. sylvestris* (Scots pine) 63, 215, 230
Piscine, see Swimming pool
Podophyllum hexandrum 244
Pointe-à-Gaz 44
Pointe-au-Pic 23, *27, 29,* 41, *43,* 53, 60, 63, 291, 294
Polygonatum biflorum 248
Polystichum braunii 247, 248
Pont des Quatre Vents 196
Pool Room 179, 180, 182, 196
Pope, Alexander 188
Poplars / *Populus*: *P. balsamifera* (balsam popar) 274; *P. canadensis* (Carolina poplar) *298; P. nigra* 'Italica' (Lombardy poplar) 53, 54, *55,* 72, 96, 99, 113, 123, 124, 127, 142, *147, 152,* 174, 176, 182, 194, 211; *P. tremuloides* (aspen) 37, 142, 144, 312

Port Orford cedar (*Chamaecyparis lawsoniana*) 214
Potager *59*, *60*, 293-8
Potentilla fruticosa 253; *P. nitida* 78
Price, Sir William 167
Primula 86, 157-60; *P. alpicola* 286; *P.a.* var. *luna* 163, *261*, *284*, 286; *P.a.* var. *violacea* 284; *P. anisodora* 264, 289; *P. aurantiaca* 286; *P. aureata* 85; *P. auriculata* 283; *P. boothii* 'Alba' 203; *P. bulleyana* 284, 286; *P. burmanica* 286, *289*; *P. capitata* 282, 289; *P. cernua* 243, 286; *P. chionantha* (*sinopurpurea*) 284; *P. clarkei* 283; *P. cockburniana* 286; *P. cortusoides* 286; *P. darialica* 284; *P. denticulata* 283; *P.d.* 'Alba' 97; *P. elatior* (oxlip) 284; *P. farinosa* 278, 284; *P. flaccida* 286; *P. florindae* 148, 149, *158*, *261*; *P. frondosa* 284; *P. gemmifera* 286; *P. glomerata* 282, 289; *P. heucherifolia* 286; *P. ioessa* 284, 289; *P. japonica* 157-60; *244*, *248*, 286; *P.j.* 'Miller's Crimson' 286; *P.j.* 'Postford White' 286; *P.* 'Johanna' *261*, *281*, 283; *P. kisoana* 286; *P.k.* 'Alba' *214*, *232*, *235*, 286; *P. laurentiana* 284; *P. luteola* 283, *286*; *P. marginata* 224; *P.m.* 'Amethyst' 86; *P.m.* 'Beamish' 86; *P.m.* 'Kesselring's Variety' *71*, *85*, 86; *P.m.* 'Linda Pope' 86; *P.m.* 'Prichard's Variety' 86; *P.m.* 'Stonecrop Blue' 86; *P. mistassinica* 284; *P. modesta* 284; *P. oreophlomis* section (*farinosa* subsec. *auriculata*) 282-3; *P.* 'Peter Klein' *261*, *281*, 283; *P. poissonii* 286; *P. polyantha* 157-60; *P. polyneura* 286; *P. prolifera* (*helodoxa*) 286; *P. x pruhonicensis* 'Lady Greer' 264; *P. pulverulenta* 286; *P.p.* Bartley Hybrids 286; *P.* 'Raynald' 289; *P. reidii* var. *williamsii* 286; *P. rosea* 283; *P. saxatilis* 286; *P. secundiflora* 286; *P. sibirica* 203; *P. sieboldii* (*Sakurasoh*) 230, 286; *P. sikkimensis* 286; *P. sonchifolia* 282; *P. veris* (cowslip) 284; *P. vulgaris* ssp. *sibthorpii* 116; *P. waltoni* 283, 284, 289; *P.* 'Wanda' *114*, 116, *278*; *P. warshenewskyana* 283, 284; *P. whitei* 282
Prunus cistena 163

Pteridophyllum racemosum 278
Pulmonaria angustifolia ssp. *azurea* 247, 248
Puschkinia libanotica 302, 305
Pylam powder 179, 188
Pyrola rotundifolia 247, 248, 261, 262

R

Ramonda myconi 79, 86
Ranunculus crenatus 247
Rattlesnake plantain (*Goodyera* spp.) 41
Ravine 144, 241-8, 311, 312
Reale, Cono 76-8, *82*, 86, 88, 216, 218-20, 232, 264
Red maple 142
Red pine (*Pinus resinosa*) 37, 42, 134
Reeve, John Fraser 22, 23, 25
Reflection pools, Pigeonnier 175, 182; terrace (*Bassin Bleu*) 72, 76, 82, 93, *106*, *311*
Rez-de-chaussée (Pigeonnier) 188, 200
Rheum palmatum 244, 248; *R.p.* 'Atrosanguineum' 244, 248
Rhodochiton volubile 203, 317n. 31
Rhododendron yakushimanum 211, 248
Rhubarb 128, 131, 133
Rhus typhina 216
Richards, John 284
Rivière-du-Loup 22
Rocaille 72, 75-6
Rodgersia 155, 187, 311; *R. aesculifolia* 147, *148*, 149, 235, 243, *246*; *R. pinnata* 243, *244*, *246*, 248; *R. podophylla* 184, *223*, *235*, 238, 243, 248; *R. tabularis*, see *Astilboides tabularis*
Rondel 120, 124-7, 133; Lombardy 142, 144
Rope bridges 155, 167-70, 179, 182, 215, 238, 286
Rosa / Rose: Penzance rose 101; *R.* 'Bishop Darlington' 101; *R.* 'Bonica' 101; *R. glauca* 101; *R.* 'Gloire de Dijon' 101; *R.* 'Kiftsgate' 100; *R. rugosa* 293; *R.r.* 'Alba' 81
Rose Garden *93*, *95*, *97*, *99*, 100-102, 155, 167, 251
Rotunda 190, *191*, 196

Royal Botanical Gardens (Kew) 167, 203
Royal Mughal Gardens (New Delhi) 152
Rozon, Gilbert 204
Rudbeckia maxima 116
Rupina-La (Central Nepal) 85, 167, 203
Ryan, Cynthia 319

S

Sackville-West, Vita 94
St. Irénée 230
St. Lawrence River 20, 22, 27, 35, 41, 50, 54, 56, 60, 63, 149, 276, 291, 293, 294, 303
St. Siméon 23
Saito, Satoshi 213
Sakaguchi, Ann Gerber 214, 224, 230
Sakaguchi, Hiroshi 214-15, 216, 224-7, 229-30
Sakurasoh, see *Primula sieboldii*
Salad Garden *63*, *64*
Salix purpurea (purple osier) 152
Sambucus canadensis 'Aurea' 235
Sanguinaria canadensis forma *multiplex* 97, 243, 316n.12
Savill Garden (Windsor) 241
Saxifraga (saxifrage) 79, 85, 86; *S. apiculata* 85; Kabschia 86; mossy 261; *S. x urbium* 264
Schilling, Tony 167, 203, 283, 317n.22
Schivereckia podolica 80
Schubert 194
Scilla mischtschenkoana 269; *S. siberica* 114, 116, *257*, *269*, *278*, *291*, 306
Scots pine (*Pinus sylvestris*) 63
Sedum middendorfianum 86
Serviceberry, see *Amelanchier*
Sewell family 31
Sewell, Isabel (later Bonner) 23
Sewell, Jonathan 23
Shadbush 142, 196, 312
Shade Borders 157-67, 251, 261
Sheep laurel (*Kalmia angustifolia*) 50
Shi-shi-otoshi 211, *213*, 247
Shirley poppy 296, 298
Shortia galacifolia 211, 238, 274, 278

Shute (Wiltshire) 67, 133
Siberian iris (*Iris sibirica*) 100, 142, 149
Sigunian-Shan (Western Szechuan) 243, 286
Silene alpestris 'Flore Pleno' 80
Sissinghurst (Kent) 94, 124, 173, 184
Skidmore, Owings and Merrill 60
Smith, Charles *173*, *192*, 192-3, *248*, 317n. 29
Smith, William 23
Smithsonian Institution (Washington DC) 131
Snakeroot (*Cimicifuga racemosa*) 157, 158, 159, 160
Soldanella 261; *S. carpatica* 274
Solomon's seal (*Polygonatum biflorum*) 157, 159
Sorbus americana (mountain ash) 157
Spingarn, Joel 76
Spruce (*Picea*) 134, 142; black spruce (*P. mariana*) 37, 41; white spruce (*P. glauca*) 37
Spruce budworm (*Choristoneura fumiferana*) 19, 41, 46, 163, 214, 261, 295, 312, 316n.6
Stevens, Bessie 30-31
Stonecrop (Cold Spring, NY) 71, *76*, 78, 85, 86, 100, 101, 107, 174, 176, 261
Stream Garden 130, 141-52, 157, 167, 171, 196
Sugar maple 141, 142
Sunset Hill 18, *19*, 53
Sweet peas 296, 298
Swimming pool (piscine) 59, 63, 67, 138, 291, 293, 300-301
Symphyandra hoffmannii 238
Syringa (lilac) 97; *S.* 'Palibin' 88; *S. prestoniae* (*S. reflexa* x *S. villosa*) hybrids *144*, 152

T

Tagetes tenuifolia 295
Taj Mahal 173, 174
Tapis Vert 56, 59, 71, 72, 82, 83, 88, 93, 94, 97, 99, 106-13, 134, 155, 216, 291, 315

Thalictrum 187; *T. aquilegifolium* 116, *251*, *253*, *258*; *T. coreanum* (*ichangense*) 238; *T. diffusiflorum* 238; *T. flavum* 167, *258*; *T. kiusianum* 223, 224, 238
Thermopsis caroliniana 134, 306
Thompson & Morgan 120
Thuja occidentalis (white cedar) 67, 72, 94, 126, 141, 173; *T.o.* 'Tom Thumb' *64*
Thuja Allée 128-33, 138
Thymus lanuginosus 102
Tiarella wherryi 187
Tilia cordata (little-leaf linden) 64, 173, 176, 179, 184, 187
Tillotson, Will 101
Tintinhull (Somerset) 184, 317n.39
Tragopogon pratensis 306
Tree, Anne & Michael 67
Trenet, Charles 204-6
Tricyrtis latifolia 244, 248
Trillium grandiflorum 'Flore Pleno' *262*
Trollius 'Alabaster' 163; *T. ledebourii* 286
Tropaeolum peregrinum 163, 203, 257; *T. speciosum* 257
Tsuga canadensis 'Cole's Prostrate' 211, 235-8; *T. sargentii* 224
Tsukubai 232
Tulipa (tulip) *159*, *184*; *T.* 'Ancilla' *187*; *T. batalinii* 269; *T.* Greigii hybrids 187; *T.* 'Mariette' *157*; 160, 163; *T. tarda* 187; *T. turkestanica* 187; *T. urumiensis* 187; *T.* 'West Point' 163
Turtle (fountain) *123*, 133
Twinflower (*Linnaea borealis*) 50, 261

U

Un Jardin Extraordinaire (book) 318n.41, 319; (song) 206, 318n.33

V

Vegetable garden, see Potager
Verey, David 101
Verey, Rosemary 50, 101, 102; *The Englishwoman's Garden* 67, 133

Verrocchio, Andrea del 28
Viburnum 97; *V. trilobum* 163

W

Wakehurst Place (Sussex) 167
Waldsteinia ternata 235, *243*, *246*, 247, 248
Watercourse *123*, 133
Waterfall 213, 215-24, 233, 235, 238, 247, 311, 312
Water Gardens 179-82
Water lilies 94, 133
Water Staircases 176, 179, 180-2
Watkins, Jane 203
Welch, Marianne Cabot (author's daughter) 213
Wessel, William: sculptures 194, 211, 247
West, Jim 101
Wheelwright, Mary Cabot 29
White cedar 19, 46, 47, 63, 106; see also *Thuja occidentalis*
White Garden 17, 59, 68, 80-88, *93*, 94-9, 107, 108, 251
White spruce (*Picea glauca*) 37
Willow 134; arctic 142; weeping 216, 230
Winterthur 114, 116
Wolong Valley (Szechuan) 149, 243
Woodland Garden 86, 95, 241, 243, 248, 258, 261-89, 315

Z

Zinn, David *200*, 204

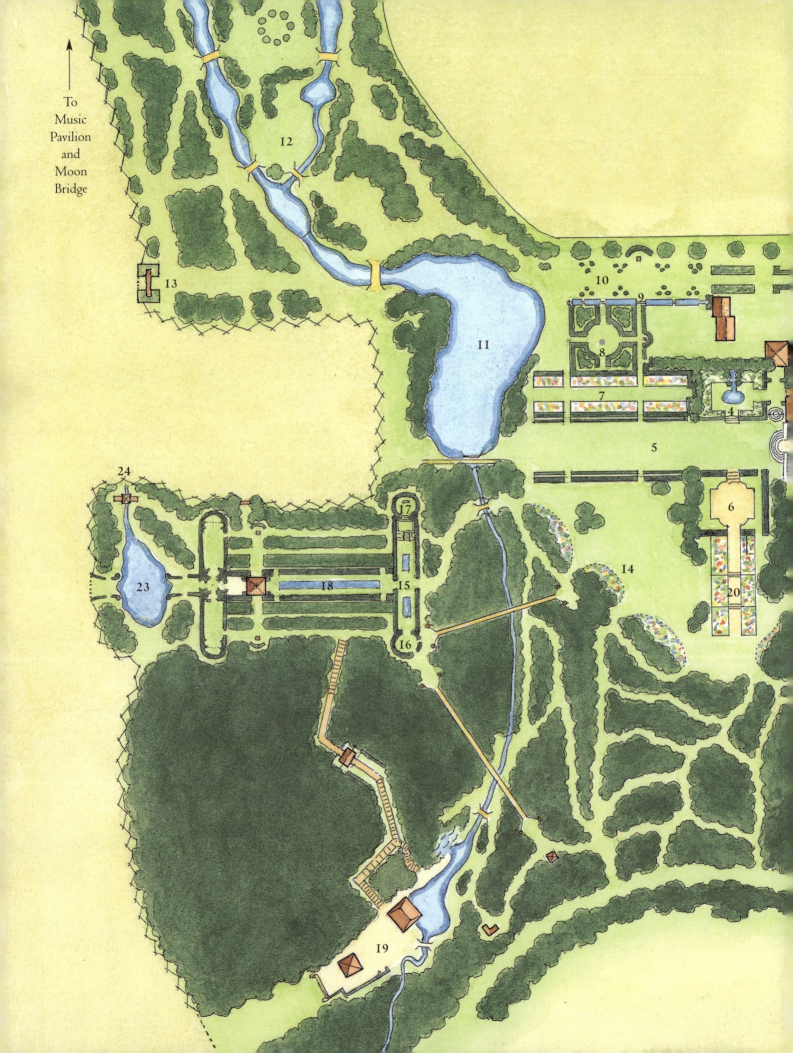